The Ethical Formation of Economists

T0382731

Economists' role in society has always been an uneasy one, and in recent years the ethicality of the profession and its practitioners has been questioned more than ever. This collection of essays is the first to investigate the multifaceted nature of what forms economists' ethical and economic views.

Bringing together work from international contributors, *The Ethical Formation of Economists* explores the ways in which economists are influenced in their training and career, examining how this can explain their individual ethical stances as economists. The book suggests that if we can better understand what is making economists think and act as they do, considering ethicality in the process, we might all be better placed to implement changes. The intent is not to exonerate economists from personal responsibility, but to highlight how considering the circumstances that have helped shape economists' views can help to address issues. It is argued that it is important to understand these influences, as without such insights, the demonization of economists is too easily adapted as a stance by society as well as too easily dismissed by economists.

This book will be of great interest to those studying and researching in the fields of economics, ethics, philosophy and sociology. It also seeks to bring an ethical debate within and about economics and to cause change in the practical reasoning of economists.

Wilfred Dolfsma is Professor of Business Management & Organisation at Wageningen University, The Netherlands. He is the author of numerous books and articles, and was Editor-in-Chief of the *Review of Social Economy* and is Associate Editor for the *European Journal of Management*.

Ioana Negru is Reader in Economics in the Faculty of Economic Sciences at Lucian Blaga University, Sibiu, Romania. She is a member of Reteaching Economics and the Skidelski Group for Economics Curriculum Reform.

SCEME Studies in Economic Methodology
Series Editor:
Matthias Klaes
University of Dundee, UK

Keynes's Economic Consequences of the Peace
A Reappraisal
Edited by Jens Hölscher

Development and Financial Reform in Emerging Economies
Edited by Kobil Ruziev

The Ethical Formation of Economists
Edited by Wilfred Dolfsma and Ioana Negru

For more information about this series, please visit: www.routledge.com/
SCEME-Studies-in-Economic-Methodology/book-series/SCEME

The Ethical Formation of Economists

Edited by Wilfred Dolfsma
and Ioana Negru

Routledge
Taylor & Francis Group

LONDON AND NEW YORK

First published 2019 by Routledge

2 Park Square, Milton Park, Abingdon, Oxon, OX14 4RN

605 Third Avenue, New York, NY 10017

Routledge is an imprint of the Taylor & Francis Group, an informa business

First issued in paperback 2020

British Library Cataloguing-in-Publication Data
A catalogue record for this book is available from the British Library

Library of Congress Cataloging-in-Publication Data
Names: Dolfsma, Wilfred, editor. | Negru, Ioana, 1974– editor.
Title: The ethical formation of economists / edited by Wilfred Dolfsma and Ioana Negru.
Description: Abingdon, Oxon ; New York, NY : Routledge, 2019. | Series: SCEME studies in economic methodology | Includes bibliographical references and index.
Identifiers: LCCN 2018056871 (print) | LCCN 2018058773 (ebook) | ISBN 9781351043809 (Ebook) | ISBN 9781138487062 (hardback : alk. paper)
Subjects: LCSH: Economists—Professional ethics. | Economics—Study and teaching—Moral and ethical aspects. | Economics—Moral and ethical aspects.
Classification: LCC HB74.5 (ebook) | LCC HB74.5 .E839 2019 (print) | DDC 174/.4—dc23
LC record available at https://lccn.loc.gov/2018056871

ISBN: 978-1-138-48706-2 (hbk)
ISBN: 978-0-367-72725-3 (pbk)

Typeset in Bembo
by Apex CoVantage, LLC

Contents

Contributors

George F. DeMartino is Professor of Economics in the Josef Korbel School of International Studies, University of Denver, USA, where he has served as Associate Dean of Graduate Studies and now co-directs the MA in Global Finance, Trade and Economic Integration. In 2018, he served as President of the Association for Social Economics. He writes extensively on the intersection of economics, justice, and ethics and has served on the World Economic Forum Global Agenda Council on 'Values in Decision-Making' and has presented his work at Davos.

Wilfred Dolfsma trained as an economist and philosopher and is Professor of Business Management & Organisation at Wageningen University, The Netherlands. He was editor-in-chief of the *Review of Social Economy* and is associate editor for the *European Journal of Management*. His articles have been featured in the *Journal of Economics Issues, Journal of Evolutionary Economics, Journal of Economic and Social Geography, Journal of Business Ethics, The Information Society, Technological Forecasting & Social Change* and *Research Policy, Technology Analysis & Strategic Management*. For further information, see www. wilfreddolfsma.net.

Craig Duckworth is Associate Dean at the Ulster University, London branch campus, UK. He has lectured in economics for over 20 years and holds a Ph.D. in Philosophy from University College London. His research interests are in philosophy of economics, with a particular interest in economics and ethics. He is currently researching the role of commitment and incentive in economic theory.

Wim Groot is Professor of Health Economics and Professor of Evidence Based Education at Maastricht University, The Netherlands. He is also Professor of Evidence Based Education and Labor Market Policy at the University of Amsterdam. He is currently a member of the board of governance of the Dutch Patient Federation, a member of the ZoNMW committees 'Topzorg' and 'Uitkomstgerichte Zorg', Chairman of the Vidi committee 'Economie and Bedrijfskunde', Chairman of the expert panel of NFK, and a member of the Advisory Board Health Care of the ING Bank. For more information, see www.tierweb.nl.

Henriette Maassen van den Brink is Professor of Education Economics at the Department of Economics and Business at the University of Amsterdam, The Netherlands. She is the founder and Scientific Program-Director of the Interuniversity Top Institute for Evidence Based Education Research. She is also a Chair of the Onderwijsraad (Education Council of the Netherlands), The Hague.

Deirdre Nansen McCloskey is Distinguished Professor of Economics, History, English and Communication at the University of Illinois at Chicago, USA, where she taught until 2015. She is the author of eighteen books and some 400 scholarly articles, ranging from technical economics and statistics to gender studies and literary criticism. She has also taught in England, Australia, Holland, Italy and Sweden and holds ten honorary degrees.

Robert McMaster is Professor of Political Economy in the Adam Smith Business School at the University of Glasgow, UK. He has published extensively in journals such as the *British Journal of Management, Cambridge Journal of Economics, Economic Geography, Journal of Business Ethics, Journal of Economic Issues* and *Journal of Institutional Economics*, among others. Together with John Davis, he co-authored *Health Care Economics*, published by Routledge in 2017.

Andrew Mearman is Associate Professor of Economics at Leeds University Business School, UK, where he holds the position of Director of Student Education for the Economics Division. He has published extensively in journals on teaching, methodology of economics, realism and heterodox economics. He also recently co-authored a book of interviews with leading (heterodox) economists. In addition, he serves on several journal editorial boards and is a Trustee of the Association for Social Economics. He recently became a member of the Green House think tank.

Jamie Morgan is Professor of Economic Sociology at Leeds Beckett University, UK. He co-edits the *Real World Economics Review* with Edward Fullbrook. He has published widely in the fields of economics, political economy, philosophy, sociology and international politics. His recent books include *Realist Responses to Post-Human Society: Ex Machina* (ed. with I. Al-Amoudi, Routledge, 2018) and *Brexit and the Political Economy of Fragmentation: Things Fall Apart* (ed. with H. Patomäki, Routledge, 2018).

Ioana Negru is Reader in Economics in the Faculty of Economic Sciences at Lucian Blaga University, Sibiu, Romania. Her current research interests revolve around scientific pluralism, the philosophy and methodology of economics, the economics of gift and philanthropy, the methodology of Austrian and Institutional Economics, the methodology of macroeconomics, ecological/green economics and sustainability. She is a member of Reteaching Economics and the Skidelski Group for Economics Curriculum Reform.

Patrick O'Sullivan is Professor of Business Ethics at Grenoble Ecole de Management, France. In recent years, he has carried out considerable research in the areas of intersection between ethics, political economy and management studies. He is a regular visiting professor at the University of Parma and holds a research professorship at Thammasat University Bangkok. He played rugby union for many years before becoming a rugby referee.

Alice Nicole Sindzingre is Visiting Lecturer at the School of Oriental and African Studies (SOAS, University of London, Department of Economics) since 2003. She is also Associate Researcher at the CEPN (Paris-North Economics Centre, University Paris-13, France), and at the LAM research centre ('*Africas in the World*', National Centre for Scientific Research/CNRS-SciencesPo-Bordeaux, France). She was formerly Senior Research Fellow at the French National Center for Scientific Research (CNRS). She taught in 2008–2010 at SciencesPo-Paris and in 2010–2014 in the department of economics of the University Paris-Nanterre. In 2005–2008, she wrote the monthly column on the theories of economic development in the French newspaper *Le Monde*. She has also served as a consultant for governments and international organisations. She has been a member of the Core Team of the World Bank World Development Report 2000-1 on poverty. She has conducted research on development economics, political economy (including extensive field-work, mainly in West Africa) and epistemology. She has published articles in academic journals and books on a large range of topics, including international trade, foreign aid, poverty traps, the theory of institutions in relation with development, and the epistemology of economics.

Edward R. Teather-Posadas is a Ph.D. candidate in Economics at Colorado State University, USA. He is currently completing his dissertation on justice, ethics and rhetoric in economic theory and history. In 2017, he was awarded the Warren J. and Sylvia J. Samuels Young Scholar prize, and, in the same year, he was appointed a CORE-Teagle Fellow of CORE, a not-for-profit organization of leading economists devoted to new ways of teaching post-crash economics.

Mark D. White is Chair of the Department of Philosophy at the College of Staten Island/CUNY, USA, where he teaches courses in philosophy, economics and law. He is the author of seven books and the editor or co-editor of nearly twenty more.

Stephen T. Ziliak is Professor of Economics and Faculty Member of the Social Justice Studies Program at Roosevelt University, USA, Conjoint Professor of Business and Law at University of Newcastle, Australia, and Faculty Affiliate in the Graduate Program of Economics at Colorado State University, USA. He is the author or editor of three books and more than 120 articles and essays.

1 Introduction

Wilfred Dolfsma and Ioana Negru

Ethics is the study of Good or "the study of one's proper interactions with others. It is the analysis of right and wrong" (Wight, 2015: 4). Recent debates in the economy have attempted to renew the interests in ethics and its role within economic theory. This voyage into knowledge has brought to attention the classic authors who proposed an economic and moral theory, but also modern authors who have sustained economics as a moral science, such as Amartya Sen, Kenneth Boulding, Anthony Atkinson and George DeMartino. As Boulding states (1968: 2), "No science of any kind can be divorced from ethical considerations". Although economics has moral and ethical roots, many economists do not allow for ethics within their analysis, and very often ethics in economics is conflated with the ethics of economists. This book is an attempt to resurrect interest in the ethics of *economists* and to advance a moral conception of the economic science. In principle, the book does not recognize the separation between normative and positive economics or the Humean distinction between *is* and *ought* and proposes that most policy analyses are pervaded by ethical frameworks and value judgments of various sorts. Ethics is part of the institutional framework in which economic activity develops and takes place. The reason elimination of ethics from economics failed with the growth of 'scientism' in economics is precisely because policy analysis needs an ethical framework in order to be done (Wight, 2015).

Following an established classification, there are three major ethical frameworks in economics: utilitarianism, deontology and virtue-ethics. Utilitarianism or consequentialism is the dominant ethical framework in economics and the economic policymaking domain. Utilitarianism as a philosophical paradigm was inspired by the Greek philosophical tradition. A hedonist approach to value was formulated at the beginning of the fifth century BC by Arystip from Cyrene and 100 years later by Epicurus, who continued the intellectual tradition of Leucip and Democritus. The doctrine established by Epicurus in the second century BC has influenced known philosophers and works, such as Hobbes's *Leviathan*, Hume, Helvetius and Holbach and the writings of Jeremy Bentham and the elaboration by John Stuart Mill. The essence of Epicurus's thinking is that the rejection or acceptance of preferences needs to have as a criterion pleasure, happiness or pain. Classical Utilitarianism as presented by

Jeremy Bentham (1780) has as its basis the Utility principle, which states that an action is right or correct to the extent it determines an increase of the happiness of all parties affected by it. The basis/foundation of this principle is that pleasure and happiness are two categories that possess intrinsic value, while pain is intrinsically undesirable. A utilitarianist follower is someone who accepts the principle of utility and is concerned with the maximization of the value of the universe, i.e., utility and the consequences of each action.

Deontology or Kantian-based ethics has as a founding principle that of duty and the belief that there are deontological constraints to our actions that arise from reason; individuals need to refrain from actions that are seen as wrong or mistaken or actions that violate the freedom of others. Deontology is concerned with the ethical behavior of economists as professionals. Deontology as such places an emphasis on avoiding the violation of certain ethical norms and is imbued with responsibility for one's own errors and actions rather than the errors of others. For instance, there are situations when, because of uncertainty, there is a need to recognize the limits of predictions, and economists have to be aware of the limitations of economic policies and their implications. Deontology has the impact of an institution: it regularizes the behavior of individuals and guides them toward respecting certain moral rules. This system is concerned with the existence of moral principles that guide human action/ economic action and the acceptance of moral rules that can become universal. The Kantian view of the individual is that of an independent, autonomous agent who makes rational and ethical decisions (Wight, 2015). According to Wight (2015), Kantian ethics states that one should be able to universalize his/ her actions, and one should always treat others as important ends in themselves. One of the main criticisms raised against deontology is that duties might conflict and harm other parties (Staveren, 2007; Wight, 2015). We contend that if moral rules and principles are self-assumed by autonomous/rational individuals, this will make the acceptance of morality less rigid, and it will be converted into individual actions.

Virtue-ethics strives for excellence in character, moral fulfillment and the continuous cultivation and development of moral features. It contends that although humans are submitted to errors and temptations, individuals can surpass such issues and can develop and cultivate their virtues and become better human beings and citizens. In an Aristotelian framework, individuals are social beings, shaped by social context, family and other social institutions, who need to be educated and taught/inspired by moral principles and values (Wight, 2015). The main criticism brought to virtue-ethics theory is that circumstances shape action (Wight, 2015), although one cannot separate action from character.

Economists can learn and operate within all these moral frameworks (cf. Dolfsma, 2006) there thus is, or can be, ethics *in* economics (cf. Figure 1.1). This book is, however, particularly focused on the ethical behavior of *economists* and thus mainly concerned with deontology and professional economics ethics. To make clear what we mean by this and at the same time show where our volume of excellent essays contributes, Figure 1.1 visually distinguishes between

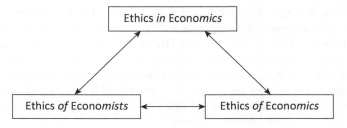

Figure 1.1 Of Ethics and Economics

three aspects of the relation between the domains of ethics and economics that are all too often conflated.

Economics is often blamed for a number of things. It is blamed, a.o., for having no conceptual space for ethical concerns. This is obviously untrue, even for the (fragmenting) mainstream. Neoclassical economics is based firmly on a legitimate ethics framework – that of consequentialist or utilitarian ethics. Indeed, quite a few scholars who have contributed to consequentialist ethics' development, including Mill and Bentham, are often viewed as economists. Some critics of economics who claim it does not have an ethical view actually mean to say, perhaps, that the utilitarian view is an inferior or inappropriate ethics.

What we have more sympathy for here is the view that in economics it has been too common not to consider the ethical impact of the insights developed and distributed by it on economies and societies. There is an ethics *of* economics (cf. Figure 1.1) that a positivist approach to economics has all too often claimed it may not need to be concerned about. Overly convinced about their own insights and not engaging in discussions with different views inside the economics discipline itself, or from other areas, economists have often laid the blame for negative consequences with policymakers. They will see their advice diluted in policies actually implemented, and economists cannot be bothered by 'non-economic' indicators of how the effects of economic policy are to be assessed. Even effects on the income distribution of different policies tend to be ignored.

This has led to a situation in which the ethical capabilities *of* economists themselves (cf. Figure 1.1) are at times questioned and hence the thought that, for instance, an oath for bankers and other employees in the financial industry forcing them to take a particular (!) ethical stance might make them less likely to show the kinds of behaviors that are believed to have led, in part, to the financial crisis of 2008–9. We are not saying such an oath is unwanted and will not have the expected effect, but the premise that this may be all that is needed to prevent a future financial crisis is not necessarily true. The explicit argument in this volume of essays is that the conclusion that economists have no ethics unless one is forced upon them is an unwarranted one.

Economists might independently develop an ethical view more or less derived, perhaps, from their upbringing or from the communities in which they have are still living. This volume claims, and we believe shows, that there are economics-specific experiences that economists may have undergone that will have affected their ethical views. In this volume, some of the most important of these experiences are discussed at some length. In doing so, the authors at times venture into discussing the other two aspects of where and how economics and ethics rub against each other.

The first two chapters of this book attempt to discuss the education and training of the 'ethical economist': what it means to train and educate an ethical economist and what is needed for economics to become an ethical profession. DeMartino's chapter falls within the domain of economists' ethics and deals with the essential question of how we can change economic pedagogy to accommodate progress in professional economics ethics. Professional economics ethics helps with the understanding of complex economic systems, the fallible nature of economic and human knowledge and the fact that even good economists sometimes act badly, with consequential errors. DeMartino argues, analyzing pedagogical reform in both undergraduate and postgraduate training, that ethical training necessitates a new curriculum. Following behavioral ethicists, economists need more than just exposure to ethical virtues and principles; they need analytical sophistication and practical wisdom/phronesis, the use of case studies of complex situations with students and training with applied economists. The main solution proposed by DeMartino is that of internships, apprenticeships and immersion of economists in the communities they hope to serve – the main example being the experience of development economists with The Exposure and Dialogue Program (EDP) initiated by Karl Osner in the 1980s.

Mearman and McMaster endorse DeMartino's prudential and precautionary ethical principles but go further than this by arguing that ethical economics has to be more than harm avoidance and has to entail *care* that centers on the relation between care-giver and care-recipient. The authors argue that standard, mainstream economics, despite contrary efforts, is *value-laden* and predicated on a particular ethical and philosophical understanding, i.e., *utilitarianism*. In considering how one might, via teaching, create the ethical economist imbued with care, the authors consider the nature of economic textbooks and examine curriculum governance frameworks, ending with a discussion of the Trolley Problem as a device to introduce ethics in the economics classroom.

O'Sullivan examines the philosophical arguments for the removal of normativity and normative analysis from economics and what the implications of this issue are on the personal responsibility of economists. The roots of economics are discussed alongside its origins as a branch of Applied Ethics when economic questions were considered to be inherently ethical. Contrary to the common knowledge that the marginalist revolution brought a separation of ethics and economics, O'Sullivan argues that the real break of ethics from economics took place with Milton Friedman's (1953) work, *Essays in Positive Economics*. Value judgments have been banned from economics. O'Sullivan advances a Myrdallian critique of Friedman's work, discussing the methodological impossibility of a value-free economics. The solutions proposed by O'Sullivan are a return of ethics to economics, a development of a greater sense of personal responsibility for economists and education for economists and business studies students in moral and political philosophy.

Duckworth presents an argument regarding DeMartino's *Economist's Oath* (2011), sustaining the view that the standard account of professional economics ethics fails to engage orthodox economics in a meaningful debate. The harm-based thesis and moral character approach are insufficient to ensure progress regarding a professional ethical code for economists. The result of this debate is "unproductive deadlock". In Duckworth's view, Iris Marion Young's social connection theory of personal responsibility could offer support for DeMartino's thesis. According to Young, individuals must be politically aware, and individual virtues generate a collective responsible action. The implication of Young's ideas for the economics profession is that only *collectively* can economists assume responsibility for the progress of the discipline and societal outcomes and policies.

White contends that economists use two standard tools to evaluate whether an action has good and right consequences: the Pareto improvement and the Kaldor-Hicks compensation test. White advances the Kantian deontological view and brings into discussion the issues of rights, dignity and duty and contrasts this with utilitarianism. Utilitarianism and economists in general do not accept a strong conception of rights. White, using case studies such as anti-trust laws and externalities, recommends that economists should balance both rights and utility considerations in economic theory, practice or policy.

Sindzingre brings into debate the issue of experiments and filed experiments, including randomized controlled trials (RCTs) and the epistemological and ethical aspects they raise. The issues are epistemological because they address the validity of extension of results and causalities from the experiment to wider social and ethical scales, as the experiments are introduced as having a 'more true' quality and relevance for policymakers. Sindzingre argues that it is crucial such methods be questioned in developing countries, where such experiments are designed by donors, on whom developing countries depend for their financing of such methods. The author concludes that the ethical dimension of RCTs appears to be negative and under-addressed by the designers.

Ziliak and Teather-Posadas examine the ethics of econometric research and the categorical mistake made by some economists when considering that ethics is to be left for business, government and policymakers and not for the econometrician. The authors advocate the practice of ethical pluralism and the use/teaching in economics of all types of ethics, from ethics of outcomes to procedures and virtues. Discussing three main limitations of econometric analysis, the authors argue that there is insufficient attention granted to ethics in econometric research and reflect on the following central problems: null hypothesis significance testing, RCTs and frequentist probability theory applied to one set of data. Ziliak and Teather-Posadas conclude with some suggestions for change, including that economists be schooled in ethics at both undergraduate and postgraduate levels, as well as in the avoidance of RCTs and the rejection of statistical significance and Fisherian tests.

Groot and Maassen van den Brink reflect on economists (who work in academia) and their role and influence in the media. The authors see economics as a science that aims to give practical recommendations for a better society. Their thoughts are that most economic research barely makes an impact. For instance, success for a scientific article means an article cited by more than ten other scientists. But for most researchers, the outcome is pure oblivion! According to the authors, economists have a duty to share their perspectives through the media, enhancing the value of the discipline for society. Also, media presence represents a source of accountability for economic researchers. Groot and Maassen van den Brink make recommendations for the qualities needed for an economist appearing in the media and, finally, a code of conduct for media behavior.

Morgan brings to the fore the economic policymaking and positive-normative divide: economists follow a positive agenda of scientific explanation, claiming objectivity while being normative as policy advisors. Economists have not been helped or trained to think of responsibility. The elimination of philosophy of social science, methodology and ethics from economists' education has as an outcome a narrow curriculum that does not foster thinking about value and judgments. The author contends that economists are "limited", and that economic responsibility has become elusive. For economists to become responsible again, the discipline must become a social science again, and economists should reconsider expertise and then address policy recommendations. Without public dialogue and competency in research, economists cannot claim credibility in policymaking.

Deirdre McCloskey, in the final chapter, offers a succinct reflection on the range of contributions in this volume and about the way in which the ethical perspectives of economists is shaped through the experiences they have encountered during their professional lives.

References

Boulding, K.E. (1968), "Economics as a Moral Science", Presidential Address delivered at the Eighty-First Meeting of the American Economic Association, Chicago, IL, December 29, 1968.

DeMartino, G. (2011), *The Economist's Oath*, New York: Oxford University Press.

Dolfsma, Wilfred (2006), " Accounting as Applied Ethics: Teaching a Discipline", *Journal of Business Ethics*, 63(3): 209-215.

Friedman, Milton (1953), "The Methodology of Positive Economics" in: M. Friedman, *Essays in Positive Economics*, Chicago: University of Chicago Press, pp. 3-43.

Van Staveren, I. (2007), "Beyond Utilitarianism and Deontology: Ethics in Economics", *Review of Political Economy*, 19(1): 21–35, January.

Wight, J.B. (2015), *Ethics in Economics: An Introduction to Moral Frameworks*, Stanford, CA: Stanford University Press.

2 Training the 'ethical economist'

George F. DeMartino

Introduction

How might economic pedagogy change were the economics profession to commit itself to the advancement of professional economic ethics? I posed the question in *The Economist's Oath*, which appeared in 2011. At the time, the question seemed just a little far-fetched. Most economists had given the matter no thought whatsoever; the leading economic associations the world over paid virtually no attention to their professional ethical responsibilities; and professional economic ethics as a field of study did not exist and certainly appeared to be a non-starter.

Since then, the ethical terrain in economics has shifted. Leading economic associations are beginning to grapple with what they should do to promote ethical behavior among economists. Several are now following the lead of the National Association of Forensic Economists (NAFE) in adopting codes of ethical behavior to guide their members. As I write this (in April 2018), the venerable American Economic Association (AEA), perhaps the most important economic association in the world, is poised to adopt an aspirational (non-binding) code of conduct for its members, better thought of as a statement of ethical principles, and Britain's Royal Economic Society has formed an ad hoc committee to investigate whether it, too, should adopt a code. The AEA draft currently available commits economists to values that are widely recognized by other professions as central to professional practice, including honesty, transparency, disclosure of conflicts of interest, civil and respectful dialogue, and "equal opportunity and equal treatment for all economists regardless of age, gender, race, ethnicity, national origin" and other attributes. Importantly, the draft states economists have not only an "individual responsibility" for their behavior but also "a collective responsibility to promote responsible conduct in the economics profession" that includes "developing institutional arrangements and a professional environment that promote free expression concerning economics" (draft available at: www.aeaweb.org/resources/member-docs/draft-code-of-conduct). What is particularly notable about the statement is that since its inception in 1885, the AEA has been dismissive of the idea of professional economic ethics and, in particular, of a code of conduct for economists.[1]

The AEA's about-face reflects many factors, including important changes in the leadership of the organization and a series of events that brought the profession unwanted attention. The film *Inside Job* (released in 2010) and subsequent research (see Flitter, Cooke, and da Costa 2010; Carrick-Hagenbarth and Epstein 2012) demonstrated that leading academic economists in the period prior and subsequent to the emergence of the global financial crisis (GFC) of 2008 who took policy positions regarding financial regulation often failed to disclose their own significant ties to the financial industry when publishing their work or providing expert testimony in legislative hearings over bills that affected their clients. Until that episode, it is safe to say that the profession had never engaged the question of when economists should disclose possible conflicts of interest. Then, in 2017, Alice Wu published a study of over a million anonymous posts to the Economics Job Market Rumors message board that demonstrated a startling degree of misogyny among economists using the site. The research was quickly reported in the *New York Times* (Wolfers 2017) and other major outlets. To its credit, the AEA Executive Council (under the leadership of President Alvin Roth) took the important step of constituting an Ad Hoc Committee to Consider a Code of Professional Conduct – and it is that committee that crafted the draft of a code and is recommending its formal adoption.[2] To get a sense of the extent of the rupture with past practice, we should consider the outcome of a proposal to the Executive Council in 1994 for a code of conduct. With Amartya Sen presiding over the meeting, the Council rejected the proposal out of hand. One member quipped, "Sure, we'll have a code – its first principle should be 'don't predict the interest rate!'" The Council members laughed at the joke, and the discussion was terminated.

At the same time, new literature has begun to emerge examining the ethical challenges associated with economic practice. Economists perform a broad range of activities, and the challenges they confront vary depending on context. That breadth and diversity are in evidence in the new *Oxford Handbook of Professional Economic Ethics* (DeMartino and McCloskey, eds.), which appeared in 2016. The *Handbook* comprises over 35 essays that explore a wide range of economic practice and the ethical questions that arise in each.

So the question of how we should train ethical economists has significance today that it lacked just a few years ago. At a minimum, the profession is coming to recognize that economic practice is more ethically fraught than it had presumed, and that inattention to ethical matters had contributed to a situation in which some or perhaps many economists were violating widely recognized precepts of ethical professional behavior. Presuming the profession aspires to do better, we can now hope for a reasonable and even productive conversation about economic pedagogy, especially – but not only – at the graduate level.

Professional ethics – *not a code*

What should training in professional economic ethics entail? The response that perhaps comes to mind for those economists favorably disposed to some ethical training for graduate students is likely to be a one-off session that identifies and warns aspiring economists about acceptable and unacceptable behavior. In this view, ethical training entails acquainting students with lists of professional dos and don'ts. In the economist's mind, when and how to disclose conflicts of interest; the urgent need for honesty and transparency in data gathering, manipulation, reporting, and sharing; the inappropriateness of misogynist, racist, or other bigoted sentiments; and the need to avoid plagiarism just about cover the scope of professional ethics. By bringing these issues to the attention of PhD students, the profession meets its ethical obligations.

This thinking is badly flawed (DeMartino and McCloskey 2016). It reflects a conceptual mistake in which the economist conflates professional economic ethics with a code of conduct. The two are and should be recognized as distinct. Professional economic ethics is not a set of commandments or a checklist. It is something much more important and consequential. Professional economic ethics refers to a practice of critical inquiry into the myriad ethical questions that arise in the context of and as a consequence of economic practice. It refers to new conversations over the full range of ethical challenges economists necessarily confront in their work – among economists, between economists and other professionals, and, critically, between economists and those economists purport to serve through their professional practice. It would require new journals, texts, newsletters, and/or bulletins targeting ethical questions. It would entail research by highly trained economic ethicists focused broadly on the ethically fraught nature of economic practice and conferences featuring lively debate on the ethical substance of economic practice, ranging from the most routine and prosaic to the most exceptional and dramatic cases. Organizing the new field would be the questions, What does it mean to be an ethical economist, and what would it mean for economics to be an ethical profession?

One point about the distinction between codes and professional ethics deserves particular emphasis. In the mind of the typical economist who conflates professional ethics with a code, its intent is to prevent morally compromised agents from doing bad things. But to achieve this objective, the code must entail sanctions – penalties the agent takes into consideration when deciding how to behave. Without sanctions, the argument goes, the code will do nothing to improve behavior while giving outsiders a false sense of professional propriety. A non-binding code would provide cover for charlatans and frauds to do evil. And since there is no easy or reliable way to enforce a code of conduct for economists – and since most economists would not countenance state regulation of the profession – we are better off with none.

The problem with this logic is that professional ethics is not, in the first instance, about preventing crooks, frauds, and charlatans from acting badly. Professional ethics is about helping virtuous practitioners do good in a complex world where what it is right or good to do is often uncertain. One central problem is that today most professionals and most economists work in institutions where they confront tangled webs of relationships that appear to push and pull them in contradictory ways. An economist working for a government agency or a consulting firm or an NGO has obligations to supervisors, peers, and subordinates and may also have obligations to "clients," third parties who may also be affected by the economist's actions, the institution's funders, and others. Sometimes these obligations may all line up in the same direction, but other times they may conflict, leaving the economist to fret over whether her obligations to clients should override her duties to the institution's funders or her superiors or third parties. Professional ethics is intended to speak to those in these kinds of situations who believe in what they profess – who seek to do good work defined as work with integrity, work they themselves can believe in. At present, many economists believe they are not able to do good work (see DeMartino 2011, chapter 3).

This view of professional ethics suggests the severe limitations to codes of conduct. Helping a virtuous economist do good under complex conditions entails something other than listing dos and don'ts since, in many contexts, there are no suitable, clear-cut, definitive decision rules. An aspirational code may assert "respect the integrity of those you serve," but that dictate does not mechanically decide the matter when it conflicts with equally important warnings, such as the imperative to avoid harming those you serve and others. Whether or not a profession adopts a code, and whether or not that code is aspirational (as is the proposed AEA code) or binding and backed by sanctions, the need for professional ethics as a tradition of critical inquiry remains. The watchwords of professional ethics are education, elucidation, and aspiration – not regulation, legislation, or condemnation. From this perspective, professional ethics is something to be cultivated at every juncture of practice, including engaging non-specialists who must rely on the profession about the ethically fraught nature of the work, training of new initiates to the field, and continuous interrogation of one's own conduct (and the conduct of one's peers), with an eye to continuous ethical maturation.

The question remains as to how economic pedagogy might change were the economics profession to commit itself to the advancement of professional economic ethics. With these preliminaries behind us, we can now begin to furnish an answer. Others, such as Rob Garnett (2009, 2016) and Michael Butler (Garnett and Butler 2009), have explored how undergraduate economic training might be reformed in order to prepare students for their roles as democratic citizens. Here, I will focus on graduate economic training – the training that intends to prepare students to join the economic profession. But I will begin with an examination of possible transformations in undergraduate training that are consistent with the project of meeting our professional ethical responsibilities to those we serve.

Pedagogical reform in economic training – undergraduate teaching[3]

Economists teaching introductory economics courses to undergraduate audiences affect how these students view economic expertise. Unlike most other professions, economists have the chance to train future "clients" of economic services, from political and business leaders to citizens, about the services economists supply. As a consequence, economics professors face difficult ethical questions. What sense of the field and of the profession should they try to cultivate in these students? In particular, what will the instructor attempt to convey about the power of economic theory and the capabilities of economists?

Economics professors can instill a sense of awe regarding the economist's knowledge and capacities. They can persuade their students that economic knowledge has achieved a status and explanatory power on par with the natural sciences. They can present economic methods as adequate to the task of deriving optimal policy. In these and other ways, they can persuade their audiences that economists therefore know best about economic matters, and that society should defer to their judgments.

The alternative is to cultivate in students awareness of the limitations of economic science. They can emphasize the "irreparable ignorance" (DeMartino 2017) economists are up against as they try to understand, predict, and control inherently complex systems. They can affirm the existence of the as yet unknown and the forever unknowable in their field. They can introduce their students to diverse theoretical approaches – including neoclassical, Austrian, post-Keynesian, institutionalist, behavioral, social, feminist, steady-state, Marxist, and others – so that students can come to see how these distinct schools of thought produce their own plausible insights about the economy and economic policy.[4]

Friedrich Hayek provides a reliable guide on this matter, and his warning should be taken to heart, not just by economists on the right, but across the political and theoretical spectrum:

> If man is not to do more harm than good in his efforts to improve the social order, he will have to learn that in this, as in all other fields where essential complexity of an organized kind prevails, he cannot acquire the full knowledge which would make mastery of the events possible. . . . The recognition of the insuperable limits to his knowledge ought indeed to teach the student of society a lesson in humility which should guard him against becoming an accomplice in men's fatal striving to control society.
>
> (1978, 34)

The desire to demonstrate professional competence to students is certainly one factor generating a mismatch between economic teaching and economic research. The economics taught in the undergraduate curriculum, David Colander argues, emphasizes a "simple system" model of the economy that yields an "economics of control" approach to policy. The simple system approach to theory presumes what Colander calls the "holy trinity" of rationality, greed, and equilibrium that allows the economist to predict agent behavior and the outcome of their interactions from first principles. The approach generates the impression that economists have sufficient knowledge to generate effective policy with predictable outcomes. This story remains the centerpiece of the economics curriculum today. "It is a control story in which there is a knowable social optimum that government policy is designed to achieve" (Colander 2005, 254).

In contrast, contemporary mainstream economic theory has joined various heterodox traditions in moving away from this simple model of the economy to an understanding of the economy as an irreducibly "complex" system. The complex system approach is predicated on an alternative and less determinant trinity of purposeful behavior, enlightened self-interest, and sustainability (2005, 251). The complexity view understands the economy to encompass emergent properties at the macro level, path dependencies, discontinuities, multiple equilibriums, and the like. In place of the illusion of control, the complex system view yields a "muddling through" policy approach in which the economist works as an inductive social mechanic, perpetually experimenting and then evaluating and adjusting strategies and always attentive to surprise and anomalies.

The effect of these methodological innovations on economists' self-conception as policy designers is profound. Rather than imagining themselves to be "*infinitely bright . . . with full knowledge of the system design,*" they now recognize themselves as "*reasonably bright . . . with limited knowledge of the system*" (Colander 2005, 251; emphasis in original).[5]

Over the course of its history, the economics profession has sought to extend its influence over economic policy formation (DeMartino 2011, chapter 4). Undergraduate teaching, I submit, has served as a critical arena in which to pursue that objective. As Paul Samuelson famously put it, "I don't care who writes a nation's laws – or crafts its advanced treaties – if I can write its economics textbooks." The quip points to an important truth – that what economists teach influences how non-economists think about the capacities of economics and economists and amplifies their voice in matters of public policy. But the pursuit of that influence entails the conflict that Colander points to. Other economists are less temperate in their critique. In the view of Deirdre McCloskey (1990), for instance, the profession has purposely cultivated a public that believes it has magic elixirs to solve economic problems, and it happily sells them at exorbitant fees. This state of affairs is untenable. The profession faces an acute obligation to correct this conceit and to deflate its students' and the public's mistaken presumptions about what economists can know, do, and control.

The foregoing suggests the need for reform of undergraduate economic training on ethical grounds in order to enhance the capacities of students to make informed economic judgments, to understand their obligation as democratic citizens to engage critically economists' claims and policy prescriptions, to know what to ask and not ask of economists and to know how to interpret what economists offer in response, and to hold economists accountable for their work. The economics of control approach should be abandoned in the curriculum just as it is being abandoned in research since it promotes a reassuring but dangerous fiction concerning the profession's knowledge and abilities. The fiction threatens to enhance the authority of economists to unwarranted levels and legitimize irresponsible economic interventions.[6]

Pedagogical reform in graduate training

An economics profession that embraces professional ethics would encourage its graduate programs to take steps to ensure students are equipped with an under-standing of the ways in which virtuous economists sometimes act badly, are immersed in the particular ethical questions that arise in professional economic work under the supervision of practitioners, and are provided with guidance and institutional resources when they come up against challenges they are ill-equipped to manage on their own.

New research – behavioral ethics

At present, there is an interesting parallel between behavioral economics and the new field of behavioral ethics. Researchers in both fields are attempting to ascertain how people behave and make sense of their behavior in scenarios with moral content and in artificial (laboratory) settings that mimic day-to-day life. Behavioral ethicists are not moral philosophers parsing the right way to live. They typically do not presume that there is one appropriate ethical pre-cept that should guide decision-makers. Instead, they attempt to ascertain the norms agents espouse and then explore whether those agents act in accordance with their own norms. Recent findings are illuminating and even disturbing. According to leaders in the field Max Bazerman and Ann Tenbrunsel (2011), agents typically expect that they will do the right thing when confronted with moral dilemmas, violate those norms in the moment of decision-making, and then fail to recognize their moral lapses after the fact. Bazerman and Tenbrunsel offer the concept of ethical "blind spots" to convey this pattern. A central idea is "bounded ethicality," which "comes into play when individuals make deci-sions that harm others and when that harm is inconsistent with these decision makers' conscious beliefs and preferences" (Bazerman and Tenbrunsel 2011, 5).

The pattern is troubling: agents who deceive themselves about the appro-priateness of their behavior do not learn and therefore do not mature as moral agents. After the fact, agents instead often concoct explanations for their behav-ior that let them off the moral hook. Bazerman and Tenbrunsel explore pro-cesses of "ethical fading" in which decisions or dilemmas that are ethically fraught come to be defined by the agent facing the dilemma as simpler, ethi-cally neutral decisions. Within a corporation, for instance, an ethical issue such as the marketing of a dangerous product may be reframed as a simple "business decision" and assigned to the accounting department. The ethical nature of the issue fades from view. Ethical fading also occurs when agents apply double standards, giving themselves moral leeway that they would never extend to others. Agents also make quick, intuitive decisions based on their emotions and then manufacture moral rationalizations for their behaviors. They also often are influenced by groupthink, in which collections of agents (such as members of a profession) converge on particular ways of seeing the world, defining problems, and making sense of the group's obligations, privileges, and duties. Once established, groupthink is very difficult to overcome. Neophytes are socialized to the mores of the profession by their elders. In all these instances, there may be no self-opprobrium or cognitive dissonance or moral learning when a virtuous actor acts badly.

Behavioral economists have much to offer the emerging field of behavioral ethics. Indeed, there is substantial overlap between the methods employed and questions explored by behavioral economists and ethicists. How might this research help the economic profession better understand the behavior of its own members, and how might it also contribute to the cultivation of ethical awareness and behavior within the profession? These questions are no doubt more attractive to many economists than are questions about the right ethical norm to guide agents' behavior in the economy since they allow for empirical investigation of the sort economists are already equipped to pursue. A profession committed to promoting ethical behavior ought to promote research into the field of behavioral ethics, with its own members serving as research subjects. The findings should then be taught to economic graduate students to heighten their self-awareness as presumably virtuous but nonetheless suggestible moral agents.

New curriculum

Ethical training for economists would require a new curriculum at the graduate level. In this regard, economics could learn much from fields like law that have struggled with how best to incorporate ethical training into a professional curriculum. Economics might very well have to experiment with the curriculum, learning from failures and successes, on its way to devising successful programs that achieve wide respect among economists and economics students alike. Fortunately, we can draw on the experience of other professions (such as law) and the broad literature that now examines effective pedagogies of ethical practice (e.g., Rhode 1992; Daly, Green, and Pearce 1995; Luban and Millemann 1995).

As the behavioral ethics literature suggests, training the ethical economist requires something more than exposure to ethical principles and problems. Indeed, some evidence suggests that training restricted to moral principles can induce more unethical behavior (Bazerman and Tenbrunsel 2011). Ethical education requires a rethinking of the manner in which the profession conceptualizes what it is that is to be taught and learned and how. The ethical economist needs analytical sophistication, as incompetence can reflect unethical behavior. But she also needs to acquire *phronesis*, or practical wisdom, so that she can translate her analytical competence into interventions that are apt to help those she serves. Practical wisdom also entails attending to the limits of one's science and one's own expertise. It involves self-awareness, the ability to recognize external pressures to compromise one's principles, such as by conforming to the judgments of those in authority when one has good reason to dissent (Kuran 1995), and the fortitude to resist such pressures, especially when others will bear the consequences of one's moral lapses. An emphasis on practical wisdom places the *student* and not just the *subject matter* at the center of the educational enterprise.

The acquisition of practical wisdom can begin in the classroom. Case studies of actual complex situations in which economists have found themselves can prepare students for the challenges that await them. Well-designed simulations that raise difficult technical, practical, and ethical questions of the very sort economists might face in their careers can supplement case work. Equally important is the identity of the instructor. Practitioner-led seminars can draw on the experiences of established economists who have made their careers outside of academia and provide a degree of realism in the training that academic-led seminars may not be able to deliver. Indeed, several respondents in the nonacademic employers' survey commissioned by the AEA Commission on Graduate Education in Economics (COGEE) in 1988 argued for bringing accomplished applied economists into the classroom to share in the instruction of economic graduate students (DeMartino 2011). The proposal makes particular sense in the context of a professional economic ethics that recognizes the multiplicity of skills and competencies the ethical economist must have at her command.

Internships, residencies, and immersions

Adequate training in practical and ethical wisdom requires something other than classroom training, however. It requires directed exposure to the field of applied economics under the guidance of trained specialists who can help the student grasp the complexities of the milieu she enters. Achieving this goal might require student immersion in both the "supply" and "demand" sides of the market for economic practice.

The economist in training needs to acquire the *craft* of economic application. Developing one's craft comprises experience in the institutions that supply economic expertise – the places where applied economists work and in which economic interventions are contemplated, drafted, and pursued. The student needs to learn firsthand what kinds of challenges well-meaning economists face in the bureaucracies and politicized arenas where they struggle to make a difference. How do routine office politics affect the economist's ability to do her work? In the public sector, how do partisan politics interfere as she attempts to forecast, advise, counsel, and prescribe? How do veteran economists in such environments maintain (or sacrifice) their integrity in the face of the various opportunities, pressures, and constraints they face? What do they do when asked posthaste for a complicated report or forecast that would require days or weeks of work were it to be done properly? What do they do when the only data available are unreliable for the kind of study required of them? Classroom discussion of these issues may be too remote to do much good. In contrast, witnessing these problems firsthand in the context of the workplace is apt to capture the student's attention and motivate her to find a resolution to a degree that classroom exercises cannot replicate (Luban and Millemann1995; Venter 1996).

The economist in training also needs to be immersed in the kinds of communities that need and will be served by economic expertise. She needs to identify and cultivate the skills and sensitivity that will enable her to learn about the specific economic, cultural, political, and social institutions that bear on economic affairs in these communities. She needs to decipher the amorphous but consequential norms and conventions (such as conceptions of fairness) that community members share and that affect how they respond to incentives and constraints. She needs to gain access, even if imperfectly, to the community's aspirations, anxieties, and mores; their human and physical resources; and other characteristics that enable and/or inhibit economic practices and bear directly on the possibility and prospects for the success of economic reform. What are the most pressing social problems, and what risks and sacrifices are appropriate in addressing them – not in the eyes of a detached, dispassionate professional economist but in the eyes of the community itself?

These arguments call for protracted immersion of the economist in training in the communities she hopes to serve to allow for direct observation and extensive dialogue. Immersion – in the form of internships and apprenticeships – could promote the ability to translate abstract economic concepts into practice. But it must also engender phronesis that allows the student to understand the limits of economic theory and the wisdom of pragmatic adjustment and compromise when situations on the ground contradict blackboard schematics. The immersion must be structured to inculcate cultural sensitivity and ethical sensibilities. The new initiates to the profession need to develop the ethnographic skills of the anthropologist. For economics departments, this proposal would require the implementation of strategies to continue training and guidance during student placements. Placements must be treated as fundamental to the training of the economist as is the core curriculum. Otherwise, they would come to be viewed as a period in which students mark time awaiting their freedom when they can move on to more important activities.

Architects, engineers, and other professionals are required to serve extended apprenticeships before licensing that allows them to work independently; school teachers must serve as interns under the observation of an experienced mentor before completing their degrees. Economists, too, need such an instrument in order to impart the kinds of wisdom and judgment that are essential to ethical economic practice, but that are virtually ignored today in graduate economic training. Graduate programs could create linkages with the providers and users of economic services that place their students in guided internships and apprenticeships. Institutions ranging from public sector, development, and multilateral agencies to economic consulting firms and nongovernmental organizations in developed and developing countries could create opportunities for placements that provide economists in training with a kind of exposure that the classroom, at its best, cannot offer.

Over the years, several economists have made suggestions of this sort. In his comprehensive study, Bowen (1953) cited the need for internships for economists. Coats (1992, 349) echoed this sentiment:

> [The] best way to develop creativity, tacit knowledge, and connoisseurship is through learning by doing, and, to this end, internships in business, banking, and government during graduate education, possibly as a requirement, would help to narrow the perceived gap between what is and what should be taught and learned.

Colander (1998) has called for consideration of the creation of two tracks in economic training: one for those who intend to make their careers in the research university and another for those who seek to apply their expertise in other venues (see Colander 1998). And, more recently, Jeffrey Sachs has expressed concern about the failure of the profession to prepare its members for the "clinical" challenges they will face, especially in the field of development:

> Economists are not trained to think like clinicians, and are rarely afforded clinical experience in their advanced training. A graduate student in an American Ph.D. program in economics may very well study the development crisis in Africa without ever setting foot in the country or countries under study.
>
> (2005, 78)

A promising approach: the exposure and dialogue program

Some NGOs have created opportunities for economists and other development experts to participate in immersions in the communities they target in their work. The most important of these is the "Exposure and Dialogue Program," or EDP, developed by Karl Osner in the 1980s, when he was an official with Germany's Federal Ministry for Economic Cooperation and Development. Osner created an exposure project for his colleagues at the Ministry; in 1987, he augmented the immersion component of the program with structured dialogues between the development officials and members of the host communities. In recent years, the EDP has blossomed into an ambitious set of initiatives and institutions, such as the German Association for Exposure and Dialogue Programmes (Chen et al. 2004, 10; see also the "Epilogue" to that report, written by Osner).

The goal of the EDP is to break down the barriers between those who provide and those who are targeted by economic development initiatives to personalize as "subjects" in their own right those who are the intended beneficiaries of these interventions. The program entails three components: exposure, reflection, and dialogue. Each component is taken to be vital to achieving EDP's goals, which are defined as "*transferring the know how* of innovative people-based self-help-organisations *from the South to the North* for fighting poverty in the South by shaping pro-poor policies in the institutions of development cooperation in the North" (Chen et al. 2004, 87; emphasis in original).

A particularly important EDP began in 2003 in India (see Chen et al. 2004). The "Cornell–SEWA–WIEGO EDP" involves two women's organizations and several economists from Cornell University. The Self Employed Women's Association (SEWA) of India is a 700,000 member organization that organizes self-employed women in India to secure full employment, self-reliance, and independence. The organization's members are among the poorest of the poor, owing in part to the obligations they face to perform household labor while also seeking outside remuneration (often in the informal sector). SEWA began conducting EDPs in 1991; this work is organized by SEWA's technical branch, the SEWA Academy (SEWA-World Bank 2006). SEWA conducted its first EDP with the World Bank in 2003 when it placed 10 development expert "guests" in homes of its members.

A second partner in this EDP is Women in Informal Employment: Globalizing and Organizing (WIEGO). WIEGO is an international policy network of researchers, activists, and practitioners working on issues facing the working poor in the informal economy. At present, WIEGO's secretariat is located at Harvard University, and its work is coordinated by Dr. Marty Chen, a specialist in South Asia regional studies. Cornell University provided a natural partner for this EDP, owing to the presence on its faculty of economist Ravi Kanbur. Kanbur had helped to initiate and also participated in a SEWA EDP when he served as the Director of the World Development Report team that authored the *World Development Report 2000/2001* subtitled "Attacking Poverty." The three parties structured the Cornell–SEWA–WIEGO EDP to establish understanding and dialogue between neoclassical labor market economists and the poor. In its words,

> the basic objective of the Cornell–SEWA–WIEGO EDP at SEWA is to start a dialogue between mainstream economists, SEWA activists, and WIEGO researchers around key assumptions of neo-classical economics – and neo-liberal economic policies – which "trouble" ground-level activists and researchers working on issues of employment and labor.
>
> (Chen et al. 2004, 96)

Like other EDPs, the program involves placing development experts with host members of SEWA for very short visits. In this case, six SEWA members opened up their homes to participants for two nights. Researchers from WIEGO and economists from Cornell worked, ate, and slept alongside host family members. The immersion was followed by two days of dialogue at the SEWA Academy, one half-day of which involved discussion with the host women, while the remainder involved SEWA facilitators and officials, the founder of SEWA (Ela Bhatt), the Cornell economists, and the WIEGO researchers (Chen et al. 2004, 11).

One might be forgiven for skepticism. How could such a short visit have an appreciable effect on the participants? It is therefore striking to read the personal and technical reflections of the economists who participated. Labor economist Gary Fields reports that his immersion changed his understanding of the minimum wage in the context of the community he visited. During his visit, SEWA representatives met with officials at the Gujarat Commissioner of Labor's Office "to establish a minimum wage for kite-makers" and "to establish a Provident Fund for bedi workers [tobacco rollers]" (Chen et al. 2004, 36). Fields sat in on the meetings and was profoundly affected:

> Because of what I saw on the ground, my professional judgment about minimum wages and supplementary benefits changed. With the standard labor economics model in mind, I had worried that the minimum wage might hurt the very women it was meant to help, because of job losses. In this context, though, the minimum wage does not act as a wage floor. It acts as an aspirational target. . . . Set in this way by negotiators who take full account of possible job losses as well as earnings gains, the minimum wage and Provident Fund are meant to help all of the women in their respective occupations, and not, as is often the case in other contexts, insiders at the expense of outsiders. This kind of "wage" increase is something that I favor. Without this experience on the ground, that is not something I would have said two days earlier.
>
> (Chen et al. 2004, 36)

For Marty Chen, insights like these represent the most important outcome of the EDP. The EDP is crucial for enabling economists to begin to understand that the abstract, deductive modeling and statistical testing upon which their science depends are insufficient to grasp the nature of the problems facing the poor. The worlds the poor inhabit are marked by complexities economists tend to suppress in the pursuit of explanatory simplicity, universality, and tractability. They often ignore features of social life that do not lend themselves to quantification. This impulse comes to economists naturally by virtue of their training.

Participation in the EDP creates opportunities for economists to face up to the limitations of this kind of knowledge. It alerts them to the value of the ways of knowing of anthropologists, who revel in the particularities of the contexts they encounter. In Chen's view, the natural antipathy of economists to such ways of knowing can lead to consequential error. For instance, it leads economists to neglect questions pertaining to the quality of data. Economists often employ data gathered for one purpose in other contexts where they are inappropriate, without awareness of what is at stake. In contrast, anthropologists understand how hard it is to gather good, reliable data. They are therefore much less willing than economists to invest any particular data set with the authority to settle theoretical questions or determine policy interventions (author interview with Chen Nov. 13, 2008).

The work of Ravi Kanbur reveals the transformative power of the EDP immersions (see Kanbur 2016). In a series of papers written over the years that he has been involved in EDPs, he has explored in a respectful way the distinct worldviews economists and community advocates and activists bring to bear on matters pertaining to economic policy. Kanbur (2001) argues that the two groups disagree on three fundamental issues: aggregation, time horizons, and market structure and power. Economists tend to what Kanbur calls the "Ministry of Finance" view of economic affairs. This perspective takes a bird's-eye view of the economy that involves extensive aggregation, reflected in the importance placed on measures such as GDP/capita. Economists tend to take a long-term view of the effects of economic policy, which encourages them to tolerate substantial short-term adjustment costs. Finally, economists tend to presume a competitive model when analyzing an economy – one that discounts the presence of economic power. In contrast, community advocates impose what Kanbur calls the "Civil Society" perspective. This is a "worm's-eye" view that emphasizes the disaggregated impact of economic interventions and pays particular attention to inequality by gender, ethnicity, race, and region in assessing policy. The Civil Society view emphasizes the salience of short-term rather than long-term policy effects because vulnerable communities often cannot weather economic dislocation of any duration in hopes of subsequent improvements. Finally, this perspective recognizes that markets often are the site of local monopoly power; indeed, this perspective is attuned to the presence of power in social relationships at all levels of analysis, and so it finds the economist's emphasis on perfect competition to be extraordinarily naive (Kanbur 2001; also see Kanbur 2007, 2009).

The EDP experience has promoted a mutually beneficial dialogue between development economists and the communities they target in their work – one that, for the economists, has resulted in greater understanding, respect for the poor, and, especially, humility. Kanbur argues that the EDP has encouraged him to realize that "the greatest weakness of economics is that it doesn't recognize or understand its own weaknesses." One learns from the EDP that "one needs both kinds of knowing: the deductive and the attention to particulars, and to context. The experience changes the way you relate to other economists and other professionals; you become more careful about your models, about what they capture and what they miss" (author interview with Kanbur May 18, 2009). Kanbur emphasizes the enduring effects of the EDP; he and his colleagues are now less apt to presume and to impose the competitive market model in their policy work. They are also less apt to default to high levels of aggregation at the expense of disaggregated analyses and to overlook the short run in policy assessment.

The transformative effect of the EDP suggests the pedagogical value of longer immersions for students who are placed in targeted communities during their graduate training. The EDP format is certainly too demanding of host families to permit long stays. The challenge for the economics profession is to explore and establish institutional means for placements that are manageable for communities but also pedagogically useful for students. The world of NGOs represents one possible avenue for institutional collaboration that could create such immersion opportunities. One can also imagine the creation of new organizations – "Economists without Borders," for instance – that seek to achieve the dual purpose of serving communities' economic needs while also providing on-the-job training for economics graduate students. Such programs would not necessarily require students to travel far, or even leave home, since many universities today have established "service learning" programs that seek to contribute to the well-being of their host communities.

Conclusion

How does the profession move from its current stance on ethics training to the kinds of initiatives discussed here? The critical steps can be taken by individual PhD programs, where small experiments in pedagogy can be undertaken at low cost. The AEA has a role to play in this regard, establishing conduits for reporting on best practices and even incentivizing programs through grants or other support to take steps to introduce ethics training. The AEA already sponsors the annual Conference on Teaching and Research in Economic Education. That venue provides opportunities for pioneers in professional economic ethics to present their ideas and practices to peers. The various journals on economic teaching and pedagogy also provide space for exploration of new ideas and initiatives, provided their editorial boards recognize ethical training as a legitimate and even important area for future research and innovation.

The central point is that introducing ethical training does not require heroic efforts, large expenditures, or readjustments in what graduate programs or the economic associations do. It bears repeating that professional ethics entails a sustained, careful, and critical conversation, and that is something the economics profession already knows how to sustain. It does not require a huge new infrastructure to police the profession or enforce a particular conception of what it is right for economists to think and do. Professional economic ethics is politically agnostic. Professional ethics training can and probably should emerge piecemeal, through trial and error. Fortunately, training the ethical economist will benefit from the parallel moves in the profession now underway to reckon with its professional obligations. The further the economic profession goes in engaging its ethical duties, the greater will be the need and opportunities for new initiatives that target the cultivation of ethical sensibilities and practice in the profession.

Notes

1   See the historical account of AEA thinking on professional codes of conduct in DeMartino (2011, ch. 4).
2   A range of other economic associations in the US and beyond have by now adopted codes. An incomplete list of economic organizations with codes can be found here: https://georgedemartino.com/econ-ethical-codes-of-conduct/.
3   I draw liberally here and in the subsequent section on (and reproduce some text from) DeMartino (2011, ch. 12), which explores some of these ideas in greater detail.
4   See the symposium in the *International Journal of Pluralism and Economics Education* (2011, vol. 2, no. 1) on "Contending Perspectives, 20 Years On: What Have Our Students Learned?"
5   Perhaps the most prominent 20th century advocate of an experimental approach to policy is Albert O. Hirschman. See Grabel (2017) for an elucidation and application of Hirschman's approach to contemporary policy and institutional innovations in global financial governance.
6   Economists can also affect the moral sensibilities of their students, for better or worse, as they teach economic theory. Research has demonstrated that by teaching the neoclassical assumption of rationality as narrow, self-interested behavior, economists might unwittingly cultivate that personality trait in their students (see Frank, Gilovich, and Regan 1993; Bowie 1991; Gintis and Khurana 2008).

References

Bazerman, M.H., and A.E. Tenbrunsel. 2011. *Blind Spots: Why We Fail to Do What's Right and What to Do About It*. Princeton: Princeton University Press.

Bowen, H.R. 1953. "Graduate education in economics," *American Economic Review Supplement* 43 (Part 2) (September): 1–223.

Bowie, N.E. 1991. "Challenging the Egoistic Paradigm," *Business Ethics Quarterly* 1(1): 1–21.

Carrick-Hagenbarth, Jessica, and Gerald Epstein. 2012. "Dangerous Interconnectedness: Economists' Conflicts of Interest, Ideology and Financial Crisis," *Cambridge Journal of Economics* (January).

Chen, M. *et al.*, eds. 2004. "Reality and Analysis: Personal and Technical Reflections on the Working Lives of Six women," Cornell-SEWA-WIEGO, April. Available at: www.arts.cornell.edu/poverty/kanbur/EDPCompendium.pdf

Coats, A.W. 1992. "Changing Perceptions of American Graduate Education in Economics, 1953-1991," *Journal of Economic Education*, 23(3): 341-352.

Colander, D. 1998. "The Sounds of Silence: The Profession's Response to the COGEE Report," *American Journal of Agricultural Economics* 80(3): 600–607.

———. 2005. "What Economists Teach and What Economists Do," *Journal of Economic Education* 36(3): 249–260.

Daly, M.C., B.A. Green, and R.G. Pearce. 1995. "Contextualizing Professional Responsibility: A New Curriculum for a New Century," *Law and Contemporary Problems* 58(3/4): 193–211.

DeMartino, G.F. 2011. *The Economist's Oath: On the Need for and Content of Professional Economic Ethics*. New York, Oxford.

———. 2017. "The Specter of Ignorance in Economics," Unpublished Paper Delivered at the Annual Meetings of the Association for Social Economics (ASE), at ASSA Meetings, Chicago, January.

DeMartino, G.F., and D.N. McCloskey. 2016. "Introduction, Or Why this Handbook?" in DeMartino, G.F., and D.N. McCloskey, eds. *The Oxford Handbook of Professional Economic Ethics*. New York, Oxford: 3–10.

Flitter, Emily, Kristina Cooke, and Pedro da Costa. 2010. "Special Report: For Some Professors, Disclosure Is Academic," Reuters. Available at www.reuters.com/article/2010/12/20/us-academics-con icts-idUSTRE6BJ3LF20101220

Frank, R.H., T. Gilovich, and D.T. Regan. 1993. "Does Studying Economics Inhibit Cooperation?" *Journal of Economic Perspectives* 7(2): 159–171.

Garnett, R.F. 2009. "Liberal Learning as Freedom: A Capabilities Approach to Undergraduate Education," *Studies in Philosophy & Education* 28(5): 437–447.

———. 2016. "Ethics and Learning in Undergraduate Economics Education," in DeMartino, G.F., and D.N. McCloskey, eds. *The Oxford Handbook of Professional Economic Ethics*. New York, Oxford: 714–733.

Garnett, R.F., and M.R. Butler. 2009. "Should Economic Educators Care About Students' Academic Freedom?" *International Journal of Pluralism and Economics Education* 1(1/2): 148–160.

Gintis, H. and R. Khurana. 2008. "Corporate Honesty and Business Education: A Behavioral Model," in P.J. Zak, ed. *Moral Markets: The Critical Role of Values in the Economy*. Princeton, NJ, Princeton University: 300–327.

Grabel, I. 2017. *When Things Don't Fall Apart: Global Financial Governance and Development Finance in an Age of Productive Incoherence*. Cambridge, MA: MIT.

Hayek, F. 1978. *New Studies in Philosophy, Politics, Economics and the History of Ideas*. London, Routledge.

Kanbur, R. 2001. "Economic Policy, Distribution and Poverty: The Nature of Disagreements," *World Development* 29(6): 1083–1094.

———. 2007. "Development Disagreements and Water Privatization: Bridging the Divide," WP 2007–09, Cornell University, Department of Applied Economics and Management.

———. 2009. "A Typical Scene: Five Exposures to Poverty," WP 2009–06, Cornell University, Department of Applied Economics and Management.

———. 2016. "Exposure and Dialogue Programs in the Training of Development Analysts and Practitioners," in DeMartino, G.F., and D.N. McCloskey, eds. *The Oxford Handbook of Professional Economic Ethics*. New York, Oxford: 697–713.

Kuran, T. 1995. *Private Truths, Public Lies: The Social Consequences of Preference Falsification*. Cambridge, MA, Harvard University.

Luban, D., and M. Millemann. 1995. "Good Judgment: Ethics Teaching in Dark Times," *Georgetown Journal of Legal Ethics* 9(31): 31–87.

McCloskey, D.N. 1990. *If You're So Smart: The Narrative of Economic Expertise*. Chicago, IL: University of Chicago.

Rhode, D.L. 1992. "Ethics by the Pervasive Method," *Journal of Legal Education* 42(1): 31–56.

Sachs, J.P. 2005. *The End of Poverty*. New York: Penguin.

SEWA-World Bank. 2006. *Exposure and Dialogue Programmes: A Grassroots Immersion Tool for Understanding Poverty and Influencing Policy*. Ahmedabad, India: SEWA.

Venter, C.M. 1996. "Encouraging Personal Responsibility: An Alternative Approach to Teaching Legal Ethics," *Law and Contemporary Problems* 58(3/4): 287–296.

Wolfers, Justin. 2017. "Evidence of a Toxic Environment for Women in Economics," *New York Times*, August 18. Available at: www.nytimes.com/2017/08/18/upshot/evidence-of-a-toxic-environment-for-women-in-economics.html

Wu, A. 2017. "Gender Stereotyping in Academia: Evidence from Economics Job Market Rumors Forum," December. Available at SSRN: https://ssrn.com/abstract=3051462 or http://dx.doi.org/10.2139/ssrn.3051462

3   Teaching future economists

Andrew Mearman and Robert McMaster

Introduction

The recent global economic crisis has had and is having well-documented impacts on growth and prosperity, employment, equality, poverty, and so forth. Yet it also represents, albeit less dramatically, a major potential crisis for the *economics discipline* (Harcourt, 2010). Economics has received criticism along several dimensions. Despite a conventional methodology of predictivism and claims of scientificity, economists largely failed to predict or explain the crisis. One of the charges was that the very character of economists was culpable. Whilst analyses of the financial crisis focused on the hubris of the financial sector, others laid the same accusation against economists. Contrary to Keynes' aspiration that they be "as humble as dentists" (CW IX, 2013a, p. 332), Fourcade et al. (2015) discuss ironically the 'superiority of economists'. Similarly, other critics, including the film *Inside Job* (2010), DeMartino (2011), and Epstein and Carrick-Hagenbarth (2012), have focused on the professional *ethics of economists*. Earle et al. (2017) speak of an "econocracy", which is profoundly undemocratic by virtue of its obscure technicalities that exclude the bulk of the population from its theoretical machinations, yet the logic of this "econocracy" shapes everyday lives.

One possible explanation for any unethical behaviour could simply be blindness to ethical issues. Economists are not able to consider the ethical dimension because they have not been trained to do so. Typical economics degree courses do not engage with ethics, and where they do, such as those in Philosophy, Politics, and Economics, there is a danger of separation between the disciplines. Most seriously of all, economics is treated as a subject in which ethical questions cannot be asked or answered. Degree courses, at best, begin with a brief discussion of the distinction between positive and normative and an eschewal of the latter. Unfortunately for the economics graduate, this leaves them poorly equipped to address many of the challenges facing them in life and work. Government economists, for example, are required to consider the ethical and political implications of their analyses (DeMartino, 2011). Economists within business cannot ignore corporate social responsibility dimensions of their decisions. However, economics training provides little basis for their doing so (DeMartino, 2011).

This, of course, has not always been the case. As Heilbroner's (1999) famous text made clear, great economists such as Smith, Mill, Marx, and Keynes were 'worldly philosophers', who thought about economic problems in a complex, interdisciplinary way. Included in their armoury was an understanding of ethics. Consequently, rather than making claims to exclude the normative, there was a recognition that economic questions were inherently ethical. This message has been made subsequently by, for example, Gunnar Myrdal (1969), who recognised the value-ladenness of economic language. However, the message has largely been lost. One reason for this was that the great thinkers were confined to footnotes, or errors. *A fortiori*, alternative perspectives in economics that embrace this wider vision of the discipline have been crowded out by a narrow, formalistic mainstream. In our view, in terms of creating ethical economists, these were serious mistakes. Thus, in order to create future economists who take ethics seriously, these trends must be reversed. This chapter considers how this might be done.

The rest of the chapter is organised as follows. In the next section, we offer a picture of current economics teaching, particularly in relation to ethics. Here, we argue that for various reasons, ethics is largely absent from most economics teaching; and this reflects its broader malaise. We suggest that a more pluralist approach to economics might provide greater scope for its inclusion. In the third section, we draw on the insight of George DeMartino in outlining the evolution of the ethical underpinning of standard economics from the Pareto principle to a "maxi-max" approach, which relegates the calculus of harm. From here, we argue that an ethical economics has to be more than harm avoidance and consider *care*. The fourth section initially discusses the nature of care and then moves to considering the different options for teaching ethics in economics. We offer a sketch of an approach to the economics curriculum that might allow future economists to engage fully with an ethics of care.

Current economics teaching

Before laying out how future economists might be more ethical, and specifically how an ethics of care might be embedded within the discipline, it is necessary to sketch the state of the art. We approach this in two ways: the first is to briefly consider the nature of standard economics textbooks, and the second is to examine curriculum governance frameworks.

Mainstream introductory textbooks emphasise at the outset that 'thinking like an economist' involves the recognition of the separability of the positive from the normative. Thus, Hume's dichotomy – the delineation between facts and values – is assumed to be not only conceptually feasible but also necessary and sufficient and therefore *desirable* for a *scientific* economics. Textbook after textbook emphasises how economics, and therefore the professional economist, deals with the positive domain (for example, see Lipsey and Chrystal, 2015; Samuelson and Nordhaus, 2010; Sloman et al., 2015; Taylor and Mankiw, 2017). The subject matter of economics is confined to the search for objective and scientific solutions to the problem of addressing unlimited wants with scarce means. The source of these unlimited wants is never questioned, or even the focus of any reflection. The unsuspecting student is expected to absorb and accept and thereafter devote their efforts to addressing increasingly sophisticated mathematical problems as expressions of economic issues (for example, see Colander's (2007) surveys).

Yet by signalling this position, the standard approach adopts a value-laden platform. By taking unlimited wants as a given, the mainstream, in effect, condones the forces generating and shaping wants. Moreover, wants are conflated with needs, and the meaning of both is confused.

From here, the introductory economics textbook invokes a further substantial value-laden view: equilibrium is desirable. In the search for the optimal solution to the issue of the combination of unlimited wants and scarce resources, the maximisation of net benefits as a sustainable equilibrium, where there is no endogenous force for change, is unquestioningly deemed as good. Moreover, the standard conception of individual behaviour, *Homo economicus*, is, according to Myrdal (1969), imbued with hedonism (behaviour is motivated by the pursuit of pleasure and the avoidance of pain) and therefore demonstrates a particular value set.

In *Objectivity in Social Research*, Myrdal (1969) argues that the morphology of mainstream economics reveals particular values and moral philosophy. In doing so, Myrdal identifies natural law philosophy, which suggests that the natural order of things is desirable. In economics, the core concepts introduced to students in ECON 101, such as equilibrium and markets, are assumed to be the 'natural' order of things. On this, we are reminded of Nobel Prize winner Oliver Williamson's (1975: 20) almost biblical declaration: "In the beginning there were markets".

Students are quickly introduced to the notion that markets possess the power of self-equilibration. It is not a massive leap of logic to configure the state as a malign force where its actions, whether by accident or design, intervene to impede this natural order. This reflects a well-known critique of mainstream texts (for example, Earle et al., 2017). A wide range of commentators have argued that contemporary standard economics is associated with certain policies and approaches to policy. For instance, Zuidhof (2014) is among those who argue that "thinking like an economist" is framed by, and infused with, neoliberal ideology given that textbooks view markets in naturalistic terms. Zuidhof argues that where there is a positive efficiency basis for state provision, as in the provision of public goods, the textbook preference remains for the state employing the market mechanism where possible, such as so-called internal markets in the provision of public services.

Zuidhof's case resonates with Mirowski's (2010) critique of the response of economics texts to the financial crisis. In reference to a popular US introductory text, he (2010: 31) acerbically observes:

> Simply augmenting his existing textbook with another chapter defining CDOs (collateralised debt obligations) and some simple orthodox finance theory would do the trick. No second thoughts for us foxes, thank you.

In our experience, textbooks, at best, introduce the financial crisis using the standard principal-agent approach – for example, chapter 37 of Mankiw and Taylor's 2011 introductory text (McMaster, 2015). This portrays the crisis as an episode of information asymmetry and moral hazard and therefore easily within the corpus of mainstream theory. A possible interpretation from this train of argument, therefore, is that the financial crisis does not represent any fundamental problem of the prevailing (Anglo-American) economic system, merely the outcome of disequilibrating influences that prevented efficient market clearing. Successfully address these sources of disruption and normal service will be resumed, presumably. If our interpretation is correct, then it is difficult to contest Myrdal's argument.

The second approach, curriculum governance frameworks, enables some appreciation of the evolution of economics teaching. In the UK, for example, economics curricula are evaluated against the Subject Benchmark Statement for Economics (SBSE). It provides a context and a set of guidelines for the delivery of degree programmes. It defines 'what can be expected of a graduate in the subject, in terms of what they might know, do and understand at the end of their studies' (SBSE, 2015: 1). While what is taught is ultimately left up to departments – and is therefore contingent on their composition – the SBSE provides a context for what is allowable and indeed encouraged.

In the wake of the financial crisis, it was hoped by many that the newest incarnation of the SBSE (published in 2015) would be radically different from previous versions. However, Mearman et al. (2018a) argue that it in fact represents little change and remains rather narrow in terms of its treatment of other economic perspectives. Specifically, they argue that the document is very weak on the sociopolitical dimension of economics, including its treatment of ethics. Whilst the document names ethics as one discipline to which economics *links*, *any* notion that economics is *inherently* ethical is absent. The SBSE contains no reference to morality. References to welfare are present but omit explicit discussion of welfare as being utilitarian or that there are alternative conceptions of well-being. Indeed, the latter is treated as synonymous with income and wealth (2.1). More broadly, the SBSE avoids any suggestion that economics is inherently value-laden. Indeed, the only use of the word 'value' conjoins with what employers may want in graduates (3.1, 5.2). The absence of 'value' is further evidence of the SBSE's weak pluralism: the concept is, after all, foundational to economics.

Approached in this way, economics is not a moral, ethical, political, or social discipline *per se*. One way to have dealt with this matter more effectively would have been to become more pluralist by incorporating heterodox economics perspectives. Another way would have been to consider more explicitly the educational goals economics teachers have – one of which might be to equip graduates to make better-informed decisions. However, as Mearman et al. (2018a) argue, the SBSE failed to do this as well.

Another way to capture the state of the discipline is to survey current teaching. This, however, is beyond the scope of the chapter (see Colander, 2007 for interesting surveys in the US). Nonetheless, one development worth noting is the much-heralded Curriculum Open-Access Resources in Economics project, better known by its potent acronym, CORE. At its centre is a large introductory undergraduate e-book called 'The Economy', which itself comprises nineteen units on a range of topics. Hence, CORE (2016a) describes itself as an e-book course. Indeed, some uses of CORE treat it as one module or course within a suite of others taught at the introductory level. Additionally, though, CORE is a curricular framework to be elaborated, whose delivery and outcomes are contingent on specific context.

CORE has made strong claims about its innovative nature, both in terms of its updated content and its pedagogy (see Birdi, 2016). Yet as Mearman et al. (2018b) argue, like the SBSE, CORE falls short in terms of its treatment of pluralism and underlying educational philosophy. They also show that in terms of ethics, CORE does little better. It does acknowledge the existence of institutions, power, and conflicts in society (cf. CORE, unit 5, 2015c). Nonetheless, CORE maintains Pareto efficiency and market solutions as the standard, which implies the adoption of the normative biases of the role of scarcity (Watson, 2011) and liberal economics (Myrdal, 1930). Further, CORE's treatment of power is limited, meaning that the fairness of outcomes is engaged with only superficially. For example, CORE mentions briefly the gender pay gap and educational levels between men and women. But it offers no hint at the social construction of gender and its effects on the economy. Nor, more importantly, does it discuss how women tend to perform certain economic jobs in economies where wage bargains are affected by culturally and historically specific notions of fairness (Power et al., 2003).

Overall, we have seen that two of the most recent developments in economics curriculum design offer quite poor treatments of ethics within economics. Is this merely intransigence on the part of economists? No. As discussed, it reflects the dominant treatment of the discipline, which neglects non-mainstream approaches and their historical antecedents. One reason given for this neglect is that economics has progressed methodologically towards one centred on mathematically formal, methodologically individualist equilibrium models. These have greater scientific cache. In turn, this reflects the continuing influence of logical positivist philosophy in the discipline. Key here are the contributions of Lionel Robbins and Milton Friedman. On the one hand, as Ozanne (2016) explores, Robbins' arguments against cardinal utility meant that questions of power and its effect on distribution were excluded. Friedman (1953) instead argued for a positive economics free of value judgements. As with logical positivism, the influence of these two thinkers' positions has long outlasted the credibility of their arguments.

The upshot of all this is that economics teaching is dominated by a narrow approach, concerned with drilling its students in techniques and core theory, which it is held to be necessary for students to learn to become economists. Indeed, given the state of postgraduate curricula, the claim is probably true for academic economists. However, of the students who study economics at university, the proportion who elect to undertake academic research is modest (for example, Colander, 2007; Earle et al., 2017). So what sense does it make to organise undergraduate curricula around their needs? Perhaps this is only really comprehensible as part of a strategy to reproduce the profession in a particular, mainstream form. Hence, the system produces students who are expert technicians but unable to think independently about real problems: they are well trained but poorly educated. The absence of ethics from their curricula is, then, neither a surprise nor confined to ethics. It encapsulates a wider malaise. The next two sections will consider how to do things differently, beginning first by addressing ethics in economics.

Economics and ethics

Of course, as we argued earlier, the standard approach insists that it is entirely objective by virtue of the positive-normative distinction. Nonetheless, the facts-value dichotomy has been subject to sustained critique in much of philosophy (for example, Putnam, 2002), and there have been important critiques from within economics. We have already noted Myrdal's (1969) argument; other important examples include Kenneth Boulding (1969) and Amartya Sen (1987).

In his 1968 American Economic Association presidential address, Boulding (1969) delivered an excoriating critique of neoclassical economics' irreconcilable reliance on the Pareto principle as a test of welfare while simultaneously claiming to be a value-free science. For us, in effect, Boulding identifies the Schrödinger's cat of economics: it is concurrently value-laden and value-free. Boulding consistently argued that science is a social activity, which therefore resides in a community (of scholars, for example). According to Boulding, all communities are founded on cultures that provide guidance on right and wrong, legitimate and illegitimate. Hence, science cannot be separated from ethical values; it is value-laden. Economics is no exception. For Boulding, the Pareto principle is an unconvincing approach to well-being, as it biases the *status quo*. By relying on it, economics is at risk of opposing all change on the basis that it may be costly to a wealthy individual despite benefitting a poor one.

Similarly, Sen (1987) analysed standard economics' embeddedness in utilitarianism and consequentialism. By being rooted in a particular philosophical tradition, economics cannot avoid values and making judgements based on a value frame. Sen's case has parallels with Myrdal's earlier contention. Mainstream economics' roots in utilitarianism and hedonism strongly suggest that it cannot be value-free in the way presumed by standard economics textbooks. While this can solicit particular policy preferences, it does not necessarily apply consistently. For instance, market socialists at the centre of the Calculation Debate, such as Abba Lerner, nested their arguments in Walrasian general equilibrium (Hodgson, 2001). More recently, Mirowski (2013) argues that the pre-crisis consensus in macroeconomic thinking belied an intimate relationship with neoliberalism, and Dow (2015) writes of the cocktail of ideology, belief, and power in portraying austerity as a rational policy option emerging from allegedly objective and impartial analysis.

DeMartino's (2011) pioneering work on the need for an ethical code for economists reveals how prominent mainstream economists' policy advice was and is embedded in a particular ethical approach, which appears to represent an evolutionary change from the Pareto principle. DeMartino identifies this as the utopian "maxi-max" decision-rule. The rubric compares alternatives solely on maximum possible benefit. In effect, potential harm does not feature since the decision rubric completely discounts the possibility of the risk of failure in any of the alternatives under review. This seems inimical to the Pareto principle, at least in application, as it abandons Pareto's emphasis on the avoidance of change that imposes any cost on any individual. For DeMartino, "maxi-max" represents an

> extraordinarily aggressive [approach] since it considers just the one desideratum of maximum possible payoff in policy choice. It is, therefore, a thoroughly utopian decision rule.
>
> (2011: 145)

Therefore,

> Maxi-max yields an attitude to policy making that is hubristic and ideological rather than humble and pragmatic.
>
> (DeMartino 2011: 151)

Among the examples DeMartino identifies are the application of Monetarist doctrine by the Pinochet regime in Chile during the 1970s and the rapid process of privatisation and deregulation in post-Soviet Russia. Central in this process were prominent US economists, such as Lawrence Summers and Jeffrey Sachs. The "shock therapy" recommended and administered was based on a series of assumptions about economic gains from competitive markets vis-à-vis the endemic issues of inefficiency and corruption of the Soviet era. No consideration was given to the risks of failure following from, for example, an insufficient legal system or of harm in such a short transition. Indeed, the authors of shock therapy argued that the gains of competition would be diminished if the transition phase was prolonged (DeMartino, 2011).

While DeMartino's case is aimed primarily at professional economists whose research informs policy, or those directly providing policy advice, he does acknowledge that teaching is highly significant in shaping the understanding of the discipline and in the reproduction of a particular value-based direction.

We endorse these arguments. Standard economics is value-laden and predicated on a particular ethical and philosophical understanding. DeMartino's stress in advocating a professional ethics in economics reflects an important driver of the Hippocratic Oath in medicine: *primum non nocere* – first, do no harm. The avoidance of cost – in the broadest sense – and the exercise of two principles, prudential and precautionary, form the corpus of DeMartino's ethical benchmark for economists and therefore the educational provision of economics.

The prudential principle urges the professional economist (or policymaker) to engage in an assessment of potential harm from the execution of some proposal. DeMartino (2011: 187) argues:

> Sustained attention to the prudential principle in economics would go some distance toward improving professional economic practice. It would encourage the profession to jettison utopian maxi-max interventions for more moderate and safer strategies.

DeMartino is sensitive to the possibility that the prudential principle could foster a conservative paralysis founded on the Pareto principle and, accordingly, the toleration of injustices associated with the *status quo*. He argues that economists should engage directly with communities in guiding deliberation over the possible courses of action. This, to some extent, is enshrined in the precautionary principle, which, again drawing from medicine, revolves around the notion of informed consent. Of course, this has its own issues, such as what 'informed consent' means in the context of a large body of people. Here, like Earle et al. (2017), DeMartino advocates economic democracy as a mechanism for tempering the potentially harmful impact of the imposition of so-called expert advice and of paternalism, in that the autonomy of the individual is privileged. This requires economists to "integrate themselves deeply" into communities and to educate those communities (DeMartino, 2011: 190). This is no easy task to realise, but DeMartino's argument highlights the ethical responsibilities of economists as both policy advisors and educators, the latter in endeavouring to ensure that communities possess capabilities and capacities to deliberate over economic projects.

For us, there is much to recommend DeMartino's analysis and advocacy. It invokes a Kantian sense of duty on the economics academy and profession that has been largely absent and, as a consequence, has arguably led to extensive injury and damage to individuals, communities, and perhaps even the planet. Moreover, there is a strong sense of justice running through DeMartino's argumentation. As a profession, economists are morally obligated to at least act in ways that do not further disadvantage or harm those who are vulnerable.

We find this a compelling moral imperative. Nonetheless, this demands a degree of empathy, which is underdeveloped in DeMartino's approach. We believe that an emphasis on avoidance of harm under the auspices of the prudential and precautionary principles is a necessary but not sufficient condition for the ethical economist. In the following section, we argue for greater cognisance of care in economists' ethical composition.

Towards the caring economist?

Care is essential to the functioning of society (Engster, 2005), and as Julie Nelson (2016: 12) observes, "The place of care in the economy is everywhere". Yet, with the exception of feminist economics, economists of all hues at best tend to overlook this insight (for example, Davis and McMaster, 2017; Nelson, 2016). If care is acknowledged, it is frequently conflated with altruism or an externality, neither of which suitably captures the properties of care (Davis and McMaster, 2017).

In this section, we initially investigate the meaning(s) of care and briefly consider the ethical dimensions. We then turn to outlining the implications for teaching economics and encouraging the development of the ethical economist.

What is care?

Care is ambiguous and complex. It may manifest as attentive interest or concern as well as actions arising as a result of such attention. Care, therefore, has philosophical properties, through ethical considerations; a psychological aspect, through emotional attachments and motivations; and labour/work dimensions, through the functional delivery of care activities (for example, Engster, 2005; Tronto, 2013). Care is therefore challenging to define. A well-cited approach is provided by Joan Tronto, who advocates a broad definition:

> On the most general level, we suggest that caring be viewed as *a species activity that includes everything that we do to maintain, continue, and repair our 'world' so that we can live in it as well as possible.* That world includes our bodies, ourselves, and our environment, all of which we seek to interweave in a complex life-sustaining web.
>
> (Fisher and Tronto, 1990: 40; cited in Tronto, 2013: 19, original emphasis)

Some critics contend that the definition is too broad and could include almost everything (Held, 2006). Without wishing to be drawn into such a debate, we note that Tronto responded to this line of criticism, arguing that the breadth of the definition reflects an attempt to establish an appreciation of care as overarching and within which contingent and specific instances, activities, and acts may be embedded. Tronto's emphasis on breadth is compatible with Nelson's allusion that care is "everywhere" and indeed Held's (2006: 3) own observation that "care is a truly universal experience. Every human being has been cared for as a child or would not be alive".

For our purposes, the ethical aspects of care are of most relevance. The literature conceives of care in phases, with each phase aligned with a particular ethical quality (Tronto, 2013). Thus, for example, Tronto discusses "caring about" as a recognition of unmet caring needs, which invites the ethical property of attentiveness and benevolence. This may lead to the second phase of "caring for", with the ethical aspect of responsibility and perhaps benevolence. The third phase, "care giving", invites competence as an ethical dimension and perhaps also beneficence. "Care receiving" is the fourth phase and, according to Tronto, is associated with responsiveness as an ethical characteristic. Tronto finally discusses "caring with" as a distinct phase. This is the most complex, involving respect, trust, solidarity, and so forth. It is here that commitments to justice feature. Held (2006) also acknowledges the compatibility of care and justice. Indeed, the latter is an integral part of the former. In doing so, she attempts to differentiate care from other ethical frames and therefore promote a particular care ethics. For Held, deontology's emphasis on universalism is too rigid and potentially disregards context and relationships. Utilitarianism neglects motive and virtue, and virtue ethics over-emphasises individual dispositions at the potential expense of relationships and mutual dependency – the focus of care. Nonetheless, she argues that virtue ethics and care are complementary, in that caring involves specific dispositions, such as compassion and sympathy.

From a different analytical entry point, Daniel Engster's (2005) work provides significant insight. Accepting a broad definition of care, Engster presents three essential aims of caring: individual survival, development, and social reproduction.

Individual survival relates to care for the self and close others in addressing basic biological needs, such as food, water, shelter, and, additionally, rest, basic medical treatments, and comforting contact for children. Development involves enabling others to achieve sufficient, or what Engster terms "basic or innate", capabilities to function in society. He identifies a range of capabilities, including emotion, movement, speech, reason, imagination, ability to affiliate with others, and such like.[1] The third aim – social reproduction – is tailored to assisting others in avoiding pain or in relieving suffering, such that they may enhance their capabilities to live life as well as possible. Engster recognises that this overlaps with the first two of his aims, but that the emphasis on pain – broadly conceived – is a source of differentiation.

In order to realise those aims, Engster identifies three ethical qualities: attentiveness, responsiveness, and respect. As with Tronto, for Engster, attentiveness resonates with empathy, where empathy refers to the ability to comprehend the feelings of others by virtue of similar experience. He claims that attentiveness "usually" involves empathy in anticipating the needs of another. Second, responsiveness is framed in terms of engaging in a dialogue with the recipient of care. The ability to listen and react is important. Engster maintains that diminished responsiveness is likely to impair the effectiveness of caring. Finally, respect refers to the notion that others are worthy of attention and responsiveness. In Kantain tones, this implies that others should be treated in ways that do not humiliate or degrade. In effect, ensuring dignity is integral to caring.

While a considerable amount of the foregoing has been neglected by much of the economics literature, the so-called father of economics anticipated much of the nature and ethics of care and caring. In the *Theory of Moral Sentiments*, Adam Smith devotes a chapter to care and employs the term in the title of

Chapter 1, Section 2 (Part 4). While Smith offers no explicit definition of care, from his work, it is evident that care coalesces with affection and virtue, the latter in the form of attentiveness, benevolence, beneficence, sympathy (as in fellow feeling), and kindness. Smith's notion of care, whilst underdeveloped, acknowledges the complexities of care embodied in acts and emotions. For Smith, care is profoundly relational; his emphasis anticipates much of the recent care literature. He discusses care in terms of concentric rings projecting from the self. Care as other-regarding extends to one's immediate family or kin – with greater sympathies directed at children – and then on to familiar others (Davis and McMaster, 2017).

Moreover, Smith identifies important feedback in these elements of care. He states:

> Nature, which formed men for that mutual kindness so necessary for their happiness, renders every man the peculiar object of kindness to the persons to whom he himself has been kind. . . . Kindness is the parent of kindness.
>
> (2000 [1759]: 331)

This represents a direct challenge to the standard assumption of universal scarcity. Indeed, Smith suggests the opposite. Demonstrating kindness – and hence caring – stimulates further kindness (and care). We feel that such insight is integral to the morality of economics and, accordingly, there is a moral imperative to embody this in the teaching of economics, to which we now turn.

Implications for teaching economics

Good teachers know their objectives. For Bertrand Russell, "Before considering how to educate, it is well to be clear as to the sort of result which we wish to achieve" (1992: 413). Teachers are well acquainted with the notion of learning outcomes; however, often these reduce to command over a mechanical technique or knowledge of a particular principle. At a course or programme level, one might see broader objectives, such as 'demonstrate an understanding of x' or 'evaluate critically key concepts within y' and such like. These objectives in turn reflect an (often implicit) educational philosophical position held by the teacher or designer of the teaching unit.

In economics, this underlying philosophical position has often been 'instrumental' in nature. Students are to be trained in an 'economic way of thinking' to learn key concepts and techniques that, in principle, are applicable in reality. One such instrumental objective (as noted in the second section) might be to reproduce economics as it is, or at least to produce the next generation of researchers. However, interviews with teachers of economics (see, for example, Bowmaker, 2010) suggest that they believe they are giving their students insight and real, practical knowledge in order to make a positive difference to the world. Also, some teachers believe they are liberating their students from false beliefs:

> I think one of the really important functions of economics in general is to knock down silly ideas. It is not just in government that silly ideas surface and become popular. You can pick up [a newspaper] any day and find a lousy idea in it.
>
> (Solow, 1999: 289)

Instrumentalist philosophy is prevalent in economics and lends itself to the maxi-max rubric discussed earlier. There are, though, alternatives. Liberal philosophy (Bridges, 1992) aims to create autonomous, critical thinkers able to reach their own judgements. In contrast to instrumental approaches, then, a liberal education would not emphasise 'facts' or 'knowledge'. Rather, it would try to help students develop critical faculties of mind. However, some 'critical pedagogues' would argue that liberal education views the learner as an empty vessel to be filled, whereas, for them, the student must fill themselves (see Hicks, 2004: 18). These thinkers, inspired by Paolo Freire (1970), emphasise a student-centred approach, stressing the critical evaluation and re-evaluation of common concepts via a process of *conscientisation*. Thus, students learn by examining their own circumstances. Such an approach is inherently problem-based.

In terms of teaching ethics, a case can be made for it using any of the philosophical positions. If the goal is to change society, or if it is to create ethically trained economists, this creates reasons for teaching this. However, if this goal clashes with the wider ones of training in specific concepts, this may create tension. Also, if the teacher adopts the instrumental position, students may simply end up recognising that there are ethical implications, perhaps knowing some competing theories, but not being able to apply them to new contexts. Herein lies the advantage of a liberal approach: it aims to develop capacities rather than knowledge. However, its weakness is that it therefore does not require ethics to be taught. It does seem consistent, though, with the aim of developing capacities, that students should be exposed to problems that are multifaceted and that contain an ethical element. This would certainly be the case if students were to start from their own positions, as in critical pedagogy. One of the first questions one might ask of a student is whether their current situations are fair. This acts as an obvious entry point for discussing how and why they got where they are and hence, for instance, the role of luck; and also for asking whether that is a fair process or outcome.

These principles can be applied to teaching ethics in economics that encapsulates care. Bluntly, if it is a training goal within an instrumental education to create caring students, this can be done by designing the appropriate training tasks. For example, students can be presented with case studies that elicit care about a person, region, country, etc. Assessment tasks could be designed to reward care, perhaps by awarding credit for co-operative acts in group settings.

However, this may not create care as a graduate attribute, as might be imagined by liberal educators. For this to be achieved, students need to apply themselves, perhaps to real cases, and reach their own judgements. This might be best achieved by using cases from their own lives, as advocated by radical pedagogy.

There may be a more thoroughgoing approach to creating caring students. Noddings (1984, 2005, 2015) argues that education for an ethics of care is very different from 'character education', which relates most closely to liberal education, noted above. Noddings' argument is that character education – and indeed utilitarian, deontological, and virtue ethics – is individualist. Care, though, is inherently *relational*. For Noddings, relations within a classroom are crucial. That applies to relations between classmates, and also between the teacher and their students. Interactions between classmates (and their teacher) need to be caring themselves. According to Noddings (2013: xviii), "To develop as caring persons, young people need to have supervised practice in caring". Educational institutions should create an open supportive learning environment – not 'safe spaces', but sites in which students will be sensitively challenged. Teaching technique, therefore, must involve 'confirmation', i.e. creating an environment in which students are encouraged rather than just criticised. In these ways, students can develop critical skills and the confidence to use them. However, Noddings' approach dictates that care requires repeated contact, which implies seminar teaching and contact time. This might conflict with the liberal stress on autonomy.

Another implication of such a thoroughgoing approach is that it demands care across the curriculum (Noddings, 2015). Noddings objects to liberal arts because, by being modular and non-linear in its arrangement of student learning, it creates disconnections between different subject areas. This can create silos, in which issue x is covered by subject A, meaning that subject B can ignore x. This is evident in economics, in which the subject is related to ethics and, as in the SBSE, draws on ethics. That means that economics can easily avoid addressing ethics, or care, by pointing elsewhere. Of course, economics students seldom encounter a course dealing specifically with ethics. Indeed, there is some research, albeit twenty or so years old, that suggests that even if they do, they are unlikely to analyse care. For example, in an interesting survey of the teaching of business ethics, DeMoss and McCann (1997) conclude that a gendered rights-based approach dominates the curriculum. This demonstrates traits of patriarchy, or maleness, individual autonomy, rationality, and equality. The authors argue that this effectively crowds out a more feminine care-oriented approach, which has a stronger emphasis on mutual dependency and emotion. Moreover, DeMoss and McCann claim that their survey evidence suggests that a majority of students would prefer a more care- than rights-oriented approach, and that the business ethics curriculum should reflect this.

There are, of course, alternative approaches within ethics of care. Noddings' approach is ambitious, in that her ideas would be challenging in coordinating ethics across the curriculum. More importantly, others argue that Noddings' approach to care is demanding, in that authentic care centres on immediate, repeated, personal (dyadic) relationships of a specific type. In particular, for care to be authentic according to Noddings (1984, 2005), the care-giver must be engrossed and motivationally displaced from the self to the other. Moreover, in order for there to be a completion of care, the recipient of care must be receptive and responsive to the care-giver. In this way, Noddings focusses on the virtues of caring rather than the practices of care. Care is therefore conditional on motivational displacement, engrossment, and receptiveness. Yet, for us, Noddings' emphasis on a dyadic relationship between care-giver and the recipient disregards the context of the caring relationship and potentially ignores other parties that may influence the caring relation. More generally, Noddings' emphasis overlooks the social embeddedness of caring processes, which may involve multiple networks consisting of socially embedded individuals (see, for example, Davis and McMaster, 2017).

Thus far, we have discussed only guiding principles in an education aimed at creating caring students. Now we move on to consider concrete examples of teaching. As an intermediate position, we first consider how teaching economics pluralistically can support teaching an ethics of care. First, we claim that is part of a *duty of care* of economics teachers that they teach pluralistically given the educational benefits of doing so. As argued by many (for instance, Mearman et al., 2011), pluralism can help students better understand a complex world, solve more effectively practical problems, develop analytical skills, make more nuanced comparisons, grow critical thinking skills, and perhaps even understand mainstream economic concepts better.

Further, pluralism has a direct impact on ethics. As already discussed, approaches alternative to the mainstream have clear ethical bases as well as traditions of considering the social and political economy of ideas, policies, and events. They also demonstrate how the mainstream itself contains an ethical viewpoint, as discussed in the third section. These ethical stances can be used as entry points into the discussion of different perspectives (see Resnick and Wolff, 2012), as well as helping students understand complex ethical dilemmas. This in turn may help boost problem-solving capacities. It may also help students understand actual past decisions in terms of the ethical drivers of them. That could lead to surprising outcomes – for instance, to a discussion of behavioural biases in decision-making. Was a decision made because of bad ethics or because a person was engaging their automatic decision-making (a la Kahneman's System 1 versus System 2 thinking)? Alternatively, was a decision made simply because of a weak institutional structure or because of the power relations within which it sits? Again, these questions demand a pluralist approach.

The Trolley Problem

It is common to use problems, ethical dilemmas, and case studies, both real and imagined, to teach ethics. Such cases reveal hidden ethical positions as well as power relations, legal structures, etc. They can also be designed flexibly to allow students to engage with the detail of cases, reflect these nuances in their thinking, and react to changes. Problems, if designed well, can also be stimulating, leading to engagement and active and hence deeper learning (see Forsythe, 2010).

Many of these themes can be discussed via the classic Trolley Problem, popularised by Foot (1978). In this, a train or tram is approaching a fork in the track. Down one branch is a single person; down the other are multiple (usually five) people, all stuck or bound to the track. If the train continued along a particular branch, the person/people there would be killed. At the junction, there is a set of points. At the points is the 'switchman', who can determine which fork the train will travel. The ethical question is, down which fork does the switchman send the train? One of the teaching purposes of the exercise is to demonstrate the difference between consequentialist and deontological ethics and to help students grasp these notions. In the canonical case, the consequentialist will usually choose to save five people by redirecting the train to the track with only one person. Further, the consequentialist draws no distinction between doing and allowing harm, whereas the deontological ethicist would judge doing harm to be worse.

That approach serves the instrumental purpose of demonstrating the difference between the theories. However, the exercise can be richer than that – for instance, by demonstrating that there is no right answer to the problem. For example, there is uncertainty about whether the train will definitely hit the five if one does nothing: perhaps its fuel will run out, or someone else might intervene. This is pedagogically important because it challenges some students' demand for certainty. That can be developmentally important, moving students from dualist to pluralist thinking (Perry, 1970). Crucially, some of the scenarios and objections above have been raised by students in class, showing their critical thinking capacities are being exercised and developed.

Further, one can change the terms of the game. Indeed, the literature is full of variants (see Thomson, 1985). For instance, as discussed, normally, the consequentialist would argue for the single person to die rather than the five. However, if the five people are mass murderers, the calculus may change. Some of the possible variants are relevant specifically to economics students. One might argue that if the single person is rich and the five are poor, the train should be diverted to save the one and sacrifice the five. In choosing this, one might make an assumption that the rich person is more productive. That could lead into a wide discussion of, *inter alia*, the sources of wealth and the processes of income distribution. That in turn could lead to a conscientisation of the students as they consider scenarios in which they or people they know, or are aware of, are on the tracks. Less dramatically, one could choose a scenario in which someone sacrifices their job to save five others – sack someone with no dependents to save someone else with dependents, for instance.

In addition to these issues of wealth generation and distribution, also of relevance to economics students are questions of valuation. If the sole person is rich but retiring, how does one value their future income stream? Should one apply discounting to their future income? It is well established in literature on cost-benefit analysis that these questions are difficult and inherently ethical (see, for example, Ackerman, 2009). Similarly, if we replaced the five people with an extremely valuable car, that may change the calculus again; for if the train hit the car, it could derail and kill many more than five people. In a further twist, the game can be made more personal. For instance, one can ask whose car it is. Does that even matter? Even more dramatically, one might ask what difference it would make if the single person tied to the track was related to the switchman – perhaps their own child.

What are the implications of the Trolley Problem for an ethics of care? A clue lies in the debate on the problem between doing and allowing harm. It is argued by some that by diverting the trolley you do harm rather than allow it. Further, consider the fat man variant of the game, in which one attempts to stop the train by pushing a fat man onto the track, thereby hoping to save five people by sacrificing one. Whilst the consequentialist would usually argue to push the fat man, for the deontologist this would be wrong, as the fat man would otherwise not have been harmed. As discussed, DeMartino (2011) advocates an economist's oath similar to the Hippocratic, in which one does no harm. Further, the care ethicist would also reject pushing the fat man. By actively pushing a person to their death, an individual would not be acting in a caring fashion; they would be doing harm and, moreover, disrespecting the individual's dignity.

The Trolley Problem reveals several other intriguing issues for a caring ethics. As noted in the section "What is care?", for much of the literature, care centres on the relationship between care-giver and recipient. It is not difficult to envisage a Noddings-inspired approach to care ethics justifying the saving of one person and the sacrifice of five on the basis of a care-giver being "motivationally displaced" by their caring responsibility for the one individual, assuming, of course, that this individual had been the recipient of care from the care-giver in the recent past. Even under Adam Smith's conception of care, the identity of the potential care recipient is central to the considerations of caring.

The situation is much less ambiguous in circumstances where all trapped individuals are unknown to the would-be rescuer. In this case, Tronto's (2013) identification of unmet caring needs highlights the shared predicament of those bound to the rails. Therefore, a would-be care-giver would be confronted with the responsibility for addressing as many unmet care needs as possible. Indeed, Engster's (2005) stress on individual survival as an aim of care also suggests the sacrifice of the one to save the five. To some extent, this scenario rather resembles a consequentialist calculation of unmet caring needs and assumes that each individual has the same needs. Moreover, the invocation of responsibility has decidedly Kantian deontological overtones. Yet the care literature identifies attentiveness and empathy as significant ingredients of care. We may empathise with the plight of the sole individual, but ultimately we have to acknowledge the limitations in our ability to provide care.

That said, care is contingent. What if the five individuals were elderly and the sole individual was young? Would this invite a recalibration of the identification of caring needs? Are issues of gender, wealth, and productivity of relevance? Engster's (2005) aims of care – individual survival, development, and social reproduction – may provide an informative platform for ethical decision-making. For example, if the sole individual is a renowned scientist and the five others are criminals, does this shape a carer's thinking, action, and ethical responsibility? Under such circumstances, could saving the one be justified on the basis of Tronto's (2013: 19, original emphasis) overarching definition of care as "*a species activity that includes everything that we do to maintain, continue, and repair our 'world' so that we can live in it as well as possible*"? Care here can also be seen as an attempt not only to limit harm but also to do good in a future-oriented manner. By saving the scientist, the carer at least hopes that the act will contribute to the greater good.

Conclusion

This chapter has considered how, via teaching, one might create the ethical economist; specifically one with an ethics of care. Practising economists, particularly in government, must show awareness of ethics. Further, economists stand accused of acting without due attention to ethics, contributing to many major harms, including the global financial crisis. We are reminded of Kaletsky's (1995) scathing critique of the award of Lucas's Nobel Prize for the theory of rational expectations. Writing in *The Times*, Kaletsky states:

> The economic damage done around the world by this one abstruse theory . . . is probably comparable to the destruction wrought by a major war.
>
> (cited in Smith, 1997: 110)

However, for various reasons, current economics teaching has largely jettisoned ethics; and recent reforms have done little to correct this movement. Nonetheless, it is possible to develop the ethical, caring economist if one sets out to do so.

We have argued that economics is self-deceiving in maintaining its cloak of objectivity. Therefore, it outwardly demonstrates a misleading façade of value-neutrality. Science is value-laden, and logic suggests that economics cannot be the exception to this. Drawing from DeMartino, there is an appealing argument that the standard approach has evolved from Paretian to a utopian maxi-max rubric. From an ethical perspective, this invites the exercise of DeMartino's prudential and precautionary principles. We strongly endorse this but argue that this does not go far enough to ensure the development of ethical economists. The ethics of care should have a prominent role in the education of economists.

Once this decision has been made, the economics teacher would deliver different materials and do so differently. Teaching would involve explicit consideration of ethics and of care. This may well involve the consideration of real or hypothetical cases that allow for open, active, deep learning. This process may also require deployment of pluralism, not least from a duty of care for students' learning. This chapter has considered various initiatives for promoting an economics embedded in an ethics of care, from the design of entire curricula to the augmentation of a traditional philosophical dilemma, the Trolley Problem. These are just some possibilities, but they demonstrate that if the will is there, there is scope for the formation of ethical economists via teaching.

Note

1   Engster distances his notion of capabilities from Nussbaum's (2011) list. He is sensitive to the elitist critique of Nussbaum. Nonetheless, he considers his approach to be consistent with Nussbaum's "innate equipment . . . necessary for developing more advanced capabilities, and a ground for moral concern" (Nussbaum, 2000: 84, cited by Engster, 2005: 52).

References

Ackerman, F. (2009) The new climate economics: The stern review versus its critics, in J. Harris and N. Goodwin (eds.), *Twenty First Century Macroeconomics: Responding to the Climate Challenge*, Edward Elgar: Cheltenham.

Birdi, A. (2016) *CORE: A Brief Guide to Its Pedagogical Method*, CORE Project: London.

Boulding, K. E. (1969) Economics as a moral science, *American Economic Review*, 59: 1–12.

Bowmaker, S. (2010) *The Heart of Teaching Economics: Lessons from Leading Minds*, Edward Elgar Publishing: Cheltenham.

Bridges, D. (1992) Enterprise and liberal education, *Journal of Philosophy of Education*, 26(1): 91–98.

Colander, D. (2007) *The Making of an Economist, Redux*, Princeton University Press: Princeton.

Davis, J. B. and McMaster, R. (2017) *Health Care Economics*, Routledge: London.

DeMartino, G. (2011) *The Economist's Oath: On the Need for and Content of Professional Economics Ethics*, Oxford University Press: Oxford.

DeMoss, M. A. and McCann, G. K. (1997) Without a care in the World: The business ethics course and its exclusion of the care perspective, *Journal of Business Ethics*, 16: 435–443.

Dow, S. C. (2015) Addressing uncertainty in economics and the economy, *Cambridge Journal of Economics*, 39: 33–47.

Earle, J., Moran, C. and Ward-Perkins, Z. (2017) *The Econocracy: The Perils of Leaving Economics to the Experts*, Manchester University Press: Manchester.

Engster, D. (2005) Rethinking care theory: The practice of caring and the obligation to care, *Hypatia*, 20: 50–74.

Epstein, G. A. and Carrick-Hagenbarth, J. (2012) Dangerous interconnectedness: Economists' conflicts of interest, ideology and financial crisis, *Cambridge Journal of Economics*, 36: 43–63.

Foot, P. (1978) The problem of abortion and the doctrine of double effect, in *Virtues and Vices and Other Essays*, University of California Press: Berkeley, CA.

Forsythe, F. (2010) *Problem-Based Learning, Handbook for Economics Lecturers*, Economics Network: Bristol.

Fourcade, M., Ollion, E. and Algan, Y. (2015) The superiority of economists, *Journal of Economic Perspectives*, 29(1): 89–114.

Freire, P. (1970) *Pedagogy of the Oppressed*, Continuum: New York and London.

Friedman, M. (1953) *Essays in Positive Economics*, University of Chicago: Chicago.

Harcourt, G. (2010) The crisis in mainstream economics, *Real World Economics Review*, June.

Heilbroner, R. (1999) *The Worldly Philosophers: The Lives, Times and Ideas of the Great Economic Thinkers*, Touchstone: New York.

Held, V. (2006) *The Ethics of Care: Personal, Political, and Global*, Oxford University Press: Oxford.

Hicks, D. (2004) Radical education, in S. Ward (ed.), *Education Studies: A Student's Guide*, Routledge: London, pp. 134–148.

Hodgson, G. M. (2001) *How Economics Forgot History: The Problem of Historical Specificity in Social Science*, Routledge: London.

Kaletsky, A. (1995) in J. Smith (1997) *Full Employment: A Pledge Betrayed*, Macmillan: Basingstoke, p.110.

Lipsey, R. and Chrystal, A. (2015) *Economics*, 13th edition, Oxford University Press: Oxford.

Mankiw, N. G. and Taylor, M. P. (2011) *Economics*, 2nd edition, Cengage Learning, EMEA: Andover.

McMaster, R. (2015) The "illusion" or "paradigm blindness" of economics: Ethical challenges to economic thought from the financial crisis, in T. H. Jo and F. S. Lee (eds.), *Marx, Veblen, and the Foundations of Heterodox Economics: Essays in Honor of John F. Henry*, Routledge: London.

Mearman, A., Berger, S. and Guizzo, D. (2018a) Whither political economy? Evaluating the CORE project as a response to calls for change in economics teaching, *Review of Political Economy*, 30 (2): 241-259.

Mearman, A., Guizzo, D. and Berger, S. (2018b). Is UK economics teaching changing? Evaluating the new subject benchmark statement, *Review of Social Economy*, 76 (3): 377-396.

Mearman, A., Shoib, G., Wakeley, T. and Webber, D. (2011) Do pluralist curricula make happier, better educated students: A qualitative analysis, *International Review of Economics Education*, 10(2): 50–62.

Mirowski, P. (2010) The great mortification: Economists' responses to the crisis of 2007–(and counting), *Hedgehog Review*, 12: 28-41.

Mirowski, P. (2013) *Never Let a Serious Crisis Go to Waste: How Neoliberalism Survived the Financial Meltdown*, Verso: New York.

Myrdal, G. (1930) *The Political Element in the Development of Economic Theory*, Harvard University Press: Harvard.

Myrdal, G. (1969) *Objectivity in Social Research*, Pantheon Books: London.

Nelson, J. (2016) Husbandry: A (feminist) reclamation of masculine responsibility for care, *Cambridge Journal of Economics*, 40: 1–15.

Noddings, N. (1984) *Caring*, University of California Press: Berkley.

Noddings, N. (2005) Identifying and responding to needs in education, *Cambridge Journal of Education*, 35: 147–159.

Noddings, N. (2015) *The Challenge of Care in Schools: An Alternative Approach to Education*, Teachers' College Press: New York.

Nussbaum, M. C. (2000) Women's capabilities and social justice, *Journal of Human Development*, 1: 219–247.

Nussbaum, M. C. (2011) *Creating Capabilities: The Human Development Approach*, Belknap for Harvard University Press: Cambridge, MA.

Ozanne, A. (2016) *Power and Neoclassical Economics: A Return to Political Economy in the Teaching of Economics*, Palgrave Macmillan: London.

Perry, W. G. (1970) *Forms of Intellectual and Ethical Development in the College Years*, Holt, Rinehart and Winston: New York.

Power, M., Mutari, E. and Figart, D. M. (2003) Beyond markets: Wage setting and the methodology of feminist political economy, in D. K. Barker and E. Kuiper (eds.), *Towards a Feminist Philosophy of Economics*, Routledge: London.

Putnam, H. (2002) *The Collapse of the Fact/Value Dichotomy and Other Essays*, Harvard University Press: Cambridge, MA.

Resnick, S. and Wolff, R. (2012) Teaching economics differently by comparing competing contesting theories, *International Journal of Pluralism and Economics Education*, 2(1): 57–68.

Russell, B. (1992) *The Basic Writings of Bertrand Russell*, Routledge: Padstow.

Samuelson, P. and Nordhaus, W. D. (2010) *Economics*, 19th edition, McGraw Hill: New York.

Sen, A. (1987) *On Ethics and Economics*, Blackwell: London.

Sloman, J., Garrat, D. and Wride, A. (2015) *Economics*, 9th edition, Pearson: London.

Smith, A. (2000 [1759]) *The Theory of Moral Sentiments*, Prometheus Books: Amherst, MA.

Smith, J. (1997) *Full Employment: A Pledge Betrayed*, Macmillan: Basingstoke.

Solow, R. (1999) Interview in Snowdon, in B. Snowdon and H. Vane (eds.), *Conversations with Leading Economists: Interpreting Modern Macroeconomics*, Edward Elgar: Cheltenham.

Taylor, N. and Mankiw, N. G. (2017) *Economics*, 4th edition, South-Western CENGAGE Learning: Andover.

Thomson, J. J. (1985) The trolley problem, *The Yale Law Journal*, 94: 1395–1415.

Tronto, J. C. (2013) *Caring Democracy: Markets, Equality, and Justice*, New York University Press: New York

Watson, M. (2011) Competing models of socially constructed economic man: Differentiating Defoe's Crusoe from the Robinson of neoclassical economics, *New Political Economy*, 16(5): 609–626.

Williamson, O. E. (1975) *Markets and Hierarchies*, Free Press: New York.

Zuidhof, P. W. (2014) Thinking like an economist: The neoliberal politics of the economics textbook, *Review of Social Economy*, 72: 157–185.

4 Economists' personal responsibility and ethics

Patrick O'Sullivan

Introduction

The question of the ethical formation of economists has been dealt with from a variety of different angles in this book, including, inter alia, a discussion of the manner in which the mathematisation of the discipline in the 20th century has been associated with a relative disappearance of concern with normative issues of ethics and policy and how such ethical discourse as has survived has been dominated by one important but narrow school of moral philosophy: utilitarianism. Economists have simply taken for granted the Pareto norm and the Kaldor-Hicks compensation principle, with almost no discussion of these and little or no awareness that there are alternatives to utilitarianism in moral philosophy. In this chapter, we shall focus on the philosophical reasons for this retreat from normative ethical discourse by economists, at least in their professional work, and we will look at what this may imply for the personal responsibility of economists as freely choosing human beings.

We will open with a brief reminder of the inescapable moral responsibility of every human being in every life situation, drawing on the work of Jean-Paul Sartre. We will then see how in the early days of classical political economy ethical considerations were a central part of the subject and indeed intimately, if often implicitly, bound up with the sense of personal moral responsibility of the economic theorists. In the 19th century, there were, of course, already rumblings of economics being a dismal, cynical, if not sinful, science, but the really decisive break between ethics and economics came in the 20th century work of Milton Friedman, who urged economists as a matter of rigorous method to ban any consideration of ethics – of normative discourse of any kind – from the science. Given the enthusiasm with which Friedman's methodological strictures on this and other points were taken up by economists (even if they did not necessarily widely accept his economics), this not only emptied economics of almost any ethical content (especially in the neoclassical mainstream) but also inevitably had an impact on economists' sense of personal moral responsibility, at least in their professional work.

We will subject this influential Friedmanite injunction to a searching critique, drawing both on the ideas of the great Swedish economist Gunnar Myrdal and on the Frankfurt School of Critical Social Theory. From there, we will move on to see that it is imperative that economics reintegrates an explicit concern with ethics into its professional practice; that hand in hand with this, economists should realise and appreciate their own personal responsibilities for the manner and implications of their theorising; and finally, that perhaps moral philosophy should (once again) be an integral part of the education of every professional economist.

A prolegomenon on freedom and personal responsibility: Sartre

Given that our specific theme in this chapter is the personal ethical responsibility of economists qua economists, it may be worth beginning with a reminder of the fundamentals of such notions and their philosophical basis. To utter any ethical or moral injunction, and indeed to utter any normative discourse addressed to human beings, presupposes that those same human beings are free to choose; that is to say that they are capable of deciding to alter in some respect their patterns of behaviour. If people were entirely devoid of freedom to change themselves and their actions, there would be no point whatever in urging people morally about anything, and normative discourse, ethics and moral reflection/analysis would be a pure waste of time. This brings us to the reflections of the great French philosopher Jean-Paul Sartre on freedom of choice. For Sartre, people are always free to choose at every moment of their adult lives; indeed from the moment they attain self-consciousness. We may not have the unbounded freedom that an absolute being might have to do absolutely anything; but within and subject to certain constraints that arise from our natural condition, each and every person always has *some* degree of freedom to make choices. Of course, some may have more freedom (more scope to exercise their free choices) than others; but for Sartre, that all are free to choose to some degree is undeniable. It is indeed incontrovertibly given to any self-reflection that is carried out in good faith.[1] From the trivia of a choice of food on a restaurant menu to more fundamental choices like those of a job or a partner for life, we know very well that however much one might like to blame others or let them make the choices for us, ultimately the choice is our own. Even letting somebody else make the choice for us is itself a choice, as Sartre so nicely put it![2]

It is just as well that it should be so because otherwise moral and ethical injunction would be completely pointless and humanity incapable of moral improvement. But what all of this means is that despite a widespread tendency to denigrate and to expel moral considerations and ethical discourse from Economics as a subject over the past seventy years, economists inexorably remain free to choose and thus personally responsible for their choices and for their actions.

The early days: ethics an integral part of economics

It is worth recalling that in the early days when economics, or political economy, as it was then called, was emerging as a separate systematic discipline, it was as an offshoot of moral and/or political philosophy. Adam Smith was in fact Professor of Moral Philosophy at the University of Glasgow (1752–1764).[3] James Mill (father of J. S. Mill), as well as writing on political economy, made contributions to the then emergent moral philosophy of utilitarianism and was a close friend of its founder, Jeremy Bentham. In fact, it was James Mill who was the first to make the fateful alliance between utilitarianism and economics in general, an association that was to prove very influential for at least a century, as we shall see. To these and many other early classical economists, political economy was in effect an offshoot of moral philosophy, a kind of Applied Ethics for business merchants and for politicians dealing with questions of economic policy (in particular with questions of international trade and commerce). In both cases, classical economists were ultimately seeking to arrive at normative guidelines for how various actors *ought* to behave if they were to serve the common good. Smith famously argued that each economic actor, in pursuing their own self-interest (and so, in particular, firms in pursuing profits), would thereby "as if by an invisible hand" promote the well-being of all in society.[4] James Mill and David Ricardo together with Smith strongly argued that politicians ought not to engage in protectionist policies but should promote free trade. In short, to the early economists, their discipline was intimately bound up with, if not part and parcel of, moral and political philosophy. Hence, moral philosophy would be an integral part of the formation of the economist, and their pronouncements on business behaviour and economic policy would therefore be a seamless extension and application of their own personal ethical views. Professional practice as an economist and well-considered personal ethical viewpoints were integrated and entirely unified.

As the 19th century progressed, this linkage gradually weakened. Even if polymaths like John Stuart Mill continued to move effortlessly between economics, politics and moral philosophy in their thought and writing, from the time of the marginalists (Jevons, Menger and Walras), economics began to strike out on its own as an independent discipline, modelling itself more on mathematical physics than on moral philosophy. It is no accident that the architect of the first marginalist mathematical model of general equilibrium, Léon Walras, was an engineer by training. Also, in the writings of the trenchant 19th century essayist Thomas Carlyle, the label "dismal science" emerged. While Carlyle has perhaps often been misunderstood on this point (he only meant that the conclusions of economists are often pessimistic but still brutally realistic), the suggestion that economics was not only dismal but could also lead to sinfulness was definitely creeping into the picture. But the really definitive break between economics and ethics and the consequent abdication of personal ethical responsibility by economists that accompanied it comes in the work of the Chicago economist Milton Friedman, writing in 1953.

Friedman: positive economics

In his 1953 work "Essays in Positive Economics",[5] Milton Friedman, in the first chapter of the book dealing with methodology, outlined certain very distinctive positions that, as Mark Blaug once put it (Blaug, 1992),[6] were to be the central influence on mainstream economists for at least a generation. One very distinctive aspect of this methodological position that certainly has had a very widespread influence both within and outside the neoclassical mainstream is the injunction to economists to banish all forms of "value judgement" – all forms of normative ethical discourse – from their economic theorising. Economics is to be a purely positive science elaborating how the world is, not dreaming about how it ought to be. Whatever other aspects of Friedman's methodology (which have also been influential), this tenet has become central to the way economists as a profession behave. It has become veritably taboo to raise value judgements or normative concerns when doing economics since value judgements are beyond the pale of rational scientific analysis and, as Friedman so nicely put it, are "about differences in fundamental values men can ultimately only fight".[7] What is less well appreciated is that this position as adopted by Friedman is based on an epistemology or philosophy known as Positivism, which is highly challengeable and has indeed long since been abandoned by most contemporary philosophers. Positivism was first expounded in a systematic way by the French 19th-century philosopher Auguste Comte, and it was popularised in the 20th century in the work of A. J. Ayer (among others).[8] According to Ayer's Verification Principle of Meaning, for any proposition (piece of discourse) to even have a meaning, it must be a (definitional) tautology or else must be empirically verifiable, at least in principle. Any discourse that does not meet one or other of these criteria is dismissed as literally nonsense (discourse that is incapable of being understood). The ultimate empiricist inspiration of such a position will be clear enough, although many empiricists before Ayer would have allowed that there can be discourse that is meaningful (capable of being understood) even if not empirically testable. Thus, while most religious discourse about God is beyond verification and so not knowledge strictly so called for empiricists, many of them would still hold it to be intelligible and so a legitimate object of *belief* (faith).

Now, normative discourse about how the world ought ideally to be precisely because it is about an *ideal* world not yet realised cannot be subjected to empirical tests; it is a matter of "value judgement". Since such discourse is clearly not tautological, it must for the strict positivist be meaningless and unintelligible to anyone other than those who happen to uphold the same value judgements (who will understand each other in a kind of echo chamber effect). Hence, while not explicitly endorsing Positivism but clearly drawing on these presuppositions, Friedman asserts (a) that all value judgements are to be banished entirely from economics, which is to become a purely positive science and (b) "about differences in fundamental values men can ultimately only fight" (Friedman, 1953: 3). There is no possibility of meaningful dialogue between those echo chambers. It is perhaps sobering and relevant to remark on how much of this outlook is reflected in the politics of populist extremists of our own day.

Be that as it may, Friedman's position has profound implications for the personal ethical responsibility of economists. Professional economists are studiously to avoid any kind of value judgement in their work even if this leads to the most dismal conclusions. Economists are most certainly not to offer normative policy advice to governments or to businesses. They are not, at least in their professional capacity, to have any normative views whatever. Decisions about what economic policies to follow are to be made by politicians (in their echo chambers). At the very most, an economist might consult for a government as a kind of agent who would explain, drawing on analysis of how economies actually work in reality, how certain policy goals might most effectively be attained.

But such a position implies a complete abdication of personal ethical responsibility by the professional economist in his/her work role. In the first place, they are not allowed at any time to bring their own ethical standpoints into play in their professional work; and even worse perhaps, they may find themselves offering detailed policy advice to governments or businesses with whose ultimate value judgements and thus policy goals they profoundly disagree. Of course, while seeking to apply the methods of positive economics over most of their professional work, many, if not most, economists find in practice that they cannot entirely suppress their moral values – they cannot entirely kill their consciences, in effect. For it should be clear that if applied rigorously, Friedman's injunction to strict value neutrality would imply a highly stressful split personality syndrome whereby economists in their professional practice (whatever that is) would be robots manipulating econometrics in a manner devoid of any moral values, while in another role as real people, they would be making free choices that derive from their own personal value judgements and ethical standpoints; and they will, *inter alia*, vote in elections or referenda about policy matters. Putting the point brutally and without wishing to make any extravagant psychological claims, when a person is put in a work situation where they have to systematically suppress their moral values and even do work that contradicts those values, that will in the long-term create huge personal stress. Such stress can only become bearable if one has recourse to what Sartre has mercilessly called the bad faith pretence that "I had no choice".

Whatever the personal pressures and contradictions to which the Friedmanite position leads, we can certainly see how it has led to a serious erosion of any sense of personal ethical responsibility among professional economists. There has been an effective abdication of moral responsibility for the consequences of their policy advice by large swathes of mainstream neoclassical economists, most particularly by those protagonists of free markets who have come to be known as Market Fundamentalists,[9] or in Europe as ultra-liberals. Consider, for example, the advice gleefully given by leading free market economists to the Eastern European economies in the aftermath of the collapse of the communist system in Eastern Europe: the so-called shock therapy, whereby those economies were to move overnight to a completely market-based system in which the role of the state would be reduced to an absolute minimum and in which all state-owned enterprises were to be immediately privatised.[10] Little or no thought was given either to the consequences this would have for those less fortunate in those societies (whether in terms of wealth or health) or to the challenges of cronyism and corruption such a sudden radical move and sell-off of state assets would lead to. It just was not the economist's job to think about these issues of fairness and/or corruption. During this event, as we now know, many less fortunate people in these countries saw their economic position and their health deteriorate seriously, in particular as a result of alcohol abuse.[11] Moreover, major Russian state enterprises were immediately and summarily privatised, sold off at prices way below their worth to an élite group of oligarchs (who, prior to the collapse, had been the kingpins of the Russian black market economy). Russia is to this day coping with the consequences. But what is poignantly telling from the point of view of this book is that these consequences *could have been avoided*. Instead of a headlong and unreflecting charge into a market fundamentalist frenzy, Russia could have instead adopted the model of a Nordic welfare state or of the European social market economy. And, of course, all those state enterprises did not need to be privatised; they could have been retained in state control while operating in a market system. This was the Chinese way. Not only was it already in place in China since 1978 (and could therefore have been copied by Russia if it so wished), it can also hardly be described as a totally flawed economic system, given China's phenomenal and stable economic growth and development since 1980.[12]

A similar insensitivity among certain mainstream neoclassical economists to the moral consequences of their policy stances can also be seen in the contemporary Eurozone. The advocates of a strict fiscal austerity are basically wedded to the view that financial markets rule and that only adherence to the strictest fiscal austerity can be compatible with the "efficient" operation of those markets. That such adherence to fiscal austerity should cause pain and suffering is perhaps regrettable, but it is also inevitable. Positive Economics (supposedly) teaches us that "*there is no alternative*", as we have been repeatedly told by Margaret Thatcher to Wolfgang Schäuble. But for those of us who have studied Sartre, as already emphasised in the prolegomenon to this chapter, of course *there is always an alternative*. Pretending we have no choice is itself a choice.

If we think the exclusion of ethical concerns and the resultant abdication of ethical responsibility by economists, both in methodological theorising and in professional practice, as I have been describing above, are morally problematic, then the importance of the ethical education/formation of economists (the central theme of this book) is clear-cut. But in order to reinforce such a definitive conclusion, which goes against the approach of so much of the economics mainstream as practised today, it will first be in order to subject Friedman's position to a searching philosophical critique; and, interestingly, one of the most powerful critiques comes from an eminent economist of similar vintage whose thought was incredibly prescient: Gunnar Myrdal.

The critique of Friedman's exclusion of ethics from economics

Before delving into economists' own critiques of Friedman's position on positive economics and value-neutrality, it may be useful to note that the positivist epistemology on which it is implicitly based (and without which it loses any cogency) is deeply flawed. According to positivist epistemology, again, any meaningful proposition must be either a tautology (a definition of words within a language) or empirically testable (at least in principle).[13] This is the so-called Verification Principle of Meaning. Yet if we apply this principle to itself, we can see that the principle is not a mere tautology. It is not just a definition of how words are used in a language; it is an assertion about the possibilities of knowledge of the world in which we live. In that case, the verification principle must itself be verifiable. To test this proposition empirically, we would need, of course, to be able to recognise a meaningful proposition when we encounter one. But how are we to do this? If one says a meaningful proposition can be recognised by its being a tautology or being testable, then we would be involved in a clear vicious circularity in our tests; we would be assuming what we were trying to prove or confirm in the empirical tests. Hence, we need some other way to recognise a meaningful proposition when we find one. One way to recognise a meaningful proposition, I would humbly suggest, is that the proposition be intelligible to another rational being. I am not saying that the proposition needs to be seen as true by another rational person or that they agree with it; I am just saying that they can simply understand the proposition even if they may not agree with it. If we thus accept intelligibility as the criterion for recognition of meaningful discourse, as opposed to unintelligible gibberish, then it is easy to see that there may be many propositions that are meaningful but neither tautology nor verifiable. "People ought not to kill except in self-defence". "People ought to strive to live together in harmony and mutual respect". These are normative propositions about an ideal world and therefore not verifiable by any kind of empirical test; but they can certainly be understood. I venture to say that you, dear reader, understood these sentences whether or not you agree with them. But in that case, *the Verification Principle of Meaning has already been falsified* insofar as I have found some meaningful propositions that are neither tautologies nor empirically verifiable. There are many other areas of discourse besides the normative that may offer examples that are neither tautological nor verifiable – for example, religious discourse (it cannot all be dismissed as unintelligible) or discourse about alternative universes in cosmology. The latter may be debatable, but it is once again intelligible.

But in the light of this epistemological proof of the untenability of the Verification Principle of Meaning, not only is the very foundation stone of Positivism destroyed, but normative discourse, as carried out in moral philosophy and ethics, can also no longer just be dismissed as meaningless. It is rather a shame that economists have not realised this since such refutation of Positivism as an epistemology as I have just outlined is certainly not original and has been well recognised by philosophers since at least the 1950s.[14]

But if the mainstream has continued to apply the banishment of normative discourse and the resultant abdication of moral responsibility in professional policy advice, there have been some economists who have rejected in various ways the Friedmanite injunction and have sought to integrate ethics into economics. Probably the first to come to mind for many economists is Amartya Sen.[15] Sen has argued that through fascination with mathematical econometric modelling, a social engineering slant has overtaken the thinking of many, if not most, economists at the expense of an approach that integrates ethical concerns when dealing with practical policy questions.[16] But precisely because the mathematical approach has made possible so many advances in our understanding of the world economy as a complex, interdependent system, that approach has drowned out the ethical concerns and obscured the fact that economics began as political economy and was originally seen as a branch of Applied Ethics (as we saw above). Sen clearly laments this and urges a revival of the tradition of political economy while also arguing that the theories of the engineering approach can provide valuable insights into contemporary reflections on ethics and moral philosophy (a position with which I would entirely concur).

A much more searching critique from within the profession that has largely been overlooked dates back to before Sen's 1987 work; I am referring to Swedish economist Gunnar Myrdal's 1959 masterpiece *Value in Social Theory*.[17] Myrdal points out that economists protest in vain about their supposed value neutrality and banishment of all normative ethical considerations from their science (or perhaps we should say discipline). He points out that every economist is inescapably involved in implicit or hidden value judgements in two ways: (a) in the selection of topics for study as an economist and (b) in the manner of the construction of the abstractions inevitably necessary for theorising. Taking the first point, topics of research in any science are hardly chosen in a purely random manner; rather, they reflect value judgements made by the researcher or by those funding the research regarding what the most urgent problems are where the research is being carried out. Across many developed and emergent countries, various types of cancer have become a leading source of mortality, and so, naturally enough, huge efforts are being put into basic medical and scientific research on this disease. Are we to abandon this research in an orgy of misguided value neutrality or are we, rather, to admit that it is morally right and proper – a good thing – that research (and research funding) *should* be devoted to alleviating a major source of human suffering? I daresay that most would agree with the latter, and that is certainly what Myrdal was defending. Research in the social sciences *should* be devoted to resolving the most pressing social problems of the day. Admittedly, there may in our own day be those who would argue that the research to be undertaken should be geared towards maximising financial returns for the researchers/institutions. That is a lamentable betrayal of the pursuit of truth as the ultimate goal of academic enquiry symptomatic of the post-modernist morass in which we trudge, but interestingly, it also embodies an inherent value judgement (of market fundamentalist stripe) about what research should be undertaken. Myrdal's first point thus remains: the very first premise of any scientific research remains a (perhaps often implicit) value judgement about what research topics are to be prioritised and funded.

Coming to Myrdal's second point, this is perhaps more subtle. Any science must make some abstraction from aspects of the phenomena it studies in order to make progress in understanding complex realities. If we seek to understand phenomena in every aspect of their real-world complexity right from the start, we will be overwhelmed. Therefore, scientists will abstract from certain aspects of complex reality that they hope will turn out to be irrelevant (or largely so) for the workings of the phenomena under study. To take a simple example, economists, when developing the theory of consumer demand, will abstract from the colour of consumers' hair. That can safely be presumed to be irrelevant unless one is looking at the market for hair dyes! That does not preclude the possibility that some scientist may in the future discover that hair colour is absolutely crucial to consumer preference patterns for all sorts of things besides hair dyes. But for the moment, in developing a theory of consumer demand, abstracting from consumers' hair colour offers a plausible but falsifiable working hypothesis. Myrdal then adds a key insight regarding abstraction patterns in the human sciences: the abstractions we construct may involve ignoring aspects of human reality that are of moral/ethical significance, and in that case, an implicit moral judgement (as to unimportance of this aspect) is being made. A telling example of this is the discussion by economists and human resource specialists of factors of production and cost-cutting economies. Economists have developed a theory of the production function in which "labour" and "capital equipment" are treated on an equal footing; they are simply arguments in a production function. This involves abstracting from the specifically human features of the labour factor for purposes of developing production theories. But while scientifically understandable, this procedure may involve hidden value judgements that will become abundantly clear when such theories are applied to deal with practical problems. Advanced countries are today engaging in a veritable orgy of cost-cutting over a whole variety of fields of production in both the public and private sectors; low-cost approaches are the order of the day. Such cost-cutting, although sometimes dressed up as increasing access to certain goods, is actually motivated by a drive to increase profitability through the leanest production methods possible, and as such, it will try to minimise the usage of factors of production and pay externally hired factors as little as possible. But whereas the ruthless quest for efficiency and cost minimisation in the use of capital equipment causes no immediate human suffering, minimising labour inputs generates unemployment, and wage-cutting dis-improves the standard of living of employees. Although it may shock many economists who gleefully talk about "churn rates" and "downsizing", such cost-cutting on the labour side generates human suffering and so *is not morally neutral*. It should be noted that we are not saying here that every act of laying off an employee is immoral. But what is inescapable and what tends to be obscured by the economist's way of constructing abstractions in the theory of production is that such acts *always* have ethical significance insofar as they affect, often profoundly, the well-being and security of other human beings. Put another way, firing employees is never ethically neutral and always involves a choice in which an employer should weigh the benefits of the firing for the company (and society) as a whole against the suffering that will be generated for the fired employee.

The upshot of Myrdal's critique is profound. It means that maintaining a strict value neutrality, as advocated by Friedman, is not only based on a deeply flawed positivist epistemology but is also, in any case, impossible to maintain. Value judgements will inevitably be present in the selection of topics to research and in the abstractions we may make from certain aspects of the human reality we study in economics and other human sciences.

Ethical value-laden economics or (should we say) political economy

If value judgements are thus inevitably present in economics and if we are to follow the call of Sen and others to return to the great tradition of political economy in which economists openly offered detailed normative policy advice, the question of how best to integrate ethical concerns into the professional work of economists naturally arises. This is at once a methodological question (at what point and how are the value judgements to appear as an economist does his/her work?) and a question of personal responsibility and education (how are economists to develop their own understanding of ethical questions in order to be better able to form their value judgements?). In this section, we will deal with the methodological question, and in the next the questions of personal responsibility.

Methodologically speaking, the key requirement, once we take on board Myrdal's points, is that economists should openly acknowledge the value judgements they are making in developing their theories. Of course, this could in many cases be embarrassing given the nature of those implicit value judgements as to what are both urgent problems and defensible abstractions. Many economists might be reluctant to have the detail of their ethical and political philosophical standpoints thus paraded in public and may even fear that their views will be taken less seriously if their ideological standpoints are thus laid bare. It is interesting at this point to note a convergence between the methodological position adopted by Myrdal on value neutrality and the Critical Social Theory tradition of the Frankfurt School, even though Myrdal is not considered a member of said school. A (or perhaps the) leading theme of the Frankfurt School is that in all social theorizing, there are implicit ideological positions imported to the analysis of social events and human interaction by the theorist. This, for the Frankfurt School, is inevitable because of constructionist epistemology. As one of its great contemporary exponents, Jürgen Habermas, has outlined, all human knowledge is constructed in the Kantian sense that in every act of perception/observation, the human mind is actively construing the data of sense in accordance with various a priori frameworks. This is inevitable because human perception can never be purely passive. Moreover, as Habermas pointed out, not only do we construct reality in accordance with a priori frameworks but those frameworks we use also invariably reflect in some way our own interests in life; and so, all too often, we see what we want to see![18] This phenomenon ranges all the way from the thirsty man who sees an oasis in the desert to bigoted (or maybe not so bigoted) people who see in the human world only confirmations of their preconceived stereotypes of certain people or problems. Arising from these epistemological insights, the Frankfurt School theorists have argued that a central task of the human sciences is precisely to unmask and lay bare the ideologies that lie behind various economic and political standpoints – both theories and practical individual/business actions or public policies. This is what Geuss has called the emancipatory function of the human sciences and scientist[19] – relieving people from their enslavement to certain ideologies (often presented as having no alternative).

It will be clear how this position converges with the first methodological injunction that follows from Myrdal's critique of what we might even call the "ideology" of positive economics. But where the Frankfurt School and Critical Social Theory in general are making a radical political point, Myrdal's intention is perhaps softer and more limited: he just wants economists to openly acknowledge their implicit value judgements.

Before we leave this theme of openness in regard to the value judgements of economists, we should mention the strange case of "welfare economics". Surely, it may be said, mainstream economics has maintained at least one area of normative discussion where in fact relevant value judgements are made fully explicit, i.e. the area known as welfare economics. In welfare economics, economists have sought, after all, to reach normative conclusions regarding questions of economic policy despite the dominant Friedmanite injunction. This they do on the basis of a normative criterion so basic that it seems innocuous and not really a value judgement at all, i.e. the famous Pareto criterion whereby any social change that leaves some people better off (with higher utility; –whatever that is) and nobody worse off represents a social improvement and so ought to be undertaken. Pareto optimality is then a social situation from which no further Pareto improvement is possible. As it happens, the analyses of welfare economics have been largely, although not exclusively, confined to demonstrations of the Pareto optimality of free market economies under conditions of perfect competition (and perfect information) and to analyses of the potential gains from free international trade and factor movement in the world economy. From the standpoint we have adopted in this chapter and this book, this is all well and good, but it remains extremely limited. First of all, the normative criterion being used, even if innocuous, is extremely narrow. There is no consideration, for example, of the distribution of gains, and this has been a glaring omission, in some cases completely compromising the otherwise valid Pareto-based normative arguments. For example, the Paretian case for free trade in the world economy is clear-cut (and predates Pareto, going back in fact to Ricardo's theory of comparative cost advantage), but the classic argument demonstrates only that global world output can be increased through free trade under conditions of perfect competition and tells us nothing about the distribution of those gains. Tragically, in our own day, sight has been lost of this fundamental point as certain countries race towards a mutually destructive protectionism that will bring Pareto dis-improvement to the world economy when in fact what may be needed is to address the question of an equitable sharing of the gains from free trade throughout the world. Conventional mainstream welfare economics has in effect remained silent on this question, and indeed the well-known Kaldor-Hicks compensation principle only serves to sidestep the distributional issues by speaking of potential Pareto improvement in cases where there may be some losers. To make definitive normative utterances on the distribution of the gains from trade would involve invoking further value judgements besides the basic Pareto norm. Value judgements about fairness and equity of distribution at world level would have to be explicitly made. That is territory into which mainstream welfare economics dares not tread, no doubt because of Friedman inspired inhibitions. It is an example of a wider criticism that can be made of welfare economics, and that is immediately obvious to any trained philosopher. The welfare economics approach is based on one very narrow norm – the Pareto norm – and this in turn is a watered down version of Bentham's utilitarian norm (the greatest happiness principle) whereby a good action is one that makes a net addition to human happiness or well-being.[20] But there is more – much more – to ethics and moral philosophy than just the utilitarian norm, let alone its narrower Paretian variant. There are moral philosophies based on natural law and notions of stewardship of natural resources that are certainly relevant to the topics of economics. There is the Kantian Categorical Imperative that, if strictly applied, would carry radical implications for the treatment of workforces. There are the ideas coming from Eastern Buddhist wisdom regarding the Middle Way and avoidance of excess in all things, which leads towards the principles of the Sufficiency Economy, as championed by Thailand.

Thus, welfare economics, as developed in the 20th century, has been but a pale shadow of the great explicitly normative tradition of 19th century political economy. It has been very restricted in scope, confined by the self-imposed straitjacket of just one very narrow norm and, as a result, practically limited regarding pronouncements on the significant challenges of the economic policy of our day (notably free trade questions). Sen has discussed these limitations in some depth and has reached the trenchantly expressed conclusion:

> The position of welfare economics in modern economic theory has been a rather precarious one. . . . As the suspicion of the use of ethics in economics has grown welfare economics has appeared to be increasingly dubious. It has been put into an arbitrarily narrow box separated from the rest of economics.[21]

Personal responsibility and the imperative of integrating ethics in the conduct of the discipline of economics

In this chapter, we have on the one hand seen that the methodological injunction to avoid normative discourse in the professional conduct of the economist's work, which to this day dominates the mainstream of economics (apart from the bizarre and increasingly disconnected enclave of welfare economics), is methodologically unsound, being based on an incoherent positivist epistemology; and on the other hand seen that in any case, economists (as any human scientists) cannot avoid value judgements in the conduct of their professional work since such judgements will inevitably be present in their choice of topics to research and in their construction of abstractions. The attempted elimination of normative discourse from the professional conduct of economists is thus methodologically impossible and indefensible.

But we have also seen that the abdication of a sense of personal responsibility for one's views and theorising that the ban on normative discourse has brought (and indeed conveniently rationalised for many economists) is also deeply problematic. It is problematic firstly at the level of the individual economist, who is expected to develop a potentially highly stressful split personality whereby in one's professional work all moral and ethical considerations are to be suppressed while in one's private life one is expected and enjoined to live by certain personal ethical standards. But it is also politically problematic insofar as policy advice potentially damaging to large swathes of people in the real world may be given under the guise of value neutrality. I have already given clear examples of shock therapy in post-Soviet Russia and austerity policies in the Eurozone. The professional (market fundamentalist) economist will simply say that it is not his or her problem to worry about such distributional or other such collateral human suffering questions as may arise from the policies recommended.

But if we revert to the Sartrean insights regarding freedom of choice with which we began the chapter, such moral indifference to human suffering is not simple indifference; it involves a moral choice to deliberately ignore and discount such suffering (without even trying dubiously to defend it as for a greater good). It is therefore deeply immoral. To illustrate poignantly the point that moral indifference can be a choice that may amount to a highly immoral negligence, please just consider the following vignette. You are walking on a beach entirely alone. You know the beach, it is safe and you can swim strongly. In the water, you see a struggling child, probably panicking in the waves and about to drown. There is nobody else around. If you ignore the child (moral indifference: not my problem, Sir), the child will very probably drown given the wave size. I would submit that if you do not get in the water promptly to save the child, you are guilty not just of moral indifference but of a *deeply unethical moral negligence*. I can already hear the objections: but that assumes this or that moral standpoint that may not be shared by all or this or that assumption about the strength of the waves (you know the beach and have often swum there) or maybe that the child wants to commit suicide (highly unlikely for a child, and, in any case, you do not know this). But I rest my case. To ignore the drowning child as "not my problem" is deeply immoral negligence; and if we start agonising over whose morals to apply or that it may be suicide, the child will have drowned before we make up our minds to act.

If these strictures and the broader argument of this chapter are accepted, where does it leave us in terms of the formation of economists? It seems to me that we can identify a number of concluding implications:

a   In the first place, it clearly echoes Sen's call that we need to **bring ethics back into economics**; or, rather, since the argument was always, in any case, present in the abstractions and ideological presuppositions of the discipline, to render the moral and ethical basis of economics fully explicit. That will not come easily partly because economists have become very attached to playing elaborate mathematical games ostensibly devoid of any moral content in their econometric playground. It will also no doubt be embarrassing for many economists to have to face up to admitting openly their ethical presuppositions.[22]

b   Having brought ethical considerations explicitly back into economics, it should follow naturally that economists will develop **a much greater sense of personal responsibility**, at least in regard to the socio-economic and political consequences of their policy recommendations. On the one hand, they should recognise that their policy suggestions have the potential to profoundly affect the lives of millions of human beings and so are suffused with moral responsibilities that they can no longer conveniently brush under the carpet. Inevitably, in considering the extended consequences for the lives of many that are implicit in economic policies, economists will have to look beyond the narrow confines of purely economic data to consider a variety of psychological, sociological, cultural and political consequences of said policies;[23] and this will bring a very welcome inter-disciplinarity into a discipline that perhaps more than the other human sciences has suffered from being confined to its own narrow, self-referential silo.

c   With ethics explicitly present and the personal moral responsibility of economists in respect of their policy recommendations centrally emphasised, it will also become important that, in the formation of economists and in their induction into the profession, there should be present a significant **education in moral and political philosophy**. This, of course, would represent only a return to its roots for the discipline, and in certain universities, at any rate, students can still study simultaneously philosophy, politics and economics for their first degree.[24] This practice deserves to become much more generalised in the education of economists.

d   This same point regarding the broadening of the education of economists can also be made, in general, with respect to business schools teaching management studies. As the scandals have mounted and the behaviour of certain segments of the financial sector has become ever more dubious and certainly self-serving, there is a nascent awareness of the importance of bringing ethical concerns into the centre of management studies (business administration) as well as economics. After all, much of the argument of this chapter regarding the influence of positivism, hidden value judgements and the degree to which affected moral indifference may often amount to seriously immoral negligence applies with equal force to the manner in which an array of management subjects (most notably corporate finance, marketing and strategic management) have developed over the past 50 years in business schools. These are not, however, our concern in this book, but the parallel between what we have argued regarding the ethical formation of economists and the imperative of integrating moral philosophy into the education of managers and business leaders is clear-cut and striking.

Notes

1 For a more detailed discussion of this point about what can be known in self-reflection by any human being, see O'Sullivan P. (1987) *Economic Methodology and Freedom to Choose*, Allen & Unwin, London, chapter 12. This book has been republished verbatim with the same title as a Routledge Revival in 2012.
2 The classic reference to Sartre's work here is Sartre J. P. (2007) *Existentialism and Humanism*, Methuen, London; passim.
3 Adam Smith's first great work was in fact on moral philosophy and ethics. See Smith, A. (1759) *Theory of Moral Sentiments,* Kincaid & Bell, Edinburgh. His much more famous *The Wealth of Nations* was published later in 1776.
4 Smith A. (1776) *An Enquiry into the Nature and Causes of the Wealth of Nations*, Methuen, London (various editions and reprints). See book 1V, chapter 2
5 Friedman M. (1953) *Essays in Positive Economics*, Chicago: University of Chicago Press. See in particular chapter 1, "The Methodology of Positive Economics".
6 Blaug M. (1992) *The Methodology of Economics* 2nd Ed, Cambridge: Cambridge University Press.
7 Friedman (1953), ibid chapter 1.
8 Ayer A. J. (1971) *Language Truth and Logic*, Pelican, London.
9 On the credo of Market Fundamentalists, see O'Sullivan P. (forthcoming) "The Capital Asset Pricing Model and Efficient Markets Hypothesis: A Market Fundamentalist Fairy Tale", *International Journal of Political Economy*.
10 Often associated with the so-called Washington Consensus, this approach was in particular defended by the American economist Jeffrey Sachs and ultimately by economists of the Chicago School, deeply influenced by Friedman, who had also pioneered such policies in Pinochet's Chile. See, for example, Sachs, J. (1996) "Achieving Rapid Growth in the Transition Economies of Central Europe", *Harvard Institute for International Development, Development Discussion Paper* no. 544. See also a very good summary of these themes at http://geohistory.today/russia-shock-therapy/ accessed 30 May 2018. On the Washington Consensus, see Williamson, J. (ed.) (1989) *Latin American Readjustment: How Much has Happened*, Institute for International Economics, Washington, DC. See chapter 2.
11 The most well known case is that of Russia, which in the early 1990s saw a sharp drop in average life expectancy. This was subsequently reversed, but it is shocking that a relatively advanced Eurasian country should experience such a phenomenon over a sustained period of years, and one in which the drop had no connection with any kind of natural disaster. For a detailed account, see Shkolnikov, V., McGee, M., & Leon, D.

(2001) "Changes in Life Expectancy in Russia in the Mid-1990s", *The Lancet* vol. 357, issue. 9260, 24 March, pp. 917–921.

12 Some flaws the Chinese system certainly has, but they have not led to economic catastrophe; and in any case, the market fundamentalist states are hardly without flaws themselves, notably in terms of inequalities and general anxiety; and ofcourse they cannot prevent economic catastrophes, such as the 1997 Asian crisis or 2008 American subprime crisis.

13 Ayer, A. J. (1971), op cit chapter 1.

14 Indeed, it was the recognition of the untenability of positivism that perplexed Bertrand Russell and led Ludwig Wittgenstein to turn to the epistemological relativism of his language game philosophy.

15 Sen, A. (2004) *On Ethics and Economics*, Basil Blackwell, Oxford. (First published 1987).

16 Sen, A. (2004), op.cit. pg 8.

17 Myrdal, G. (1959) *Value in Social Theory*, Routledge and Kegan Paul, London. See especially the succinct introduction to the work by Paul Streeten.

18 For all of this, see Habermas J. (1972) *Knowledge and Human Interests*, Heinemann, London.

19 See Geuss R. (1999) *The Idea of a Critical Theory: Habermas and the Frankfurt School*, Cambridge University Press, Cambridge.

20 This last is a hugely problematic philosophical qualification into which we need not venture here: are happiness and well-being synonymous?

21 Sen, A. (2004), op. cit pg 29.

22 How many market fundamentalists would be prepared to espouse openly, for example, the so-called ethical egoism advocated by Ayn Rand? This is effectively the moral underpinning for those who extol the pursuit of self-interest as leading to, if not actually constituting directly in itself, the greatest good. See Rand, A. (1964) *The Virtue of Selfishness: A New Concept of Egoism*, Signet Books, New York.

23 In this connection, we may note the significance of the Social Progress Index (SPI) (and indeed some of the other alternative indices to GDP) that has appeared in recent years. For the SPI, the macrolevel performance of a society in terms of development and well-being cannot be assessed purely in terms of classic but ever so narrow indicators such as GDP per capita and its growth rate. Rather, social progress (and thus the evaluation of the eventual impact of economic as well as social policies) is to be assessed using a very broadly based indicator that pays attention to a whole variety of aspects of human life in society: mortality, health and wellness, personal safety, quality of the natural environment, rights to self-expression and freedom over life choices, tolerance and inclusion. The SPI is freely available online at www.socialprogressindex.com/ accessed 01 June 2018.

24 The author admits to having been lucky enough to have studied this combination for his first degree.

References

Ayer, A. J. (1971) *Language Truth and Logic*, Pelican, London.

Blaug, M. (1992) *The Methodology of Economics* 2nd Ed, Cambridge: Cambridge University Press.

Friedman, M. (1953) *Essays in Positive Economics*, Chicago: University of Chicago Press.

Geuss, R. (1999) *The Idea of a Critical Theory: Habermas and the Frankfurt School*, Cambridge University Press, Cambridge.

Habermas, J. (1972) *Knowledge and Human Interests*, Heinemann, London.

Song, A. http://geohistory.today/russia-shock-therapy/ accessed 30 May 2018.

Myrdal, G. (1959) *Value in Social Theory*, Routledge and Kegan Paul, London.

O'Sullivan, P. (1987) *Economic Methodology and Freedom to Choose,* Allen & Unwin, London. Reprinted 2012 by Routledge, London as a Routledge Revival.

O'Sullivan, P. (forthcoming) "The Capital Asset Pricing Model and Efficient Markets Hypothesis: A Market Fundamentalist Fairy Tale," *International Journal of Political Economy.*

Rand, A. (1964) *The Virtue of Selfishness: A New Concept of Egoism,* Signet Books, New York.

Sachs, J. (1996) "Achieving Rapid Growth in the Transition Economies of Central Europe," *Harvard Institute for International Development, Development Discussion Paper* no. 544.

Sartre, J. P. (2007) *Existentialism and Humanism,* Methuen, London.

Sen, A. (2004) *On Ethics and Economics,* Basil Blackwell, Oxford.

Shkolnikov, V., McGee, M., & Leon, D. (2001) "Changes in Life Expectancy in Russia in the Mid-1990s," *The Lancet,* vol. 357, issue. 9260, 24 March, pp. 917–921.

Smith, A. (1776) *An Enquiry into the nature and Causes of the Wealth of Nations,* Methuen, London (various editions and reprints).

Williamson, J. (ed.) (1989) *Latin American Readjustment: How Much has Happened,* Institute for International Economics, Washington, DC.

www.socialprogressindex.com/ accessed 01 June 2018.

5 Social connection and the responsible economist

Craig Duckworth

Introduction

Recent discussions of professional economic ethics have centred around George DeMartino's acute contribution (DeMartino & McCloskey, 2011, see also 2013a, 2013b, 2016; DeMartino & McCloskey, 2018). Concerns about the ethical character of the economics profession predate the 2008 financial crisis. Johnson, 1937, for example, reflects interwar concerns about ivory-towered economics (see also Bartlett, 2009; DeMartino & McCloskey, 2005) and the crisis does not constitute the core of DeMartino's concerns. Policy interventions in transitional economies and the developing South were, he argues, earlier cause for alarm (e.g. DeMartino & McCloskey, 2011: 142–144). However, the 2008 crisis and its origins, as many see it, in ideological conviction and professional hubris (Desai, 2015), added momentum to the debate. For many, including, for example, Heise (2017, 2018), the financial crisis was a watershed for professional introspection among economists.

In *The Economist's Oath*, DeMartino presents arguments in favour of the ethical reform of economics and what he sees as its usual style of policy formation and implementation. A *theorist knows best* style of economic policy supports a top-down approach in which the democratic voice is largely ignored. Criticisms of this mode of policy intervention are not new. John Dewey (1927), Joseph Stiglitz (2003) and Amartya Sen (2001), to cite three well-known examples (for a more recent view, see Dow [2017], Coyle [2012]), are among those who regret the distance between the mechanisms of policy design and implementation and policy recipients. What is different in DeMartino is that he sees modification of behaviour within the economics profession itself as a way to improve the situation, rather than, primarily, theoretical or regulatory change. Deliberative democrats, for example, who share DeMartino's concerns, consider that the epistemic virtues of public deliberation recommend democratic consultation as essential for legitimate policy formation (Bohman, 1998). But DeMartino does not ask that the economist take on new ways of thinking – to think like the deliberative democrat, say. He recommends changes to economists' conduct as a way to address what he and others see as economics' ills.

A central component of his argument is a harm-based thesis that points to the too often profoundly negative implications of economic intervention.

He couples this with a character-based account of the normative basis of a needed revision of existing economic praxis (see also Dekker & Klamer, 2016, who emphasise the latter). While the harm-based aspect of DeMartino's thesis draws attention to the consequences of economists' professional conduct, the character-based dimension considers its consistency with their personal moral outlooks. The harm-based aspect provides a normative reason to introduce a behavioural code into professional economic practice, while the emphasis on character is intended to prevent this reducing to mere rule following. The notion of moral character, having its roots in Aristotelian virtue theory (for recent discussion, see Alzola, 2015), employs a conception of moral reasoning that sees it as the application of mature moral sensitivities, of practical wisdom (in particular, Aristotle, 2009: Book VI), rather than obedience to codes of conduct.

The distinction is a common one that resonates with traditional debates in moral theory, and appears in other professional contexts. Postema (1980) supports a character-based approach for the legal profession, arguing that a rigid division between personal and professional contexts, advocated classically by Montaigne (1965, Book III, Ch. 10), may be too permissive. It has been suggested, for example (Loewenstein et al., 2012, Cain et al., 2010), that disclosing conflicting interests (and in that way following a professional moral code) can be viewed as licence to offer biased advice – this owing to "*moral licensing* (the often unconscious feeling that biased advice is justifiable because the advisee has been warned)" (Loewenstein et al., 2012: 669). Encouraging the professional to reflect on the ethical consistency of his or her professional and personal ethics is one way to avoid this kind of moral derailment. A positive feature of DeMartino's thesis appears to be that he, indeed, promotes this kind of consistency by combining harm-based reasoning (with its justification for normative constraint on behaviour, associated with a professional code) with considerations that are associated with agents' personal moral sensitivity.

I argue in this chapter, however, that DeMartino cannot easily help himself to either of these positions. Harm and character-based views are found wanting when viewed in the light of certain structural features of a professional economic ethic. They produce only unproductive confrontation between this kind of proponent of professional economic ethics and (the many) economists who defend a restricted, technical conception of the profession. This negative proposition may seem dispiriting to people who, like me, see immense value in DeMartino's project. Alternative support for his thesis can be found, however, in the shape of Iris Marion Young's *social connection* theory of personal responsibility (Young, 2003, 2006, 2010, 2013, 2010). Young's thesis has implications for professional economic ethics. Applied to economics, Young demands that economists adopt a perspective that incorporates an appreciation of the role of their discipline in shaping societal outcomes. It requires economists to take an extra-disciplinary perspective that takes into account its societal consequences. In this way, Young's thesis offers a way to ground DeMartino's arguments that avoids mere intellectual standoff. Her thesis also has important implications for the place of pluralist or meta-methodological thinking in economics. While many argue for the positive benefits of a pluralist perspective, Young's thesis offers a way to see it as a professional responsibility.

Section 1 contains an outline of certain structural features of a professional ethic, drawing on the notion of an economist's oath. It provides basic ingredients for the claim, made in section 2, that DeMartino's argument stands in need of revision. Section 3 considers Young's account of personal responsibility and its implications for economics. Section 4 notes, in particular, how Young's social connection thesis entails a responsibility to adopt a pluralist stance. A final part concludes.

1. Voluntary commitment and the professional oath

In his leading contribution to the debate around professional economic ethics, George DeMartino (2011) envisions the economics initiate taking a ceremonial oath. It is revealing to consider why public oath taking might be thought a necessary gateway to the economics profession. It is, of course, a way to emulate the way that medicine and aspects of the legal and political professions, for example, incorporate respect for behavioural principles, and so a way for economics to signal corresponding intent (for a helpful account of the paradigmatic Hippocratic Oath, see Hulkower, 2016). But, more than this, the significance of oaths reflects the normative character of their specific content. One would not expect to take an oath to be punctual for work meetings, for example, or to not be routinely insubordinate. These kinds of behaviour are easily monitored, and direct and transparent incentives can be used to discourage such conduct. Oaths, on the other hand, are associated with behaviours that rely, primarily, on *self*-governance. Indeed, oaths ordinarily contain injunctions that their adoptive professions may, to their detriment, find it difficult to monitor and regulate (cf. Williamson, 2000: 601, where he suggests oaths may be a partial way to address the problem of *incomplete contracts*).

This helps us to see that the taking of an oath functions, in intention, as an institutional device. The responsibilities it entails structure behaviour so as to achieve objectives towards which professions may not be naturally inclined and that are not easy to incentivise. Sulmasy (1999) presents arguments in favour of oath taking that see them as a mark of the professional and as carrying social benefits (Sulmasy, 1999: 340–342). He does not explicitly mention their institutional role, though he does view oaths as a way to regulate individual behaviour where other monitoring devices may be ineffective: "The patient, with no recourse but trust, has a moral claim on a special degree of trust in the care to be rendered. This is what the profession of an oath provides" (Sulmasy, 1999: 341).

Importantly, in this regard, and as the economist is likely to notice, an oath is a type of *commitment device*. Familiar from a variety of contexts (Bryan et al., 2010, contains a helpful review), commitment devices bolster resolve where an agent may be tempted to do other than was planned. They are a commonplace of business economics, in which investments that are costly to undo tie a firm into a future course of action. Perhaps more apposite are their role in everyday planning behaviour (on which see Bratman, 2014, 1987), in which the device (an agreement to meet, for example) does not override but merely supports the will. It has been observed that in Ancient Greece, an oath was viewed as an act of *self-cursing* (Sommerstein & Torrence, 2014: 2). Calamity was expected to visit the person who took but failed to remain faithful to an oath. But shorn of such transcendental connotations, an oath remains a means to make the commitment to its requirements credible.[1] Note, in this connection, the publicity and ceremonial solemnity of the declaration in DeMartino's work.

Talk of an economist's oath, then, indicates the character of the requirements that DeMartino, and like-minded economists, have in mind when they recommend a professional economic ethic. They are behavioural principles for which institutional design tends not to offer effective support. They are the type of principle for which self-governance, bolstered by (credible) commitment, on the part of the individual is required. One might think this account a little too mechanistic and want to say that the effect of an oath on behaviour is more like that of a professional ethos. This would be consistent with the view expressed here, however. An ethos is arguably a means to encourage commitment; see the discussion that emanates from Cohen (1992).

Some would argue that it is the commitment, simpliciter, that the professional makes that is the very source of the normativity of the behavioural requirements contained in a professional oath. Margaret Gilbert, in her work on *joint commitment*, argues that the commitment to carry out an act with one or more persons creates an obligation to the other party to perform the promised act (2014). According to Gilbert, a commitment is a form of decision that binds future action, and that in a context of joint action generates reciprocal obligations. Gilbert is not appealing here to the causal power of commitment, its capacity to actually bind the will at a future date (a mechanism that John Elster, for example, does "not understand" [2002: 1768], and that Williamson [2000, 1979], as is well known, sees as an unreliable constraint on future choice). It is the normative logic of commitment that Gilbert is pointing to. However, while the professional context can be interpreted as an example of joint action, and so lends itself to Gilbert's analysis, it is difficult to be convinced that, in this context, the act of commitment itself provides the basis of the normativity of a professional code of conduct.

Centrally, a commitment to a professional code is conditional. It is active only as long as the person making the commitment remains a member of the relevant profession, and membership can be voluntarily annulled at any time. This is something that Sulmasy (ibid.) appears not to recognise, alluding instead to the intrinsically, career spanning nature of professional commitment. It is true that an oath communicates a long-term intention. This does not, however, preclude withdrawal, and this can take place at any time.

In her celebrated consideration of Kantian moral philosophy, Phillipa Foot (1972) points up the voluntary character of moral commitment. Whether voluntariness is a central feature of morality per se or is restricted to specific domains (such as etiquette) remains a moot point in her paper. However, for contexts in which formal normative constraints are voluntarily accepted (as in the case of professional codes of ethics), Foot's point is a powerful one. The strength of (voluntary) commitment determines the degree of attachment to the normative principles contained in a professional code. However, commitment cannot itself be the source of the code's normative purchase because commitment (being voluntary) can be withdrawn ad libitum. So an account of the normativity of the kind of principles we are considering, that traces it to the act of commitment itself, fails to accommodate its *voluntary* character. It can be withdrawn with impunity if the person leaves the profession. Commitment would not, in this context, appear to tie anyone into binding, reciprocal obligations. Taking an oath to a profession is not the same as a wedding vow.

The idea of an economist's oath captures, then, the votive character of a professional economic ethic. The vow, however, to be faithful to the principles expressed in the oath is conditional. It holds only as long as the oath taker remains an economist. It is annulled with impunity whenever professional membership is renounced. This entails that, while an oath helps to make commitment to a professional ethic credible, and so has the potential to regulate behaviour, committing to be obedient in this way does not itself entail normative constraints. While Gilbert's thesis may hold for other contexts, commitment does not entail obligation in this one.

That the commitment to a professional economic ethic is voluntary may not, at first sight, appear to be problematic for DeMartino's thesis. It is a central task of moral theory to identify what we have normative reason to choose. However, in the context of professional economic ethics, voluntariness has arguably enervating consequences for DeMartino's approach. The next section attempts to say why.

2. DeMartino and the economist's defence

DeMartino offers a harm-based argument in support of professional economic ethics (e.g. 2011: 144–153, 159–168) and supplements this with a model of personal moral reasoning that emphasises the role of practical wisdom over mere rule application (e.g. ibid.: 85–88, 2013b). Both of these aspects of his reasoning come in two forms. They are, on the one hand, theoretical and as such connected to entrenched academic conversations. On the other, they are common sense accounts that appeal to everyday intuition. They are attractive in this respect because arguments in their favour need not rely on abstruse or specialised reasoning. This seeming virtue, however, is insufficient, I would argue, to recommend the position to the profession as a whole.

Consider, first, the harm-based aspect. The content of a professional ethic is specific to each distinct profession. Durkheim (1992) early noted that the virtues of the medic are not all relevant to the lawyer, say. This implies that the value of behaviours within a specific profession derive from the contribution they make to that particular profession overall. DeMartino's harm-based argument in favour of professional economic ethics aligns with this understanding of the value of ethical practice within professions. Ethical conduct is considered beneficial because it contributes to the health of the profession. But the specificity of the benefits (that they differ between professions) indicates a key difference between the normativity of the moral principles that hold within a profession and moral principles per se. While the latter normally apply universally, a professional ethic applies only to those who are members of the profession. Moreover, this allows that the normative principles considered appropriate be relative to the practitioners' shared conception of the nature and purpose of their profession. Even a prescriptive view of the social role of professions, such as that of Tawney (1921), allows for controversy within each profession as to how its social purpose is best achieved. This suggests that putative normative professional principles do not possess moral status independently of a conception of the profession to which they are intended to apply. Indeed the conception provides a rationale for the acceptance of the principles they support. We have seen that commitment to the principles is not, *pace* Gilbert, a plausible source of normativity in this context. The normative purchase of a professional ethic is in its supporting rationale, and voluntary acceptance of the rationale depends on acceptance of the associated conception of the profession's nature and purpose. This contingency creates serious issues for DeMartino's project.

As has been noted, DeMartino uses examples of seriously harmful consequences of, for example, autocratic policy implementation and methodological conviction. There are, indeed, many ways to criticise the application of economic theory to real-world policy issues and to support the thesis that current practice is wrong and ought to be changed. However, the contingent character of normative principles in a professional context entails that these types of argument can be rejected, out of court, by those who have a different vision of the role of economics and the economist.

Paul Krugman is representative. In a review of developments in economic geography, Martin (1999: 75) notes:

> Clearly there are aspects of . . . spatial agglomeration . . . that . . . lend themselves to mathematical representation and modelling. But there are also severe epistemological and ontological limits to such a narrow approach. For one thing, it means that "messy" social, cultural and institutional factors involved in spatial economic development are neglected. Since these factors cannot be reduced to or expressed in mathematical form they are assumed to be of secondary or marginal importance and, as Krugman puts it, are "best left to sociologists."

Boettke and O'Donnell (2016) are less suspicious than Krugman of interdisciplinary and qualitative research. However, they worry that requiring the economist to consider the societal consequences of his or her discipline casts him or her as social philosopher; and this may give an economist's own values and political views freer, rather than more limited, rein. They argue for a more secure boundary between the economist as scientist and the practices of policy implementation. Tackling the institutional deficiencies associated with the latter ought not to be, they say, the role of the academic researcher.

It is possible, then, for the economist to be more accommodating than Krugman and to accept the need for, for example, greater economic democracy. The economist might see the epistemic value of public consultation, for example. Yet she might, nonetheless, reject the notion that that aspect of policy implementation ought to feed into theory formation or be the responsibility of the practicing economist. The attempt to provide a harm-based justification for a professional economic ethics that demands greater respect for cultural and geographical context, for example, or deeper notions of well-being, turns out to be a battle for the soul of the profession. Those who would defend a restrictive, technical conception of economics can reject DeMartino's vision in toto and leave no basis from which to reorient the argument in favour of professional economic ethics. The result is unproductive deadlock.

The alternative tack, as I have noted, is to argue that the personal ethics of the economist offers a foundation for professional economic ethics. On this approach, it is practical wisdom rather than the application of ready-made principles that is the wellspring of morally sound professional conduct. In a sophisticated reading of this form of Aristotelian moral theory, the individual is viewed as acquiring critical powers while simultaneously being sensitised to the normative landscape of his or her social milieu through acculturation (see McDowell, 1996: Lecture VI). On this view, the value of ethical professional conduct does not derive solely from its contribution to the health of the profession as a whole. Its value is informed by and forms part of the personal moral outlook of the person. This type of view is supported in Larry May's much discussed work, in which the person is viewed as having multiple and overlapping identities (May, 1996; Cf Sen, 2015). Integration of personal and professional moral outlooks is not, however, a stable intellectual position. Professional ethics, it is often noted, is an example of role morality (Thompson, 1986), and this idea has much force here.

Consider again the commitment that the economist undertakes when committing to accept professional responsibilities. This is, we observed, a voluntary and conditional commitment. It holds as long as the person remains within the profession. Commitment can be rescinded at any point at which the person exits. This indicates that it is qua economist that a person makes the relevant commitment. In making the commitment, the person adopts a role, and it is in that role (and only while in that role) that the person is bound to honour the commitment he or she has made. The act of commitment, we might say, creates the role for the adoptive person and, thereby, the associated identity (a conception that has Sartrean overtones, Sartre [1946]).

If this analysis is correct, it is open to the mainstream economist to point to the fundamental role-based nature of the adoption of a professional ethic. If, as would be expected, they claim that the role (in its ethical aspect) ought to extend only to integrity and transparency and nothing else, then a DeMartino style argument will be unable to provide a convincing objection. Once again, the disagreement is about the nature of economics as a discipline, and this is orthogonal to the debate DeMartino wants to have about ethics.

It seems, then, that neither harm-based nor character-based reasoning can provide a way to argue for professional economic ethics. The harm-based approach is derivative. It derives its force from a conception of the economics profession that sees existing practice as socially harmful. This can be rejected, however, by those who view economics as having more restricted objectives. The alternative way of arguing for professional economic ethics that grounds it in personal moral outlooks also fails. It is as an economist and not as a person per se that professional responsibilities are held. To the extent that this argument is convincing, it will be dispiriting to those who consider professional economic ethics to be essential to the reform of the discipline and the wider profession. There is, however, an alternative approach, one that draws on the work of the political theorist Iris Marion Young.

3. Responsibility and social connection

One reaction to the idea that economics needs a professional ethic is the view that individual economists cannot be held responsible for aggregate societal outcomes over which they have no personal control. The mechanisms that produced the Great Depression of the 1930s or the financial crisis of the first decade of this century are, on this view, too complex and the structural and behavioural patterns too intricate to blame any individual or specific group of individuals. That kind of responsibility – the kind that identifies the guilty – is not, however, the type Iris Marion Young has in mind for what she calls the *social connection* model.

Drawing on the work of Hannah Arendt (1994, 1987), Young distinguishes between *forward-looking* and *backward-looking* responsibility. Whereas backward-looking responsibility attempts to name the blameworthy, the forward-looking variety captures the type of actions a person is responsible for doing; and what a person is responsible for doing is not necessarily that for which she can or ought to be held responsible in a backward-looking sense.

To motivate the distinction, Young points out that social outcomes are the result of complex causal factors, of intricate and interrelated behaviours and events. She emphasises the fundamental role of social structure in influencing opportunities, interests and allocations in a way that shapes agents' choices and relative powers. The institutional structure, however, ought not to be reified, on Young's account. Institutions are, in important respects, a vehicle by which the micro-decisions of otherwise unconnected individuals combine to form constraints that in turn delimit other micro-behaviour. It is a conception of structure that owes a lot, quite explicitly, to Giddens and Sartre (Young, 2013: Ch 2, Sec. II) (and is not inconsistent with the methodological individualism of the mainstream economist). This conception of institutional structure forms the basis, in Young, of an account of responsibility that grounds it in *social connection*. She conceives society as a nexus whose members are responsible, in typically untraceable ways, for societal outcomes. While Arendt sees being a member of a political community as grounds for (political) responsibility, Young finds this "mystifying" (ibid.: 79). She views it, rather, as systemic. It is a person's ineluctable contribution to collective outcomes overall that is the basis of personal responsibility. Hence, no one can be held personally accountable for the collective outcomes to which he or she makes a microscopic contribution. This does not, however, provide entire exemption from personal responsibility.

It is unrealistic, Young acknowledges, to expect each individual to be singly responsible for taking actions to change, however marginally, the social structure. It is reasonable, however, for each to be responsible for the articulation of injustices and the active promotion of potential solutions through democratic devices, where such devices exist. Young's thesis is, in part, a call to greater political activism, and it is in this respect demanding, but it is not this dimension that is directly relevant to the economist.

Her proposal entails more fundamental *intellectual* responsibilities. It requires that individuals be politically awake, and so adopt an abiding evaluative stance towards social issues. It requires a perspective that embraces the complexity and interrelated character of social phenomena. For the economist, in particular, it requires an intellectual take on the profession that sees it as part of the social structure. In this way, Young's thesis applies to the economist qua person and requires an out-of-theory perspective that contextualises economics and economic practice. The social connection model of responsibility requires that the economist see her profession, and the theory it takes as its explanatory frame, as embedded in a wider social context. In her private identity, the economist must, in Young's view, consider the contribution of the economics profession to societal outcomes from a perspective that transcends that of professional economist.

While Young's argument might be characterised as a theory of justice, it is a particularly helpful way to ground the responsibilities of the economist because of its cosmopolitan character. Famously, and for many disappointingly, John Rawls' theory of justice did not extend its distributive principles of justice to the international arena (Rawls, 2001). There are, of course, many attempts to produce a less modest theory of justice with international reach (for recent discussion, see Held & Maffettone, 2016), but Young's is particularly powerful for present purposes. Her argument for a cosmopolitan account of justice does not require independent theoretical justification for international human rights or the (otherwise important) notion that shared international institutions entail shared responsibility across national borders (Jaggar, 2010). The type of personal responsibility she argues for in a domestic setting extends naturally to the international context. This is because the social connections that are, in her thesis, so consequential for individual lives naturally transcend national borders (Young, 2013: Ch 5). Adopting Young as the basis from which to argue for economists' responsibilities, then, does not land the economist with parochial concerns. Young's theory of responsibility shares economics' international landscape.

We saw that the standard approach leads to deadlock. Where a professional economic ethic derives from an estimation of the character of the economics profession as it stands, it is open to rejection on the grounds that it relies on a faulty conception of the role and purpose of economics. The standard account's attempt to achieve neutral ground from which to engage economic orthodoxy is arguably bound to fail. It relies on a conception of professional ethics that does not appeal to the person per se, but to the person in the guise of economist. But Young's thesis invites the economist onto neutral ground outside of her profession to argue as private citizen, about her responsibilities. It is not certain that the economist will be convinced by Young's argument, but it offers a basis for a conversation about responsibility that prevents the economist from taking refuge behind an existing conception of the nature of economic enquiry and the role of the economist in policy formation and implementation.

4. Young and pluralist economics

Young, then, develops a theory of personal responsibility for democratic society. It places a requirement on all to use democratic means to foment or contribute to joint action given that only joint action can feasibly alter societal outcomes. An application of her theory is the coordinated action taken to change the supply chain practices of multinational companies (Young, 2007). This is a favoured example, as it exhibits the relationship between unfairness and institutional complexity and because only in concert can individuals' actions have impact. Young's thesis is then a call to be politically active, to be like Young in her dual capacity as academic and activist. It is helpful, however, to say more about the *intellectual* responsibilities that are implicit in her thesis.

The intellectual virtues for which we are, according to Young, responsible for curating underpin or create the potential for responsible collective action. To be *primed* to act, along with others, to address perceived social unfairness, a person must be socially alert. Attention must be paid to the possibility that burdensome costs, unwarranted geographical or stratified concentrations of low expectations, skewed exposure to risk, limited opportunities and so on may have remediable institutional causes. It is a stance that must attempt to bring into relief the reasons for the normative issues that such a perspective identifies. The activist personality that Young endorses must be ever ready to engage in social critique, and this preparedness, while only implicit in Young, is necessary if the kind of society she envisaged, one populated by politically active members, is to really exist.

There are different ways to characterise the perspective a person must adopt if she is to criticise the society to which she belongs. For Young, as a critical theorist (on which see Jaggar, 2009), the appropriate characterisation of critique is to see it as historically and socioculturally embedded. While reflection on social conditions is possible, it is from within a milieu that is inescapably the critic's own. There is no pretence here to neutrality, to a detached perspective that brings into relief extant social facts from an ahistorical vantage point, bare of culture. In a seminal contribution to feminist theory, Young (1980) develops an inchoate theory of the institutional origins of gendered oppression, in which behavioural differences between sexes arise from the self-imposition of social expectations. In later work, she sees wider behaviours and attributes – "language, gestures, forms of embodiment and comportment" (Young, 1990: 86) – as shaped by institutional factors and the task of critical theory to make them "the subject of public discussion, and explicitly matters of choice and decision" (ibid.). This requires for the theorist, and the people whose behaviour is in question, a second-order appraisal of entrenched attitudes and routine ways of thinking. The idea that social critique requires apprehension of first-order thinking carries implications for economics. In particular, it has significant implications for the responsibilities of the economist in relation to pluralist controversies.

Supporters of pluralist thinking in economics encourage a meta-theoretical perspective, one that is open to alternative methodological options (e.g. Lee & Cronin, 2016). Exemplary are Sheila Dow (2009, 2013, 2016) and David Ruccio (2008). Both point to instrumental reasons for economists to adopt a synoptic methodological point of view. Where their views coincide, they recommend pluralism for its capacity to reshape a problem and so reroute enquiry. It exposes points of contact with other disciplines and so suggests where interdisciplinary dialogue might be profitable. In Ruccio's case, the *postmodern* dynamic that he claims is shaping the evolution of economic thought can only be brought into view if the discipline is placed in historical perspective. In this way, economists can avoid being slave to *paradigm shift* (Kuhn) and argue directly about the direction they think their discipline ought to be going in. Economists ought, Ruccio suggests, to

> take up the challenge of unearthing the "undecidables" and "aporias" of economic discourse, as part of a new phase of *self-conscious thought*, a new phase perhaps of society and history: that which has been labelled the postmodern. . . . Our challenge to Samuelsonian progress starts from the premise that modernism is not only an exhausted project but a destructive one. One form of damage is its silencing of theoretical disagreement.
>
> (Ruccio & Amariglio, 2003: 3–4, italics added)

Where defences of the pluralist outlook are normative, they are most naturally consequence-based. A mono-method mentality may be socially harmful owing to its tendency to mute information it cannot compute; and there is potential here for a normative basis for pluralist thinking. We have seen, however, how easy it is for the economist to be dismissive of talk of the morality of professional disregard for the social consequences of economic practice. So, as with professional economic ethics, appeals for pluralism may go unheeded by a profession that is wedded to its established techniques.

Perhaps the most profound implication of Young's social connection model for professional economic ethics is that it provides reason to think that the pluralist perspective is not only desirable but also *required*. Young's thesis, as it applies to the economist, suggests that a pluralist take on the discipline is a professional responsibility.

To see this, consider how Young's conception of social institutions encourages us to see economic professional practice itself as part of society's institutional fabric. An important aspect of what conditions choice in a societal setting is, Young emphasises, the decisions of many other people, unconnected apart from the way their decisions are channeled through social institutions. John Rawls (1972, 1993), for example, includes competitive markets among the *basic institutions* that delimit individual choice. The choices made within those markets are not, however, for Rawls, themselves institutional. Similarly, while the family is an institutional feature, choices made within families do not constitute part of the institutional setting. It is otherwise for Young. Viewing Rawls and other theorists as guilty of reifying social structure, Young sees personal choices as themselves institutional. While Rawls, then, would distinguish between the economics profession as an institution and the choices made within that institution, Young makes no such distinction. The point of view entailed by the intellectual responsibility to adopt a reflective stance towards social institutions must then, necessarily, bring into view the economics profession and its activities. From this standpoint, there is no ready-made justification for selecting a favoured version of what economics is or ought to be as a social science. Economics per se is, in view, economics in the round.

Recall that, for Young, the critical stance requires self-conscious apprehension of entrenched modes of thinking. To criticise society, we must engage in second-order thinking, and, as we have seen, this is an intellectual responsibility. The responsible economist must, then, not only *think like an economist* but must also reflect on what it means to think like an economist. The intellectual responsibilities that fall out of Young's theory imply, therefore, for the economist, a responsibility to embrace a meta-theoretical, pluralist perspective.

Conclusion

A central argument in support of professional economic ethics points to the harmful consequences of the standard approach to economic policy intervention. The risks of unintended effects may be ameliorated by, for example, greater democratic accountability. The economic profession ought, then, to commit to being more sensitive to contextual conditions. This harm-based view is coupled with an approach that emphasises the need for mature moral sensitivity on the part of the economist. This prevents a professional moral code reducing, implausibly, to the application of established rules. This seems an attractive combination. While there are sophisticated arguments in favour of harm and character-based approaches, they appeal sufficiently to intuition to provide an uncontroversial basis for a professional ethics for economists.

However, neither approach is tenable when confronted with a mainstream conception of economic intervention that views it as a technical application of value-neutral principles. Where harms are identified, it is not, on this view, the role of the economist to address them. Furthermore, the acceptance of the relevant professional responsibilities involves, fundamentally, the adoption of a role. It is possible to argue that there ought to be a requirement, when performing that role, to ensure consistency of professional and personal ethics. However, it is equally possible to argue that what is required of the economist is *only* role ethics. For the mainstream, that role need not go beyond basic standards of honesty, integrity and transparency. The more extensive approach to professional economic ethics, then, that is associated, centrally, with George DeMartino does not provide the materials for the kind of argument that is needed to transform the economics profession. The result is an intellectual standoff.

I have suggested that a way around this is to draw on the work on responsibility of Iris Marion Young. Her argument invites the economist to adopt an extra-disciplinary point of view, from which perspective economists' style of policy formation and intervention is in view. Being extra-disciplinary, it is a perspective that precludes the economist appealing to the limited, technical nature of his or her role. From the perspective of the democratic citizen, the legitimacy of the technical conception of economics is precisely the kind of thing that ought to be under review. Young's thesis suggests, moreover, a responsibility to engage in second-order thinking, thinking that takes in not only how things are but also the way in which our mode of thinking is moulded. This is a general responsibility for all members of a social system constituted by rich interdependencies. For the economist, this requires a meta-theoretical stance that embraces alternative theoretical options and methodological techniques. It entails, I have suggested, a responsibility to be a methodological pluralist.

Note

1   There is, interestingly, controversy as to whether the Hippocratic Oath was originally sacred or secular given Hippocrates' apparent atheism (Hulkower, 2016).

References

Alzola, Miguel, 2015. Corporate roles and virtues. In A. Sison (Ed.), *Handbook of Virtue Ethics in Business and Management*. Springer: Dordrecht.

Arendt, Hannah, 1994. Organized guilt and universal responsibility. In *Essays in Understanding*. New York: Schocken Books, originally in *Jewish Frontier*, No. 12, 1945.

———, 1987. Collective responsibility. In S.J.J.W. Bernauer (Ed.), *Amor Mundi. Boston College Studies in Philosophy*, 26. Dordrecht: Springer.

Aristotle, 2009. *The Nichomachean Ethics*. Oxford: Oxford University Press.

Bartlett, Robin, 2009. Code of ethics for economists. In Jan Piel and Irene van Staveren (Eds.), *Handbook of Economics and Ethics*. Cheltenham: Edward Elgar.

Boettke, P.J. and O'Donnell, K.W., 2016. The social responsibility of economists. In *The Oxford Handbook of Professional Economic Ethics*. Oxford: Oxford University Press.

Bohman, James, 1998. The coming age of deliberative democracy (survey article). *The Journal of Political Philosophy*, 6(4), pp. 400–425.

Bratman, Michael, 2014. *Shared Agency: A Planning Theory of Acting Together*. Oxford: Oxford University Press.

———, 1987. *Intention, Plans and Practical Reason*. Cambridge, MA: Harvard University Press.

Bryan, G., Karlan, D. and Nelson, S., 2010. Commitment devices. *Annual Review of Economics*, 2(1), pp. 671–698.

Cain, D.M., Loewenstein, G. and Moore, D.A., 2010. When sunlight fails to disinfect: Understanding the perverse effects of disclosing conflicts of interest. *Journal of Consumer Research*, 37(5), pp. 836–857.

Cohen, G.A., 1992. Incentives, inequality, and community. *The Tanner Lectures on Human Values*, 13, pp. 263–329.

Coyle, D.M., 2012. The public responsibilities of economists. In *Tanner Lectures*. Oxford: Brasenose College, May 18–19.

Dekker, E. and Klamer, A., 2016. About doing the right thing as an academic economist. In *The Oxford Handbook of Professional Economic Ethics*. Oxford: Oxford University Press.

DeMartino, G. (2011), *The Economist's Oath*. New York: Oxford University Press.

DeMartino, G.F. and McCloskey, D.N., 2018. Professional ethics 101: A reply to Anne Krueger's review of the Oxford Handbook of professional economic ethics. *Econ Journal Watch*, 15(1), p. 4.

———, 2016. "Econogenic harm": On the nature of and responsibility for the harm economists do as they try to do good. In George DeMartino and Deirdre McCloskey (Eds.), *The Oxford Handbook of Professional Economic Ethics*. Oxford: Oxford University Press.

———, 2013a. Professional economic ethics: Why heterodox economists should care. *Economic Thought*, 2(1).

———, 2013b. Professional economic ethics: The Posnerian and naïve perspectives. *Journal of Forensic Economics*, 24(1), pp. 3–18.

———, 2011. *The Economist's Oath: On the Need for and Content of Professional Economic Ethics*. Oxford: Oxford University Press.

———, 2005. A professional ethics code for economists. *Challenge*, 48(4), pp. 88–104.

Desai, Meghnad, 2015. *Hubris: Why Economists Failed to Predict the Crisis and How to Avoid the Next One*. Yale: Yale University Press.

Dewey, John, 1927. *The Public and its Problems*. Athens, OH: Swallow Press, 2016 edition.

Dow, S., 2017, People have had enough of experts. INET, February. Available at www.inete conomics.org/perspectives/blog/people-have-had-enough-of-experts (March 2018).

———, 2016. Economics and ethics. *ISRF Bulletin*, 11, pp. 10–14.

———, 2013. Codes of ethics for economists: A pluralist view. *Economic Thought*, 2(1), pp. 20–29.

———, 2009. History of thought and methodology in pluralist economics education. *International Review of Economics Education*, 8(2), pp. 41–57.

Durkheim, Emile, 1992. *Professional Ethics and Civic Morals*. London: Routledge.

Elster, J., 2002. Don't burn your bridge before you come to it: Some ambiguities and complexities of precommitment. *Texas Law Review*, 81, pp. 1751–1787.

Foot, P., 1972. Morality as a system of hypothetical imperatives. *The Philosophical Review*, 81(3), pp. 305–316.

Gilbert, Margaret, 2014. *Joint Commitment: How We Make the Social World*. Oxford: Oxford University Press.

Heise, A., 2018. Reclaiming the university: Transforming economics as a discipline (No. 67). Discussion Papers, Zentrum für Ökonomische und Soziologische Studien.

————, 2017. Defining economic pluralism: Ethical norm or scientific imperative. *International Journal of Pluralism and Economics Education*, 8(1), pp. 18–41.

Held, David and Maffettone, Pietro, 2016. *Global Political Theory*. Cambridge: Polity Press.

Hulkower, R., 2016. The history of the Hippocratic Oath: Outdated, inauthentic, and yet still relevant. *Einstein Journal of Biology and Medicine*, 25(1), pp. 41–44.

Jaggar, Alison M., 2010. *Thomas Pogge and his Critics*. Cambridge: Polity Press.

————, 2009. L'imagination au pouvoir: Comparing John Rawls' method of ideal theory with Iris Marion Young's method of critical theory. In Ann Ferguson and Mechthild Nagel (Eds.), *Dancing with Iris: The Philosophy of Iris Marion Young*. Oxford: Oxford University Press.

Johnson, A., 1937. The economist in a World in transition. *The American Economic Review*, 27(1), pp. 1–3.

Lee, Frederic S. and Cronin, Bruce. 2016, Introduction. In Frederic S. Lee and Bruce Cronin (Eds.), *Handbook of Research Methods and Applications in Heterodox Economics*. Cheltenham: Edward Elgar.

Loewenstein, G., Sah, S. and Cain, D.M., 2012. The unintended consequences of conflict of interest disclosure. *Jama*, 307(7), pp. 669–670.

Martin, R. 1999. The new geographical turn in economics: some critical reflections. *Cambridge Journal of Economics*, 23(1), pp. 65–91.

May, Larry, 1996. *The Socially Responsive Self: Social Theory and Professional Ethics*. Chicago: Chicago University Press.

McDowell, John, 1996. *Mind and World*. Cambridge, MA: Harvard University Press.

Montaigne, M., 1965. *Complete Essays (Vol. 1)*. Stanford: Stanford University Press.

Postema, G.J., 1980. Moral responsibility in professional ethics. *New York University Law Review*, 55, pp. 63–89.

Rawls, J., 2001. *Law of Peoples*. Cambridge, MA: Harvard University Press.

————, 1993. *Political Liberalism*. New York: Columbia University Press.

————, 1972. *A Theory of Justice*. Oxford: Oxford University Press.

Ruccio, David, 2008. (Un)real criticism. In E. Fullbrook (Ed.), *Tony Lawson and His Critics*. Ann Arbor: University of Michigan Press.

Ruccio, David F. and Amariglio, Jack, 2003. *Postmodern Moments in Economics*. Princeton, NJ: Princeton University Press.

Sartre, Jean-Paul, 1946. Existentialism is a humanism. In Walter Kaufman (Ed.), *Existentialism from Dostoyevsky to Sartre*. New York: Penguin, 1975.

Sen, Amartya, 2015. *Identity and Violence*. London: Penguin.

————, 2001. *Development as Freedom*. Oxford: Oxford University Press.

Sommerstein, Alan H. and Torrance, Isabelle, C., 2014. *Oaths and Swearing in Ancient Greece*. Berlin and Boston: De Gruyter.

Stiglitz, Joseph, 2003. *Globalization and Its Discontents*. New York: W. W. Norton & Company.

Sulmasy, Daniel P., 1999. What is an oath and why should a physician swear one? *Theoretical Medicine and Bioethics*, 20, pp. 329–346.

Tawney, R.H., 1921. *The Acquisitive Society*. London: Collins, 1961 edition.

Thompson, Paul B., 1986. Collective responsibility and professional roles. *Business Ethics*, 5, pp. 151–154.

Williamson, O.E., 2000. The new institutional economics: Taking stock, looking ahead. *Journal of Economic Literature*, 38(3), pp. 595–613.

————, 1979. Transaction cost economics: The governance of contractual relations. *Journal of Law and Economics*, 22(22), pp. 233-261.

Young, I.M., 2013. *Responsibility for Justice*. Oxford: Oxford University Press.

————, 2010. Responsibility and global labour justice. In *Responsibility in Context*. Dordrecht: Springer, pp. 53–76.

————, 2007. Responsibility, social connection and global labour justice. In Iris Marion Young (Ed.), *Global Challenges: War, Self-Determination and Responsibility for Justice.* Cambridge: Polity Press.

————, 2006. Responsibility and global justice: A social connection model. *Social Philosophy and Policy*, 23(1), pp. 102–130.

————, 2003. *Political Responsibility and Structural Injustice.* The Lindley Lecture, University of Kansas, May 5.

————, 1990. *Justice and the Politics of Difference.* Princeton, NJ: Princeton University Press.

————, 1980. Throwing like a girl: A phenomenology of feminine body comportment motility and spatiality. *Human Studies*, 3(1), pp. 137–156.

6 More harm than benefit

The ramifications of the neglect of rights in economics

Mark D. White

Economists are typically taught two standard tools to evaluate whether an action makes things "better": the Pareto improvement test and the Kaldor-Hicks test. The Pareto test is stricter, demanding that at least one party be made better off while no party is made worse off, while the Kaldor-Hicks test allows some parties to be worse off if the parties made better off "could" compensate the former – in other words, if the total gains from the change exceed the total losses. The Pareto test is preferred but is often impractical, especially in situations where scarce resources must be allocated and gains to one party imply losses to another. (Pareto improvements are more common in changes in rules and institutions that improve efficiency overall and benefit all parties.) For this reason, economists often resort to the Kaldor-Hicks test, resting satisfied that, even though some parties are being harmed, others are benefitting enough to justify it – although actual compensation is rarely arranged.

The Kaldor-Hicks test is entirely consistent with mainstream economics' foundations in the classical utilitarianism of Jeremy Bentham (1781), for whom the balance of pleasure and pain is both the chief motivator of human action and its evaluative standard for ethical purposes. A social reformer at heart, Bentham believed that actions should be undertaken that increase net happiness among those affected. This translates easily into the terms of economics, in which preference-satisfaction or utility-maximization for the individual is presented as "the good." If Pareto improvements that increase the good for some without lowering it for others are not possible, a Kaldor-Hicks improvement that maximizes the sum total of individuals' good – aggregate utility – is the second-best solution.

As the first step in a decision-making process, the Kaldor-Hicks test is useful and reasonable. A profile of the benefits and costs of a proposed action or policy is an integral component of any deliberative process, but it is only the first part, normally followed by a detailed examination of the negative impact, consideration of the parties affected, and development of plans to address if not alleviate it. Although this is taught regularly in public planning programs, economists are often left with Kaldor-Hicks efficiency as the first and last step, sufficient to justify an action simply because it increases total utility, and resting confident that any compensation will be arranged by someone else.

There are, however, serious concerns with utilitarianism as a system of moral philosophy and a tool for critical evaluation, concerns that economists are rarely made aware of in their graduate training. Although utilitarianism represents the ideal of moral equality in treating each person's utility as equal in the sum total regardless of class, gender, race, or religion, it also implies an interchangeability among persons that allows one person's pain to be traded off for another person's pleasure, as if they were mere parts of a single agent. As John Rawls (1971, 27) wrote, utilitarianism "does not take seriously the distinction between persons," treating individuals equally seriously but also equally poorly.

This is what happens when economists too quickly accept the judgment of the Kaldor-Hicks test as a stamp of approval on an action or policy that will harm some parties for the sake of benefitting others. The fact that some are benefitting by more than others lose does not justify the latter's losses, particularly if those losses, or harms, involve violations of their rights and are therefore wrongful, regardless of the net utility generated.

Harm, rights, and wrongfulness are not common terms in economic parlance, and this is a product of the wholesale adoption by the field of a simplistic version of utilitarian decision-making in the form of the Kaldor-Hicks test. But the widespread use of this test results in underappreciated if not ignored wrongful harm done in its name that affects people in the real world. In this chapter, I will use the deontological ethics of Immanuel Kant, a moral philosophy that contrasts with utilitarianism and focuses instead on dignity, duty, and rights, to explain the gaps left by the Kaldor-Hicks test and the utilitarian basis of economics in general. I will also explore the implications of the neglect of rights for standard economic concepts such as the Coase Theorem, externalities, and antitrust law, all of which may be interpreted very differently if the importance of rights were acknowledged and incorporated into economic theory, practice, and policy.

Kant and Kaldor-Hicks

There are a number of shortcomings of the Kaldor-Hicks test that some economists do recognize – especially ones that actually use the test in practice – although they fall short of the problems to be discussed here. For instance, the test normally relies on self-reported willingness-to-pay figures, which are of questionable reliability due to their tenuous link to actual predicted benefits and harms. If the reported willingness-to-pay figures can be taken as accurate, then the effect of wealth comes into play: those with more resources will be able to "pledge" more than those with fewer resources even if the latter are affected to a larger degree. (The diminishing marginal utility of money only exacerbates this problem, as the larger pledges of wealthy may be disproportionate to their actual concerns.) As Jules Coleman (1984, 662) wrote, the Kaldor-Hicks test is "normatively prejudiced in a particularly insidious way: namely, it turns out that what is efficient depends on what people are willing to pay, [which] in turn depends on what they are capable of paying. In short, the greater one's wealth, the more likely one is to increase it."

These criticisms point out the unfairness in how data is generated and used in the Kaldor-Hicks test, but they do not speak directly to the treatment of individuals under it. For that, we bring in Immanuel Kant, whose system of ethics is grounded in the dignity of individual persons and the respect thereby owed to them.[1] To Kant, each rational being is possessed of a *dignity*, an incalculable and incomparable worth, due to their capacity for autonomous choice – that is, the ability to make ethical choices despite inclinations or preferences to the contrary. This is reflected most clearly in one of the versions of his famous categorical imperative, the Formula of Respect: "Act in such a way that you treat humanity, whether in your own person or in the person of another, always at the same time as an end and never simply as a means" (Kant 1785, 429).

Although not as widely known as the Formula of Universal Law – "act only according to that maxim whereby you can at the same time will that it should become a universal law" (Kant 1785, 421) – the Formula of Respect more directly emphasizes the expectations for the ethical treatment of persons based on their inherent and equal dignity. According to this formula, one may never treat a person simply as a means to one's own end *without also* considering them as a valuable end in themselves or as a person deserving of respect. This formula can be (and certainly has been) read too strongly as to prohibit ever using another person in any way. But we use other people all the time, including merchants, customers, employees, employers, and even friends and family, all of whom do things for us (and vice versa). The crucial thing is that we treat them at the same time with respect, and the two primary ways this mandate can be violated are by coercion and deceit, both of which deny the person the ability to fully cooperate or consent to the action being taken that affects them.

Fortunately for us, the nuances of the Formula of Respect and exactly what it means to "treat humanity in a person" properly are not necessary for our purposes.[2] The operation of the Kaldor-Hicks test is the epitome of using persons simply as means: an action or policy approved by the Kaldor-Hicks test imposes harm on some persons, without their consent, *explicitly* for the purpose of generating benefit for others. In the interest of total utility or welfare, this is considered an acceptable cost, justified because the benefits are greater than the costs, but this does not justify the coerced harm on the losing parties, who are being used as means for the ends of others without being considered as valuable persons in themselves. As Anthony Kronman (1980, 238) put it succinctly, "For a Kantian, the Kaldor-Hicks test has no significance."

Actions approved by the Kaldor-Hicks test are sometimes called "potential Pareto improvements" because those who benefit can afford to compensate those who are harmed and still come out ahead (because the total gains, by definition, exceed the total losses). To the extent this compensation remains potential, of course, it has no more ethical relevance than the car thief who says he might return your Honda. It is merely a restatement of the fact that gains exceed losses in a way that makes the harm imposed on some compensable; without actual compensation, however, it is meaningless, if not insulting. ("You could be compensated, but you probably won't be.") Even if compensation were to occur, it would remain problematic if the entire "transaction" itself could not be rejected: a compensated taking is still a taking if it is conducted without consent and the possibility of refusal.

This problem with "potential Pareto improvements" made actual in the absence of consent also points out an ethical difficulty with Pareto improvement, widely considered the gold standard of evaluation in economics. The value of Pareto is presumed to rely on consent – after all, who would refuse to consent to a policy that helped some while hurting none? However, the judgments of benefit and harm on which the Pareto decision is based are made by outsiders with no knowledge of the interests of those affected (White 2009). Based on these judgments, the consent of the parties affected is assumed rather than solicited. This also applies to compensated Kaldor-Hicks actions: the compensation is imposed on the parties negatively affected by the changes and then judged to have made them "no worse off," generating the illusion of consent that satisfied the Pareto criterion. But without an option to reject the compensation and the action that generated, there is no consent, leaving only coercion, which violates the Formula of Respect.

Even though compensation does not erase the problem with obtaining consent, it would lessen the harm from Kaldor-Hicks changes. Nonetheless, economists rarely account for compensation, arguing that it is a technicality or not their responsibility, falling instead on those who will implement the change, such as government or corporate bureaucrats. This division of labor may be reasonable in theory, but in effect, it absolves economists of their responsibility to take account of all of the effects of their actions (and harms deliberately imposed can hardly be considered an "unforeseen consequence"). If compensation is to be taken seriously, it should be incorporated into any proposal submitted to a Kaldor-Hicks test, and if that test shows compensation itself to be too costly, this should be taken as a criticism of the proposal itself, not an excuse to ignore it or pass the buck. Treating compensation as an afterthought allows the economist to sweep it under the rug, compounding their moral culpability in Kaldor-Hicks decisions.

Rights and the Coase Theorem

An unfortunate effect of the utilitarian foundations of modern economics in general, and Kaldor-Hicks in particular, is that it has erased the concepts of rights and wrongs from the lexicon. Following in the spirit of Bentham's proclamation that rights are "nonsense on stilts," economists recognize rights in pragmatic terms – especially the property rights that ground the operation of the market – but only insofar as they are supported by utilitarian arguments. As Ronald Dworkin (1980, 198) wrote of economists, "The institution of rights, and particular allocations of rights, are justified only insofar as they promote social wealth more effectively than other institutions or allocations."

Dworkin argued more positively that for rights to have any meaning independent of utility, they must be able to "trump" considerations of utility:

> Individual rights are political trumps held by individuals. Individuals have rights when, for some reason, a collective goal is not a sufficient justification for denying them what they wish, as individuals, to have or to do, or not a sufficient justification for imposing some loss or injury upon them.
>
> (1977, xi)

In this sense, rights exist to protect the essential interests and concerns of the individual, based on her dignity and worth, even when such protection may conflict with the pursuit of overall welfare. A promising young student may produce the most benefit for humanity by becoming a surgeon, but she has the right to choose her own career; a landowner may increase tax revenues for his city if he develops high-priced condominiums at his property, but he has the right to build a modest home for himself instead. More relevant to the current discussion, persons harmed by a policy decision should have the ability to reject it if it wrongfully and negatively affects their interests, especially if the policy is designed specifically to benefit other parties at the expense of the former (and even if compensation is arranged).

Utilitarianism does not recognize such a strong conception of rights, and neither does economics. Calling these rights "absolute," Richard Posner argued (in Orwellian fashion) that "the economist recommends the creation of such rights . . . when the cost of voluntary transactions is low. . . . But when transaction costs are prohibitive, the recognition of absolute rights is inefficient" (1983, 70). In the spirit of Bentham, economists believe that rights that take precedence over utility are fine only if they promote utility; if not, they defeat the purpose.[3] As Dworkin stressed, however, such rights are not rights in any meaningful sense, but merely a facile repackaging of utility considerations.

The absence of a strong conception of rights that we see in the Kaldor-Hicks test has wide-ranging effects in many different areas of economic theory and policy. One example is the well-known Coase Theorem, which holds that when property rights are clearly assigned and transaction costs are negligible, the initial assignment of rights in a private legal conflict is irrelevant to the parties arriving at the most efficient solution (Coase 1960). For all its brilliance and simplicity, Ronald Coase's eponymous theorem stands as an example of how the absence of rights can mask normative problems with policy solutions (even those mandating no policy response).[4]

The problem arises not when the conditions for the Coase Theorem are met – in which case the parties in a conflict are assumed to find the most efficient solution on their own – but when they are not, particularly when property rights are not clearly assigned. In such a case, the conflict ends up before a judge, who assigns the right to determine the outcome to one of the parties (in effect, determining the outcome). According to the economic approach to law, the judge should grant the right to the party who values it the most – not because this is right or just, but because it will further efficiency and welfare, and also because it "mimics the market" in the sense that, if the conditions for the Coase Theorem held, this would be the result of private bargaining anyway.

This is consistent with the economic conception of a right as derivative of utility: rights are vested in the party who values it the most. While this may in fact be the result of private bargaining under ideal conditions, it is not a meaningful description of how rights are vested to begin with. Within a strong conception of rights, when one person's property is damaged by another person's actions, the first person has the right to specify the extent and form of compensation (within reason, as determined by the courts), a right that is derived from the property right that was violated. Even if property rights themselves are in dispute – such as a conflict between neighbors over one's excessive noise – it is a matter to be settled by examining the nature and basis of such rights, not the parties' relative valuation (which is subject to insincere self-reporting, as in the case of the Kaldor-Hicks test). Some economists argue that such a view "requires an arbitrary initial assignment of rights" (Posner 1983, 98), but it is arbitrary only from a utilitarian point of view that does not recognize the existence of meaningful rights that are not contingent on calculations of relative utility.

This neglect of rights is also reflected in the concept of *reciprocal causation* that grounds the common interpretation of the Coase Theorem. As conflicts are framed in this context, each party stands to harm the other if that party's rights are acknowledged. In Coase's own example, for instance, a railroad harms farmers whose lands the tracks go through by throwing sparks that burn crops, but the farmers would harm the railroad owners if they imposed monetary sanctions on them. As Coase (1960, 2) wrote, "The question is commonly thought of as one in which A inflicts harm on B and what has to be decided is: how should we restrain A? But this is wrong. We are dealing with a problem of a reciprocal nature. To avoid the harm to B would be to inflict harm on A." In his view, harms are reciprocal or bilateral and therefore normatively equivalent, and the only issue is to find the lowest-cost solution to the conflict.

As Talbot Page (1986, 252) notes, however, reciprocal harm confuses "a physical harm with the effects of a remedy." Even Coase's examples bear this out: they all cast one party as imposing harm on another. As Richard Epstein (1973, 165) puts it, "Coase describes each situation by the use of sentences that differentiate between the role of the *subject* of each of these propositions and the role of the *object*." Referencing Coase's example, Posner (1973, 216) argues that "most torts arise out of a conflict between two morally innocent activities, such as railroad transportation and farming," and asks, "What ethical principle compels society to put a crimp in the latter because of the proximity of the former?" This ethical principle would be the preexistence of property rights, which recognizes the unilateral nature of the harm and grants the harmed party the right to determine the outcome – which, if the conditions for the Coase Theorem hold, will be a lowest-cost solution, but as determined by the morally relevant party, which the standard economic analysis literally finds irrelevant.[5]

Wrongfulness and externalities

Coase's work was an innovative way to approach the problem of externalities, but this problem exists in large part only because economists lack a keen appreciation of rights.[6] Externalities (or spillover effects) are defined as incidental effects of a transaction on third parties not involved in the transaction and therefore unlikely to be included in the transacting parties' deliberations over price and terms. Although externalities can be positive, such as a bakery improving the smell of the air for its neighbors, economists are naturally more concerned with negative externalities involving harm. The classic case is pollution, but externalities arise from almost any social interaction with overlapping interests, including the impact of additional drivers on traffic congestion and that of homeowners refusing to mow their lawns, which affects well-being and perhaps property values among their neighbors.

Economists would treat all harms equally, as would their utilitarian forbears. In their view, harms represent negative utility, regardless of their source, and must be minimized (or optimized in conjunction with associated benefits) in order to maximize total utility. But this neglects an important dimension of harms: their wrongfulness, which depends on whether rights were violated when the harm was inflicted. Some externalities do involve the violation of rights even if those rights are not well defined in the Coasean sense: pollution wrongfully harms the interests of neighboring populations, and a negligent driver wrongfully harms the interests of other drivers they may hit. But many externalities involve no rights violations and are instead the simple result of social interaction and overlapping interests. The homeowner who does not take as much care of his lawn as his neighbors do is lowering their well-being and possibly their home values, but is not violating any widely recognized right of theirs. A driver who enters the flow of traffic at rush hour is slowing every other driver by a tiny amount, but is not violating any right they have to a commute of a certain length. And competition itself necessarily involves externalities: the manager who secures a hotly desired promotion to the exclusion of her colleagues definitely sets back their interests but, again, not wrongfully.

Economists would look at each of these examples differently, never recognizing the relevance of the absence of rights violations in any of them. In case of competition for a promotion – or market competition in general – externalities are part of a process that leads to efficiency. In the model of perfect competition, externalities between firms drive extra-normal profits to zero, resulting in an efficient market. The prisoner's dilemma of oligopolistic competition relies on externalities in the same way, without always leading to optimal efficiency. In these cases, externalities are accepted because they have offsetting benefits; in other words, the institution of competition would pass the Kaldor-Hicks test.

The aesthetically impaired homeowner creates an externality for his neighbors, but insofar as the harm involves property values, economists would consider it a *pecuniary externality* that is offset by the benefit to potential homebuyers. If the profligate homeowner's ghastly lawn leads to a $10,000 decrease in the value of his neighbor's property, that neighbor's loss is exactly and completely offset by the $10,000 gain to the eventual buyer of that property. As long as the sale of the property goes through, the change in selling price has no effect on overall utility. (The effect of the unkempt lawn on neighbors' well-being remains, of course, but is of little policy concern.)

The case of traffic congestion is the only one of the three that would prompt corrective action on the part of economists. With no offsetting benefit to increased traffic and commuting times, economists would attempt to resolve the externality. Due to the large number of anonymous parties involved – as well as the absence of any applicable notion of property rights – the Coase Theorem would not apply, and the economist would likely resort to Pigouvian congestion taxes, charging each driver a fee roughly equal to the harm they impose on other drivers. This would lead each driver to make her own decision incorporating the externalities she imposes, either accepting this cost or choosing to drive at less busy times (and avoid the extra charge).

Despite the difference in economists' responses to these three examples, they share a common element, highlighted above, in that none of them involves any consideration of the presence and importance of rights violations. Harm was inflicted in all three cases, but was the result of scarcity or proximity that led to overlapping and conflicting interests, and none of the three involves any wrongful action. Not only were the actions that led to these harms not wrongful, but they could also all be considered protected by the rights of the agents performing them. Competitors have the right to compete (within accepted rules); homeowners have the right to maintain their property as they choose (within community guidelines); and drivers have the right to use public roadways, regardless of how many other drivers are already using them.

In a social world where interactions are frequent, incidental harms are ubiquitous and often morally innocuous. To be fair, economists usually focus on the most significant cases of external harm, such as traffic congestion that affects thousands of people every day. But even with costly instances such as this, any policy proposed by economists would interfere with rightful activity even if merely by raising its cost. The very concept of rights implies that individuals are free to act in ways that do not necessarily increase total welfare and may even lower it; this is the sense in which, as Dworkin said, "rights trump welfare." Even if an action is harmful, but in an incidental and not wrongful way, the harm produced is of no moral or legal relevance to an economist who acknowledges the distinction between wrongful and nonwrongful harms.

What, then, of wrongful harms, those that violate rights? These do raise significant moral, legal, and political concerns, but for the most part economists need not worry about them because the institution of tort law is designed to deal with the infliction of wrongful harm. By setting the conditions under which one party can shift the harm they suffered to the party who caused it, tort law provides an elaborate and thorough developed method for adjudicating externalities that involve rights violations (and are therefore wrongful).[7]

Within tort law, there are two approaches, one grounded in utilitarianism and supported by economics, the other based more firmly in rights. The utilitarian view, which can be traced to the amoral legal realism of Oliver Wendell Holmes (1881), maintains that the goal of tort law is to minimize the total cost of accidents, which includes harm from accidents and the cost of taking precaution. Law-and-economics scholars (such as Shavell 1987) have elaborated on this by developing formulae for determining the optimal level of precaution that minimizes the sum of these costs. Although this is a fine goal, this approach renders moot the identities of the parties involved (in the spirit of reciprocal causation), the existence or amount of compensation for harm, and the degree of fault or wrongdoing involved. Once the optimal amount of precaution is incorporated into the rules of liability and costs are minimized, the economist is not concerned with wrongs done or whether compensation is provided – once again, recalling the Kaldor-Hicks test.

The traditional approach to tort law, based on Aristotle's idea of *corrective justice* that addresses wrongs, stands in stark contrast to the utilitarian and economic conception of tort law.[8] Rather than attempt to minimize harms and thereby maximize total utility, corrective justice attempts to address individual wrongs based on the rights and relative position of both parties. As Goldberg and Zipursky write:

> Tortious wrongdoing always involves an interference with one of a set of individual interests that are significant enough aspects of a person's well-being to warrant the imposition of a duty on others not to interfere with the interest in certain ways, notwithstanding the liberty restriction inherent in such a duty imposition.
>
> (2010b, 937)

In this view, appropriate compensation for wrongs committed, rather than optimal precaution to prevent them, is the focus, which has the benefit of avoiding the implication of the economic approach to tort that there is an "efficient level of wrongs" that balances harms with the costs of precaution. In theory, innocuous harms can be optimized (assuming the process itself does not involve rights violations), but wrongs should never be optimized – authorities should aim to eliminate them even if this is not possible in practice.[9]

Although nonwrongful externalities should be considered irrelevant to economic theory and policy, there is still room for economists to be concerned with some wrongful harms that tort law is ill-prepared to handle. Perhaps the best example is pollution, which can be classified as wrongful due to its violation of an "underlying entitlement to physical security" (Geistfeld 2014, 389), but is notoriously difficult to adjudicate in civil courts due to the absence of clear property rights (which economists call "missing markets"). In cases of wrongful harm that tort law cannot handle, traditional economic solutions such as Pigouvian taxes may be appropriate, but they should be used for the right reason: to address wrongdoing rather than optimize harm. Economists should learn from their students who scoff at hearing that economists do not aim to eliminate pollution but only to optimize it – these students implicitly recognize the moral problem with wanting to manage wrongs as if they were mere harms arising from (in Posner's words) "a conflict between two morally innocent activities."

Utility, rights, and antitrust

Another implication of the focus on utility and neglect of rights in economists' training and practice is the presumption that individual agents have an obligation to act in ways that maximize total utility. On the surface, economists respect ideas such as consumer sovereignty and the right of individuals to their own preferences, the maximization of which is consistent with overall utility-maximization provided there are no spillover effects or externalities. If I am happier wearing a blue shirt than a red shirt, and if this decision has no effect on anyone else, then I am increasing total utility by wearing a blue shirt. But my sartorial choice may have an effect on others: perhaps I wear a very ugly shirt or a shirt with a controversial political slogan that may cause serious anger among those who disagree.[10] Even though my choice of attire may cause more distress in others than joy for me – and therefore fail a Kaldor-Hicks test – it is generally agreed, even among economists, that I would have the right to wear any shirt I choose (within certain contextual standards).

This is yet another example of Dworkin's dictum that rights must trump welfare in at least some significant cases. This concept grounds most cases of individual rights, which grant persons the liberty to do things that may not maximize total utility but are not wrongful either. In the United States, for example, the Bill of Rights grants individuals the freedom to say what they want, worship whomever they want, and gather with whomever they want, even if those activities fail to maximize total utility insofar as they are social activities and may generate externalities (especially in these politically fraught times of increasingly forceful speech and protest, in which creating externalities is precisely the point).

This respect for individual rights and action in the face of utility-maximization does not always extend, however, to law and policy regarding business activity. To some extent, business owners are free to start firms in whatever area they find lucrative, produce the goods and services they choose, and price and market them as they deem fit (within basic laws prohibiting fraud and coercion). But these activities, if successful, can be understood to maximize welfare in that they generate mutually beneficial trade; if not, the venture fails and the owners adopt new strategies. In this way, the competitive process ensures that businesses contribute to aggregate welfare in the long run.

It follows that perfect competition is the ideal market structure from the point of view of utilitarian efficiency: many firms with no pricing power, producing output at marginal cost, and earning no profits above opportunity cost. Even though it is ordinarily an unattainable ideal (especially in its extreme mathematical form), more competition is generally seen as more efficient and therefore better for society. To this end, governments around the world restrict business practices they see as anticompetitive – such as collusion on terms, mergers among oligopolists, and predatory pricing – under the name of anti-trust or competition law. While some violations of this area of law are deterred by pressure or preemptive action from the authorities, others are prosecuted and punished as crimes, implying that these actions are not only harmful but wrongful as well.

This is where the focus on utility to the exclusion of rights becomes problematic in the case of antitrust: the prescribed actions may have a negative impact of total welfare, but they are not wrongful, because they violate no rights of consumers or competitors.[11] As Jonathan Baker writes in his defense of antitrust (2003, 27), its benefits arise chiefly from "deterring the harms from anticompetitive conduct across the economy," specifically by "protecting consumers against anticompetitive conduct that raises prices, reduces output, and hinders innovation and economic growth," but with no mention of wrongdoing or the violation of rights. Such behavior on the part of firms may lower total welfare, but individuals (including business owners) have the right to use and dispose of their property as they choose (within the bounds of standard criminal and civil law) even if their conduct does not maximize total utility.

After summarizing empirical studies of firm behavior, Baker elaborates on the harm from anticompetitive behavior:

> This evidence plainly suggests that in the absence of antitrust rules, anti-competitive conduct would often take place. . . . This evidence, too, suggests that absent antitrust enforcement, many industries would find ways of coordinating to the detriment of consumers and economic welfare. . . . In sum, studies of firm behavior during these four periods demonstrate that without antitrust, firms can and do exercise market power, to the detriment of consumers and other buyers.
>
> (2003, 36–38)

To be sure, colluding with other firms on pricing, merging with close competitors to increase industry consolidation, and undercutting competition with the hopes of driving them out of the market and increasing prices later all have deleterious effects on the utility of consumers (and, in some cases, competitors, especially smaller ones). But none of these actions, as rapacious and devious as they may seem, violate any widely accepted rights of consumers or competitors and are not wrongful in this sense. Consumers do not have a right to a certain (low) price, and competitors do not have the right to a certain (high) price, just as a firm does not have any right or claim on certain behavior from its consumers or competitors.[12] The only right guaranteed to market participants is the right to participate, not the right to any particular outcome; to claim such a right would imply a right to have control over another party's free choices.[13]

Considered more broadly, the labeling of such actions as "anticompetitive" is ironic because it is based on the outcome of such actions rather than their inherent nature. In truth, any action one firm engages in when competing with other firms is competitive, regardless of whether it leads to greater efficiency and higher welfare. Understanding the actions prescribed by antitrust in this way recalls our earlier discussion of competition as a process that emerges from business activity, rather than being constitutive of it, and also that the externalities of competition are generally held to be justified by its result. Antitrust defenders would argue that in this case, the harms from competition are not justified by their result because that result – lower efficiency or welfare – is itself negative. But this is the result as judged by utilitarian logic, focusing on outcomes rather than process. If instead the result is considered to be a market in which business owners are free to exercise their valid property rights, then any nonwrongful harms generated by business competition (in the broad sense) are justified. Furthermore, by implication, antitrust law is a wrongful constraint on this activity. If the activity prescribed by antitrust law involves the rightful exercise of protected rights without violating any recognized rights of other parties, prevention and punishment of that activity by the state are not justified in any context that acknowledges that rights must sometimes trump welfare.[14]

More generally, mainstream economists' perception of competition as a result to be engineered is yet another reflection of their utilitarian orientation, in which the goal of market behavior is to maximize welfare, rather than to create a process by which individuals exercise their rights to advance their interests.[15] This utilitarian mindset is also responsible for the category mistake of "market failure," which makes sense only if the market is assigned a purpose or goal against which its performance can be measured. Viewed from the perspective of rights, however, the government's role shifts from promoting conditions for maximal efficiency – often at the expense of the rightful exercise of individuals' property rights – to protecting those rights and addressing true wrongs, such as deception, fraud, and coercion (as well as assault and theft), all of which involve violations of rights.

Conclusion

When economists are taught welfare economics and the Kaldor-Hicks test without their utilitarian context, they can earn their doctorates without knowing that there are other valid perspectives on ethics (not to mention the criticisms of utilitarianism itself). Ethical systems that stress the importance of rights, such as the deontology of Immanuel Kant, are needed to temper the excesses of adherence to an oversimplistic version of utilitarian reasoning, one that too easily sacrifices the interests of the few for those of the many without adequate consideration of the rights involved and potentially violated.

This is not to say that utility has no role to play in economic theory, practice, or policy. Economists can ground their work in utilitarianism while observing common-sense constraints on their policy recommendations based on important rights, using judgment to help balance the two considerations. This is how individual choice can be modeled along Kantian lines (White 2011; White 2015b), and policy decisions can be made the same way, assuming that the constraints on action imposed by rights are taken as seriously as traditional economic constraints.[16] Failure to do this can result in harm that cannot and should not be optimized and accepted – wrongful harm resulting from the violation of essential rights that must be avoided. And the first step in avoiding it is teaching economists about rights and incorporating them into economic thinking in a meaningful and significant way. I guarantee that the benefits of doing so will far exceed the costs.

Notes

1 Most of the Kantian ethics discussed here can be found in Kant (1785); for a succinct introduction, see Sullivan (1994). The discussion of the Kaldor-Hicks test in Kantian terms is based on White (2011, 143–146).
2 For a thorough exploration, see Dean (2006) and Audi (2016).
3 Along the same lines, Kaplow and Shavell (2002) famously argued that policy and law must be designed to maximize welfare because that will maximize welfare.
4 The discussion of the Coase Theorem in the rest of this section draws on White (2011, 146–154).
5 Perhaps surprisingly, Arthur Pigou, to whose recommendations regarding optimal taxation Coase was responding, did emphasize responsibility alongside efficiency in his work; see Coleman (1980), Page (1986), and Kumekawa (2017). Also, Coleman (1980, 236) notes that Coase may not have denied unilateral causation inasmuch as he declared it irrelevant to the operation of what came to be known as the Coase Theorem; the rhetorical effect, however, remains.
6 This section draws from White (2015a).
7 For concise introductions to tort law, see Geistfeld (2008) and Goldberg and Zipursky (2010a).
8 See Aristotle (350 BCE, Book V); for modern treatments, see, for instance, Weinrib (1995) and Wright (1995).
9 This is particularly relevant in the context of criminal law, which more clearly than tort law deals with wrongs. Nonetheless, in the economics of crime, the focus is on optimizing the costs from crime to find the "efficient" level. For example, as Posner (1980, 82) wrote in response to retributivist theories of punishment that aim to make penalties "fit the crime" rather than provide optimal deterrence, "There can be no assurance that a pure system of retaliation or revenge would result in the imposition of optimal penalties. But this is not to say that there would be too much crime. There might rather be too little" (1980, 82).
10 A shirt that reads "externalities are irrelevant" may cause quite a stir in certain circles.
11 The rest of this section is drawn from White (2016).
12 These would be the "arbitrarily assigned rights" Posner claimed existed in traditional tort understanding but did not describe as such in his antitrust work (2001).

13　To be sure, there are some who claim that activity in violation of antitrust law is theft. For instance, Robert H. Lande (2013, 2351) writes that "the overriding purpose of the antitrust statutes is to prevent firms from stealing from consumers by charging them supracompetitive prices. When firms use their market power to raise prices to supracompetitive levels, consumers pay more for their goods and services, and these overcharges constitute a taking of consumers' property."

14　For more on the perspective on antitrust from property rights, see Epstein (1982). Also, the fact that antitrust sanctions are often classified as criminal penalties serves to emphasize the conflation of harm and wrongfulness. Crimes are normally understood to be wrongful harms not only to individuals directly affected but also to society as a whole. If no individuals were wronged by "anticompetitive behavior" – in other words, if no rights of any individual were violated – then the criminal law of antitrust law implies that wrong done by such behavior must be against society. However, this makes sense only in the context of a utilitarian conception of the state in which firms have a legal duty to maximize welfare.

15　I am careful to specify mainstream economists here because economists of the Austrian school are well known for their emphasis on competition as a process; see, for instance, Armentano (1990, ch. 2).

16　This is also how legal philosophers such as Ronald Dworkin (1977) envision the role of the courts: as constraining policy as enacted by legislators.

References

Armentano, Dominick T. (1990) *Antitrust and Monopoly: Anatomy of a Market Failure*. Oakland, CA: The Independent Institute.

Audi, Robert (2016) *Mean, Ends, & Persons: The Meaning & Psychological Dimensions of Kant's Humanity Formula*. Oxford: Oxford University Press.

Baker, Jonathan B. (2003) "The Case for Antitrust Enforcement." *Journal of Economic Perspectives* 17(4): 27–50.

Bentham, Jeremy (1781). *The Principles of Morals and Legislation*. Buffalo, NY: Prometheus Books (1988 edition).

Coase, Ronald H. (1960) "The Problem of Social Cost." *Journal of Law and Economics* 3: 1–44.

Coleman, Jules L. (1980) "Efficiency, Auction and Exchange." *California Law Review* 68: 221–249.

―――. (1984) "Economics and the Law: A Critical Review of the Foundations of the Economic Approach to Law." *Ethics* 94: 649–679.

Dean, Richard (2006) *The Value of Humanity in Kant's Moral Theory*. Oxford: Oxford University Press.

Dworkin, Ronald M. (1977) *Taking Rights Seriously*. Cambridge, MA: Harvard University Press.

―――. (1980). "Is Wealth a Value?" *Journal of Legal Studies* 9: 191–226.

Epstein, Richard A. (1973) "A Theory of Strict Liability." *Journal of Legal Studies* 2: 151–204.

―――. (1982) "Private Property and the Public Domain: The Case of Antitrust." In J. Roland Pennock and John W. Chapman (eds.), *Ethics, Economics, and The Law: NOMOS XXIV*. New York: New York University Press, 48–82.

Geistfeld, Mark A. (2008) *Tort Law: The Essentials*. Austin, TX: Wolters Kluwer Law & Business.

―――. (2014) "The Tort Entitlement to Physical Security as the Distributive Basis for Environmental, Health, and Safety Regulations." *Theoretical Inquiries in Law* 15: 387–415.

Goldberg, John C. P., and Benjamin C. Zipursky (2010a) *The Oxford Introduction to U.S. Law: Torts*. Oxford: Oxford University Press.

———. (2010b) "Torts as Wrongs." *Texas Law Review* 88: 917–986.

Holmes, Oliver Wendell (1881) *The Common Law*. Ed. Mark DeWolfe. Cambridge, MA: Harvard University Press (1963 edition).

Kant, Immanuel (1785) *Grounding for the Metaphysics of Morals*. Trans. James W. Ellington. Indianapolis, IN: Hackett Publishing Company (1993 edition).

Kaplow, Louis, and Steven Shavell (2002) *Fairness Versus Welfare*. Cambridge, MA: Harvard University Press.

Kronman, Anthony T. (1980) "Wealth Maximization as a Normative Principle." *Journal of Legal Studies* 9: 227–242.

Kumekawa, Ian (2017) *The First Serious Optimist: A.C. Pigou and the Birth of Welfare Economics*. Princeton, NJ: Princeton University Press.

Lande, Robert H. (2013) "A Traditional and Textualist Analysis of the Goals of Antitrust: Efficiency, Preventing Theft from Consumers, and Consumer Choice." *Fordham Law Review* 81: 2349–2403.

Page, Talbot (1986) "Responsibility, Liability, and Incentive Compatibility." *Ethics* 97: 240–262.

Posner, Richard A. (1973) "Strict Liability: A Comment." *Journal of Legal Studies* 2: 205–221.

———. (1980) "Retribution and Related Concepts of Punishment." *Journal of Legal Studies* 9: 71–92.

———. (1983) *The Economics of Justice*. 2nd ed. Cambridge, MA: Harvard University Press.

———. (2001) *Antitrust Law*. 2nd ed. Chicago: University of Chicago Press.

Rawls, John (1971) *A Theory of Justice*. Cambridge, MA: Harvard University Press.

Shavell, Steven (1987) *Economic Analysis of Accident Law*. Cambridge, MA: Harvard University Press.

Sullivan, Roger J. (1994) *An Introduction to Kant's Ethics*. Cambridge: Cambridge University Press.

Weinrib, Ernest J. (1995) *The Idea of Private Law*. Cambridge, MA: Harvard University Press.

White, Mark D. (2009) "Pareto, Consent, and Respect for Dignity: A Kantian Perspective." *Review of Social Economy* 67: 49–70.

———. (2011) *Kantian Ethics and Economics: Autonomy, Dignity, and Character*. Stanford, CA: Stanford University Press.

———. (2015a) "On the Relevance of Wrongfulness to the Concept of Externalities." *Oeconomia* 5: 313–329.

———. (2015b) "Judgment: Balancing Principle and Policy." *Review of Social Economy* 73: 223–241

———. (2016) "On the Justification of Antitrust: A Matter of Rights and Wrongs." *The Antitrust Bulletin* 61: 323–335.

Wright, Richard W. (1995) "Right, Justice, and Tort Law." In David G. Owen (ed.), *Philosophical Foundations of Tort Law*. Cambridge, MA: Clarendon Press, 159–182.

7 Experiments in economics and their ethical dimensions

The case of developing countries

Alice Nicole Sindzingre

Introduction

Mainstream economic publications consider mathematical models to be a requisite, models being viewed as a guarantee of 'scientificity'. Experiments, for their part, have become widespread in mainstream economics since the end of the 20th century, being viewed as an additional method that is particularly effective regarding the provision of this guarantee of rigour. Among such experiments, those conducted outside the laboratory ('field' experiments, 'natural' experiments), including randomised experiments (randomised controlled trials, RCTs), have gained an increasing importance in economic studies. The expansion of such experimental methods in economics raises many questions. These questions are of an epistemological nature, notably regarding the validity of an extension of results and causalities inferred (usually via econometrics) from the experiment with its specific construction to wider scales and social settings – sometimes much wider settings, such as the transposition of causalities inferred from a local experiment to an entire country. These questions are also of an ethical nature. Yet the ethical dimensions of the recurrent use of experiments by economists remain under-investigated, though they constitute crucial issues, as experiments are presented as providing results that are more 'true' not only in terms of scientificity but also in terms of relevance for policymakers – being more 'true' than qualitative methods and even more than conventional modelling and econometric techniques. These ethical issues are particularly crucial in developing countries, where experiments have become widely utilised, their results viewed as guides for policymaking and resource allocation that would be more rigorous than all other methods.

The chapter thus analyses field experiments in developing countries, including randomised controlled trials. It argues that these experiments raise many issues, with these being particularly acute in developing countries. Firstly, these issues are epistemological; these epistemological questions are simultaneously ethical, as the ontological framework of experiments is utilitarianism and a conception of persons as individualists who rationally respond to inputs such as policy variations in isolation from social or political contexts (policies being moreover viewed as binary inputs that are comparable to objects, e.g. drugs, and that can be administered to samples of human or animal populations). Secondly, these issues are ethical because experiments aim to guide policymaking. Developing countries are characterised by poverty and therefore dependence on donors' financing. The designers of experiments are most often from donor countries, and the policy space of developing country governments is limited in regard to the questioning of the results of experiments and extrapolation to policymaking, which underscores the importance of the ethical choices and responsibility of the economists who devise experiments. Similarly, because of the poverty of these countries and their vulnerability, errors in experiments' designs, causal inferences and extrapolation to public policies have more detrimental consequences in developing countries than in richer countries.

The chapter is organised as follows. Firstly, it analyses the rise of experiments in economics, and in this context, the preeminence of RCTs, particularly in development economics and policymaking in developing countries. Secondly, the chapter analyses the epistemological and ethical dimensions of a widespread use of RCTs in developing countries, in particular the ethical challenges for economists that stem from the specificities of these countries due to their poverty and dependence on external policy decisions, and shows that these dimensions appear to be mostly negative.

The rise of randomised controlled trials as the method for 'rigorous' policymaking

The expansion of experiments in economics

Experiments can be defined in different ways, e.g. as devices aiming at validating a hypothesis or general tools for acquiring knowledge. They are not new in the history of thought. Since the birth of philosophy, thought experiments have been powerful heuristics for problems where empirical verification was difficult for the deepening of a particular problem and the exploration of logical consequences that do not appear at first sight: among many examples, Erwin Schrödinger's cat, Alan Turing's test – which, interestingly, could much later be partially verified in laboratory experiments – John Rawls' 'veil of ignorance', John Searle's 'Chinese room' (Tittle, 2005, for a review).

In economics, experiments were considered as falling outside of the domain of economics during the first part of the 20th century (as economists cannot achieve the 'controlled experiments of the chemist or the biologist', Samuelson, 1948: 4), though classical theorists had reflected on the conditions under which experiments are possible. The development of experimental economics after the mid-20th century has been strengthened by the expansion of game theory, which fostered the view that economic causalities that could not be explored via traditional economic models could be reached in a more rigorous and enlightening way via experiments: games devised in order to explore a particular economic problem (trust games, ultimatum games, dictator games, etc.) may be considered particular types of experiments.

At the end of the 20th century, the use of experiments witnessed such an expansion that it gave rise to an autonomous sub-field where the method – experiments – had become the content – 'experimental economics'. Experiments have thus become a specific domain within economics ('experimental economics'), with the experimental method becoming, at the same time, one tool among others for economists. This expansion of experimental economics has been associated with that of behavioural economics, which contributed to the strengthening of the links between games and experiments, e.g. via psychological games. Interestingly, the exploration of the ethical features of economic agents has been a core subject of behavioural economics, e.g. the notion of reciprocity, other-regarding behaviour, altruism or guilt (Charness and Dufwenberg, 2006). Analysis of social preferences in the line of behavioural economics can even explore central issues of theory of ethics, such as the conditions for decision-making to be deontological (rules-based) or consequentialist (Chen and Schonger, 2016). Experimental findings are less focused on the assessment of the validity of economic theory than on the identification of domains that so far are out of the scope of economic theory (Binmore, 1999). Yet behavioural economics, as well as game theory, remains within the neoclassical framework (Berg and Gigerenzer, 2010; Sindzingre, 2017). Together with the models that underlie experiments, it relies on an 'as if' that justifies the process of reduction inherent in the activity of modelling whatever the model's departure from realism – which was explicitly claimed by Friedman (1953) (Hausman, 1992; Sindzingre, 2018). Indeed, experiments may be viewed as models, the difference being that they rely on material manipulation, where models rely on theoretical assumptions (Mäki, 2005). Beliefs and behaviour remain here conceived at the level of the individual, who, even if she may display strategic behaviour, is assumed to maximise utility and to be driven by incentives such as payoffs (gains) (Henckel et al., 2017). Such a framework allows for the possibility of experiments, as experiments can test these assumptions.

The discipline of economics became increasingly specialised from the 1960s onwards, giving rise, e.g., to health economics, urban economics, etc. Behavioural economics and experimental economics became institutionalised sub-fields in the mid-1980s (Cherrier, 2017). Experiments could have been conceived as a particular methodology, but the claim by their promoters that they represented a major scientific advance has fostered their constitution as a sub-field of economics, with economic theory and experimental economics contributing to one another (Samuelson, 2005). Experiments may indeed be viewed as having a greater epistemic power than models for the understanding of economic phenomena because they are 'versions of the real world' that are 'captured' in the laboratory rather than representations of it (as are models) (Morgan, 2005). The recognition of experimental economics within economics culminated in the Nobel Prize awarded to Vernon Smith in 2002 (together with Daniel Kahneman) for his contribution to laboratory experiments (Svorenčík, 2015). Experimental economics had from the beginning an applied dimension: an experimenter moves from the 'natural' phenomenon to its study in a laboratory via performance-based payments of experiment subjects and then to a policy recommendation (Svorenčík, 2017).The development of experimental economics can be viewed as a dimension of the rise of the sub-field of applied economics within economics, which has characterised the end of the 20th century (Backhouse and Cherrier, 2017) – as well as of the preeminence given to 'evidence-based' results in the world of policymakers (such as the World Bank). Games and experiments have in common the isolating of precise questions and claiming that they are privileged approaches for providing rigorous answers.

Experiments may be artefacts, i.e. devices elaborated by researchers in order to disentangle a particular problem and differentiate its various consequences. They may be laboratory and field experiments. Laboratory experiments are artefacts that are conducted within a particular closed setting in order to test economic theories, influence policymaking or collect data on unanticipated regularities (Roth, 1986). Field experiments are artefacts conducted outside the laboratory, in the real world; and among them, RCTs have gained a remarkable importance in the discipline of economics since the end of the 20th century. Right from the beginning, results of experiments have been used in order to make extrapolations from limited data to general claims on human behaviour or on appropriate policymaking and have therefore been subject to debates (Binmore and Shaked, 2010): e.g., in the case of laboratory experiments, debates have focused on the 'generalisability' of their results (Lewitt and List, 2007), on the latter's artificiality, or on the impossibility of the *ceteris paribus* assumption ('all other things being equal') in the quest for the isolation of mechanisms that characterises laboratory experiments.

The concept of experiments does not necessarily require the devising of artefacts, and there may be 'natural' experiments – i.e. same as 'artefactual' or 'framed' field experiments but where subjects 'naturally undertake these tasks and where the subjects do not know that they are in an experiment' (Harrison and List, 2004).The latter may be viewed as experiments in a broad sense, and their nature of experiments may be debated.They use existing states of affairs in order to isolate the specific effects of a particular nexus of economic features or public decisions and differentiate them from the effects of other nexuses or decisions, e.g. Engerman and Sokoloff (2002) on the natural experiment provided by the difference in inequality between North and South America, Acemoglu et al. (2004) on the natural experiment provided by the existence of South and North Korea, Kumar and Liang (2018) on the natural experiment provided by amendments allowing credit in Texas and the latter's effects on labour markets, Nunn and Qian (2011) on the impact of a new agricultural product such as potatoes, among many studies. Natural experiments, as experiments that contrast with laboratory experiments, have become important tools regarding the evaluation of policies or of the impact of specific events – for example, when RCTs appear to be impossible to devise (Craig et al., 2018). This is the case not only in economics but also in political science, e.g. to assess the motives of a vote (Wantchekon, 2003;Vicente, 2010; Drago et al., 2018).

The use of games as well as laboratory or field experiments witnessed a spectacular development in mainstream economists' analyses, while they may model any possible economic notion: behaviour (e.g. trustworthiness, Bauer et al., 2018; prosocial behaviour, Goette and Tripodi, 2018; or social cohesion, Stage and Uwera, 2018), policy (e.g. accumulation of public debt, Battaglini et al., 2016) or institution (such as a market, e.g. of consumer goods, Brown et al., 2018, or a labour market, Dickinson et al., 2018). The distinction between these categories has become increasingly blurred, and many studies use all of them – for example, using one of these methods, e.g. an experiment, in order to test the robustness of another method, e.g. a game (e.g. Belloc et al., 2017, for the use of a game and a laboratory experiment; Kühl and Szech, 2017, for a field experiment confirmed by a lab experiment; Karaja and Rubin, 2017, for a trust game utilised in a natural experiment). Field experiments, laboratory experiments and games may be used in the same study (as in Henrich et al., 2004, who test a variety of games 'in the field' in fifteen 'traditional' societies in developing countries).

Games and experiments are also used by heterodox economists, or economists who work on complexity or are situated at the border of mainstream economics (among many others, Schelling, 1978, on segregation; Arthur, 1994, on the 'El Farol bar problem'; Bowles, 2004, on institutions).

The rise of randomised controlled trials as a preeminent paradigm within experiments

Within this paradigm, a particular method, randomised controlled trials (RCTs), has witnessed an increasing importance from the end of the 20th century onwards, especially in behavioural and public economics. RCTs in economics are randomised experiments conducted 'in the field'. The rationales of RCTs may be viewed as symmetrical to the above mentioned experiments, as they go 'from the lab to the field', i.e. from hypotheses and procedures devised *ex ante* outside a 'natural' setting ('in the lab') to a natural environment, where the implementation of these procedures aims at producing policy recommendations that are as rigorous as those devised 'in the lab'. While experiments in their broad sense may not have the reflection of real-world problems as a first target, external validity, understood as the generalisation of results from laboratory to non-laboratory conditions (Guala and Mittone, 2005), should be an important issue for RCTs.

Randomised controlled trials were originally widely used methods in medical science and public health for the testing of the efficacy of drugs – though RCTs appear to have been promoted as early as the late 19th century in psychology by C. S. Peirce (Peirce and Jastrow, 1885). A drug, which is the subject of the experiment, is given to some populations – the 'treatment' groups – while other populations – the 'control' groups – do not receive it. This allows for the disentangling of the specific effect of the treatment. RCTs in economics and in other social sciences have extended this methodology to the isolation of some hypothesised factor: RCTs randomly sample the target of the experiment (e.g. a sample of schools if the RCT analyses the impact of a school policy); they compare a group exposed to the factor (the 'treatment' group), e.g. an economic policy, a particular event or project – all other factors being supposed to be constant, notably the two groups being comparable and sharing some basic characteristics – and a group that is not exposed to this factor; and they analyse the differences between the respective hypothesised effects of exposure and non-exposure among the two groups.

Randomised controlled trials have gained a preeminent position in economics, but also in other social sciences – for example, in political science (Vicente, 2007; Gerber and Green, 2011) – this preeminence having even been viewed by some studies as an 'hegemony' (Pearl, 2018). In particular, RCTs have become a central method since the 1980s in regard to the evaluation of public policies – for example, in the evaluation of labour markets and welfare programmes. RCTs gained a particular preeminence in development economics and promoted a microeconomic approach of development. Among many economic domains that are also issues of public policy, RCTs have been widely used in order to analyse, e.g. health and education (Dupas and Miguel, 2017), poverty (Alatas et al., 2012), corruption (Olken, 2007), tax compliance (Mascagni, 2018) and access to services (e.g. banking systems, Dupas et al., 2018; Buri et al., 2018) or the evaluation of projects and programmes related to these issues – health or education projects, anti-poverty programmes, social programmes (Premand and Schnitzer, 2018), cash transfers programmes (Armand et al., 2018), firms' training programmes (Cusolito et al., 2018), etc. RCTs have contributed to the trend that has become pervasive in the economics of development, which views development as an outcome of microeconomic problems, with some marginalisation of the macroeconomics of development in comparison with the post-World War II period.

For their supporters, RCTs are a major improvement in the scientific rigour of economics (Duflo et al., 2006; Banerjee and Duflo, 2017, for syntheses). They claim that RCTs allow overcoming risks of bias, notably selection bias (Eble et al., 2017), and that much better than all other methods – e.g. statistical models, laboratory experiments or other evaluation methods[1] – with the right sample and experimental design, randomisation can identify causal relationships by comparing the impacts of various interventions on treatment and control groups. They argue that RCTs are more 'transparent' and 'credible' than all previous methods. Avoiding the flaws of 'high theory', RCTs promote empirical economics and claim to have induced a 'credibility revolution' in this sub-field of economics (Angrist and Pischke, 2010). RCTs would be the most 'credible' and 'rigorous' of the credible methods and at the top of the hierarchy of evidence. The 'credibility' of RCTs comes from their ability to get answers without the use of prior information about structure, such as causal factors or mechanisms of operation (Deaton and Cartwright, 2016).

Economics, including economic modelling, always had the ambition to be heard by policymakers, and this is even more the case for RCTs. Right from the initial studies in the late 1990s, RCTs made it explicit that they had the goal of being a tool for policymaking – for example, regarding the evaluation of projects – and notably public policies or projects funded by foreign aid in developing countries. For example, one of the pioneer studies aimed at showing that school-based mass treatment with deworming drugs randomly phased into schools was more efficient than a treatment that was randomised at the individual level (Miguel and Kremer, 2004). RCTs are intrinsically linked to policy evaluations, and as such have ethical implications. They aim at influencing policies – they are not purely academic assessments of the world – and have the ambition to change, or 'improve', them.

The method of randomisation was promoted as a major advance in economics by economists such as Esther Duflo. The creation of a research centre, which is financed by numerous donors,[2] has helped in the dissemination of RCTs throughout developing countries (and also in industrial countries) via aid funds and making RCTs a central tool for the assessment of economic behaviour and public policies, both in the discipline of development economics and in developing countries' policies. RCTs also claim a moral superiority over all other methods in economics, particularly in developing countries, because, in their view, they are more efficient than other approaches for the alleviation of poverty and the reduction of 'human suffering' (Donovan, 2018).

RCTs in economics follow a sequence of steps that is more or less standard. Researchers start from a general question that may belong to any economic field, then design the experiment, then elaborate the sampling and randomisation that delineate the treatment groups and the control groups, then provide results of the trial, which are by definition quantified measures that are viewed as responses to the question, and finally analyse how the RCT constitutes a valid response to the general question. Indeed, as randomised experiments stem from the objective of making evaluation of policies more 'scientific', they withdraw the conduct of evaluations from 'qualitative' researchers, notably other social scientists, such as anthropologists, sociologists or political economists. Results of RCTs are typically of the form 'individuals exposed to the policy A (or participating in the programme B) are x percent more likely to become Y or to exhibit the behaviour Z' (among many examples, Martinez et al., 2018). Criteria are simultaneously academic criteria (e.g. a robust econometric analysis) and policy criteria (e.g. a policy that is the most relevant, effective or fair). For example, recurrent questions of RCTs are the identification of policies of education that are, among other criteria, cost-effective (Macdonald and Vu, 2018) or fairest (Evans et al., 2017).

The ethical implications of randomised controlled trials in developing countries

The context: the ethical challenges implied by the dependence of poor countries' policies on external decisions

Before analysing the ethical issues that experiments may raise for economists in developing countries, the specificities of these countries must be highlighted.

Firstly, developing countries are characterised by poverty and vulnerability. Many populations live at the subsistence level, and hence there are greater risks inherent in any public policy. In particular, inappropriate public policies can easily aggravate the livelihoods of populations. In poor countries, the sense of overall responsibility of the policymaker and her deontology regarding the impacts of different alternative policies, in particular on the different social groups that comprise them, is thus crucial.

Secondly, as an outcome of their poverty, developing countries are characterised by dependence on foreign aid. Domestic policies in poor countries are thus more influenced by foreign donors' decisions and by academic studies that are conducted within donor countries than decisions and studies elaborated by the governments and academics of these developing countries. This implies that it is donor governments and their economists that share a great part of the responsibilities that are inherent in the devising of public policies. Particularly since the 'lost decades' that characterised the economic growth of developing countries in the 1980s–90s (Easterly, 2001) and the associated recourse to the conditional lending of international financial institutions (IFIs, the IMF and the World Bank), poor countries have been subjected to an 'externalisation' of their policies, i.e. 'being decided in Washington or Brussels' (non-conditional financing being difficult to conceive and implement and a debated issue, Sindzingre, 2016). This externalisation of policies due to financing that is conditional to IFI policies and therefore an accountability of developing countries' governments to external donors rather than to citizens is detrimental to the ownership of policies by citizens, and hence to the effectiveness of these policies (Kaldor, 1963; Moss et al., 2006).

Equating field experiments with science, marginalising theory and other methods

Field experiments, including RCTs, exhibit epistemological weaknesses, and these are often simultaneously ethical weaknesses.

A weakness that is often underscored is arguing that the two worlds – that of experiment and the 'real world' – are heterogeneous, and that experiments have no epistemic value for the understanding of 'real' societies. This has been highlighted, for example, by Austrian economics, for which history consists in non-repeatable facts (Mises, 2003).

Other weaknesses may be underscored, however. Firstly, the conception of society that is explicit in RCTs is a naturalisation – a 'physicalisation' – of societies, in the sense that a society is viewed as more a population of individuals that share identical characteristics, their only difference being 'with/without' the treatment (policy), i.e. more a population of clones, than a community cemented by social links and rules. As in biophysics (the initial epistemic 'cradle' of experiments), this population is viewed as a biophysical system of organisms that reacts when it receives chemical inputs. Individuals as bodies driven by dynamics of chemical processes is the vision that underlies RCTs and the concepts of treatment and control groups as well as the application of RCTs to societies – a vision that is implied in words such as 'experiment' and 'trials'. Societies are viewed as juxtapositions of bodies and public policies as units that can be isolated and separated – e.g. as would be the case for the administration of a medical treatment – and as events that can affect in a similar way all members of a sampled population – as would be an identical treatment X administered to N homogeneous individuals.

Similarly, RCTs conceive individuals and groups as independent from any social and political context and do not conceive that their behaviour may be path-dependent (dependent on past events). Yet comparability is questionable between individuals who are exposed to the policy or programme, but whose characteristics are shaped by their insertion in a given context, and individuals who are not exposed to this policy, as the latter may be inserted in different contexts (different time and space).

An economist who thinks that experiments say something 'true' about 'real' societies makes a decision regarding the ontology of these societies, which economics as a social science is supposed to explain. This selection of a particular ontology – i.e. the social world can be compared with a world of individuals reacting to inputs 'as if' they could be reduced to physicochemical processes – is simultaneously an ethical decision, as in such a world norms and responsibilities are limited. Yet prior to their conception and design, RCTs do not provide a justification of such ontology.

These flawed 'physicalist' metaphorisations of societies and of the impact of public policies on the various individuals who constitute them are indeed illustrated by the difficulty in replicating experiments in economics. It has thus been found that about 40% of economic laboratory experiments fail replication (Camerer et al., 2016) – which suggests worse performances for field experiments.

Not only are individuals heterogeneous (RCTs may under-theorise the 'fallacy of averages', Subramanian et al., 2018), but this conception of public policy is also simplistic, and complex objects such as policies that affect complex concepts such as societies cannot be reduced to treatments administered to sampled populations. This conception ignores research on public policies within economics, which shows that economies and the impacts of public policies on them must be analysed as complex systems (Durlauf, 2012). Economic phenomena, both macro and micro, may be affected by non-linearities and threshold effects, which affects the relevance of public policies (Cohen-Cole et al., 2012). An outcome can be caused by a variety of factors (possibly unknown) that RCTs have difficulty detecting. As with any modelling exercise, the design of the RCT can be subject to issues of misspecification of the model (Durlauf et al., 2008). Moreover, as empirical research, if results rely on a single study, they cannot be fully credible. As shown by Ioannidis et al. (2017) via a sample of 159 meta-analyses, empirical economics research is subjected to important biases, with the majority of the average effects being 'exaggerated by a factor of at least 2' and at least one-third being exaggerated 'by a factor of 4 or more'. Similarly, RCTs are exposed to the issue of experiment as 'exhibit' rather than test. An 'exhibit', in Sugden's (2005) words, is an experimental design that induces a regularity 'combined with an informal hypothesis about the underlying causal mechanism', but which can be produced by different causal mechanisms.

Secondly, randomised experiments are said to provide 'evidence-based' assertions, which are therefore, because of this evidence, more 'scientific'; yet the nature of this 'evidence' is rarely questioned. In RCTs, modelling is equated with science and rigour; the 'internal validity' of the model – i.e. identification, specification – is viewed as enough for guaranteeing the rigour of the causal processes the RCT will highlight (Deaton, 2009). Yet the 'internal validity' and technical aspects of RCTs are subject to several weaknesses, and economists who claim RCTs' indisputable superiority do not display the quest for truth that is the basis of scientific research. RCTs claim that little prior scientific knowledge is required. Their supporters admit that a theoretical framework is necessary to indicate the experiments to be run and to provide a general interpretation, but RCTs are also conceived as a 'challenge to theory' (Duflo et al., 2006). Indeed, their focus is 'what works' rather than 'why it works' (Deaton and Cartwright, 2018). This is an ethical choice that underscores the consequentialist and utilitarian perspectives of RCTs, as it disregards the analysis of (theoretical, *a priori*) causalities that underlie the 'it works'.

Thirdly, another outcome of RCTs is that the assessment of policies or events and their impacts must be made by experts or researchers who are able to use models and econometrics – notably those of RCTs. Indeed, an RCT relies on modelling and econometrics (e.g. a technique such as 'differences-in-differences') because its foundations and the justification of its epistemic superiority are its capacity to measure, which is greater than any other method, as well as its capacity to establish correlations. RCTs claim that they could solve a recurrent problem in economics, i.e. that the measure of impact is more difficult than that of output, in particular regarding the establishment of a causal impact rather than a correlation (Olofsgard, 2014). Therefore, only econometricians are reputed to be able to build RCTs and assess their results and, more generally, to be able to assess the impacts of policies and events. RCTs thus function as exclusionary devices. Economists who rely on 'qualitative' analyses are thus excluded from this epistemic field, which has ethical consequences regarding the economists' profession. An econometric technique such as 'differences-in-differences' – the 'showpiece of the credibility revolution' claimed by RCTs – however, requires a careful design and may produce invalid results if, e.g., treatment and control groups are not comparable (Kahn-Lang and Lang, 2018). Likewise, even within the World Bank, voices have underscored that the investigation of what works and what does not regarding development policies 'cannot be monopolised by one method' (Ravallion, 2009).

The design of randomised controlled trials: ethical issues

The design of RCTs can be subjected to a variety of questionings, as shown by the vast literature on their 'internal validity'. Only the questions related to ethical issues of this design are considered here.

A central question that is inherent in RCTs is that it is the domain of policy that is their field of operation while at the same time they present themselves as an advance in the domain of research – e.g. they would ask more appropriate research questions on the concept of effectiveness or on econometric methods. RCTs thus operate simultaneously in the domain of relevance (of policies), i.e. the domain of action, and that of truth (of research assumptions), i.e. the domain of knowledge ('episteme') (Sindzingre, 2004). This induces a fundamental ambiguity regarding the tools of validation of RCTs, i.e. action (are the policy recommendations derived from an RCT effective?) or knowledge (are the assumptions that have driven the design of an RCT true?). This ambiguity plagues the credibility of RCTs and their use by economists. At the same time, RCTs claim that their credibility stems from the fact that prior information is excluded by randomisation. Yet, as shown by Deaton and Cartwright (2016), this prior information reappears in the interpretation of the results.

In addition, the design of RCTs is mostly made by Western economists and with questions that derive from the conceptual framework of neoclassical economics – i.e. the rationality of agents, their quest for the maximising of their utility, the existence of a representative agent and the possibility of averaging results – even if RCTs claim to be 'atheoretical' and to be a method of enabling findings that are not biased by theoretical *a prioris*. Yet it may be argued that this imposes a specific concept of 'rational agent' (that of Western industrialised countries) on societies that may have a different interpretation of experimental situations (e.g. a misperception of the experiment by the 'treated' individuals, Karlan et al., 2018) and of concepts such as fairness, cooperation, inferential induction or moral reasoning. Hence, the claim that a particular behaviour or a response to a particular policy might be universal, on the basis of a sampling from a single subpopulation, is not justified (Henrich et al., 2010). Similarly, it is not justified to infer the superiority of a particular policy only in terms of efficiency or provision of incentives across societies.

Equally, from their origins in the testing of medical drugs, RCTs separate the individuals who are exposed to the treatment from the others. In economics, they separate the individuals exposed to the policy, project or programme from the others. In clinical RCTs, individuals are 'randomly' singled out in order to be allocated to the 'treatment group' and to the 'control group', respectively, and RCTs assert that the ethical attitude is not to know *a priori* which therapeutic strategy is the best one. Yet in the same way as clinical RCTs, the use of RCTs for economic or policy questions induces ethical issues in regard to the selection of the individuals and the decisions regarding those who will be chosen (the 'treatment' group) and those who will be excluded from the policy or programme (the 'control' group). This 'randomness' and the ethical motives it claims have been called into question, as the very fact of receiving or not receiving a drug can change the life of an individual (Hacking, 1988). Even supporters of RCTs acknowledge that 'being surveyed can change related behaviour' as well as parameter estimates (Zwane Peterson et al., 2011). RCTs may thus give no treatment (programmes) to vulnerable individuals and withhold useful programmes or policies from the control group (Ziliak and Teather-Posadas, 2016). As shown by Ravallion (2009), some of those to whom a programme is randomly assigned will not need it, while some in the control group will, and, in contrast with clinical experiments, the designers of RCTs in the domain of economic development under-address these ethical issues. Indeed, RCTs may be criticised as being unable to handle heterogeneity (and misunderstanding exogeneity) (Deaton 2010). Similarly, it may be difficult for RCTs to take into consideration contextual variation (Ravallion, 2008). Likewise, RCTs may be affected by allocation imbalance – e.g. the treatments may be given disproportionately to one stratum (e.g. men) and not to others (e.g. women) (Ziliak and Teather-Posadas, 2016).

As shown by several studies on aid delivery in developing countries, there may be biases in the selection of the individuals who receive the aid projects. These individuals may be those who are connected to politicians, donors or NGOs, those for whom better infrastructure allows easier access or those on whom some statistical data are available. Heterogeneity across locations regarding the political acceptability of RCTs can also be a source of bias, and some social experiments may raise more ethical concerns in some settings than in others (Ravallion, 2012). These biases imply that entire populations of a given country may be ignored for geographical, political or sociological reasons (e.g. homeless people). Moreover, the quality of the collection of data and hence of results may be proportional to the funds made available to the RCTs by the government or donor. This raises issues of truth and ethics related to the conduct of the surveys and analyses and to their results. Indeed, the precision of an average treatment effect estimator can be improved either by collecting data on additional individuals or by collecting additional covariates that predict the outcome variable (Carneiro et al., 2017).

The issues regarding the extrapolation of experiments and their ethical dimensions

A series of critical points affecting experiments, and RCTs in particular, are analysed through the lens of the ethical issues they entail.

Among them are the conditions for extrapolation of the results of an RCT and for these results to remain identical if the settings of the RCT are modified. RCTs are based on the assumption that extrapolations are possible from one level – a small number, a given setting specific to a particular time and space – to another. This issue is often coined as the 'external validity' of RCTs, though 'external validity' refers, rather, to the relationship of the experiment to the 'real world' – the link between 'internal validity', i.e. the coherence of the experiment, and 'external validity' being subject to debate (Jimenez-Buedo and Miller, 2010). The notion of 'external validity' may be distinguished from the epistemic possibility of extrapolating correlations established in a given stetting to another setting – e.g. from one school to the education system, from one village to a country. These questions are debated for experiments in general, and they affect RCTs as well.

Experiments that are focused on the testing of theories tend to be more centred on 'internal validity', while those exploring empirical regularities are more centred on 'external validity' (Schram, 2005). As argued by Rodrik (2009), the issue of external validity is insufficiently taken into account by RCT studies, which devote more attention to their internal validity.

Yet in the real world, extrapolation may not be possible for a number of reasons. Firstly, extrapolation may not be possible because of the very technical design of an RCT. The small size of samples may inherently not be 'big enough' for any extrapolation (Ravallion, 2012). Also, there may be many unobserved covariates. As underscored by Deaton and Cartwright (2017), estimates apply only to the sample selected for the trial, and an extension of the results to other groups is not always justified: Deaton and Cartwright even argue that a justification must be provided for any extension to any population to which the trial sample belongs – or to any individual, including an individual in the trial – and yet such a justification is not always provided.

These intrinsic limitations regarding extrapolation have ethical dimensions, as policies applied to some populations may be derived from RCTs that were achieved on a specific and small-size sample; for example, policies (treatment) may be implemented that are inappropriate and even generate perverse effects because individuals are heterogeneous and do not form a permanently homogeneous group. RCTs indeed assume the homogeneity of a 'group' or 'population' because of their sharing of some characteristics that RCTs select (e.g. attending a given school, residing in a certain area); yet the latter mask the heterogeneity of individuals under an infinity of other characteristics.

Equally, results of RCTs may be affected by fallacy of composition. Typically, a result regarding education, e.g. that a higher level of education can improve the wages of the educated people, may not be true when extended to a whole country: levels of education impact wages, which are exogenous at the small-scale level and therefore impact the returns to skills (Acemoglu, 2010), but this exogeneity may not be true at the level of a country.

Furthermore, the possibility of making valid inferences from RCTs, in terms of both 'internal' and 'external' validity, is blurred by the issue of 'spillover effects'. RCTs randomly assign projects or programmes to some individuals and not to others and thus partition groups into 'participants' and 'non-participants', the latter being assumed to be unaffected by the programme. As shown by Ravallion (2009), if the longer term is considered, such a separation cannot be plausible in poor developing countries.

The impossibility of extrapolation also refers to the political dimensions inherent in any economic and social setting (De Janvry et al., 2010). Any human setting is organised by power relationships, social norms and institutions. These work simultaneously at various levels – from local to broader ones, e.g. kinship groups, village, region – and make extrapolation of RCTs' results risky. These power relationships also shape the very response to questionnaires and thus may induce biases in results and their interpretation. For example, local social norms and hierarchies, e.g. governing gender or age relationships, can prevent certain responses or, in contrast, make others compulsory (as shown by Boyer, 1986, regarding the refusal by Uzbek peasants to respond to simple questions if they had not received the approval of an individual situated in a higher position). Furthermore, local power relationships may expose the very implementation of a field experiment (especially if it is implemented by foreigners from richer countries) to its adaptation and manipulation by local interests. The latter dimensions are acknowledged by RCTs' defenders, but they are addressed as an issue of appropriately disentangling the provision of efforts in the treatment and control groups in a principal-agent framework (Chassang et al., 2010). The inherent existence of this 'politics of field experiments' has ethical implications for economists who design and conduct them. Indeed, an experiment can modify or destabilise existing power relationships and, more in line with a deontological perspective, thus obliges the economist to include considerations on her responsibility in the whole process, from the initial design to the recommendations derived from experiments.

Randomised controlled trials as drivers of public policies: consequentialism and its limits

In fine, economists who design RCTs have the explicit aim to shape policy-making. RCTs aim not only at 'speaking to theorists' but also at 'whispering to the ears of princes' (Roth, 1986). This aspect is particularly important, as economists in developed countries have, throughout the 20th century, increasingly claimed a central role in the designing of public policies, alleging the superior scientificity of their discipline in comparison with other social sciences – and actually claiming a status of natural science more than a social science (Fourcade et al., 2015). This increased power appears furthermore to be associated with a greater institutionalisation of this influence and the recommendation of market-oriented policies in their studies (Christensen, 2017). Yet in developing countries that are financially dependent on external aid and whose public policies have a limited capacity to counter arguments made by the academics of donors' countries, policy recommendations made by foreign academic economists can have particularly strong economic and ethical consequences.

Policymaking *per se* raises ethical issues. According to a classical distinction, the ethics of public policies can be assessed either via consequentialist approaches, of which utilitarianism is a prominent modality, or via the approach of (rules-based) deontology. For utilitarianism (theorised by, e.g. Jeremy Bentham and John Stuart Mill), an ethical attitude consists only in the production of the right consequences. Causes matter less than consequences – for example, the production of more welfare or happiness for more agents (for their part, for some libertarians, an action is acceptable provided it does not harm; and interestingly, Vernon Smith was close to libertarian views, Hamowy, 2008).

Indeed, for supporters of RCTs, the economist must be an 'engineer', able to address all complications (e.g. of the design of markets put forward in game and experimental economics, Roth, 2002), or a 'plumber' (Duflo, 2017). Moreover, defenders of RCTs argue that the policies that are based on the results of RCTs replace 'unscientific' policies by more rigorous and 'scientific' ones. In these views, rather than a theoretical framework for the understanding of human behaviour, economics is firstly a policy tool, and the main role of the economist is to advise governments in their elaboration of laws and policies. Beyond their apparent technical rationales, RCTs are thus also instruments of government (Labrousse, 2010; Jatteau, 2013). Their impact as tools of government is even stronger in developing countries because the latter are characterised by poverty and by institutions and administrations that have limited capacities. For supporters of RCTs, ethical issues mainly refer to ensuring that, e.g. the questions asked by RCTs are policy-relevant, researchers are not over-regulated and data are appropriately collected (Glennerster and Powers, 2016).

The 'economists-plumbers' must focus on 'many details about which their models and theories do not give much guidance' in order to predict what may work in the 'real world' (Duflo, 2017: 1). RCTs thus situate themselves in utilitarian and consequentialist perspectives. The complexity of social, political and economic causalities is less pertinent than the fact that the recommended policies 'work' and have the consequences these policies have targeted, notably public policies that are the most efficient and cost-effective and provide the greatest incentives for an individual behaviour said to induce the greatest collective welfare, e.g. children who attend school, teachers who do not practice absenteeism, firms that pollute less, bureaucrats who perform better, public funds that reach their targets, etc.

Consequentialist stances in the domain of policymaking seem the best possible ones in poor countries, as in such countries where many individuals live at the subsistence level, a benevolent policymaker should be interested in only the consequences (efficiency) of her policies and hence always prefer policies that 'work' over policies that do not. Yet the 'economist-plumber' overlooks the complexity of the criteria of 'policies that work', as these criteria involve not only the short term but also the long term, and involve not only the economic level but also the social and political levels. As underscored by Drèze (2018), though RCTs claim to be 'rigorous evidence', evidence refers to facts, while policy refers to political decisions, and in this matter as well as the detail of policy design, economists are not necessarily 'competent plumbers'. Moreover, in poor countries with tight fiscal constraints, the issues of 'consequences of what?' and 'consequences for whom?' are crucial. They question the narrow consequentialism of RCTs, as policies aiming at improving the welfare of a great number of individuals (e.g. via more efficient primary schools or dispensaries) can imply the reduction of the welfare of others (e.g. due to fewer universities, fewer hospitals). Indeed, for Deaton (2010), RCTs exhibit so many epistemic and ethical flaws that they should 'stay away' from the evaluation of policies and programmes. This statement is particularly remarkable, as the claim of more 'rigorous' evaluations of policy effectiveness is the core of the justification for RCTs.

Hence, for economists who devise and interpret RCTs, ethical responsibilities are much larger than the narrow focus of RCTs on incentives and efficiency. RCTs also require reflection on the overall deontology of their activity, and even more so in developing countries.

Conclusion

This chapter has investigated randomised controlled trials under their ethical dimensions through the case of developing countries. It has situated RCTs within the conceptual framework of experiments in economics and has highlighted a series of critical epistemic questions that are raised by RCTs.

It has also shown that these epistemic issues are simultaneously ethical ones, in particular because RCTs operate both at the level of academic knowledge (the question being that of truth) and action, i.e. policymaking (the questions being those of relevance and ethics). The widespread use of RCTs in developing countries entails ethical challenges for economists that are particularly crucial due to the specificities of these countries, notably poverty and dependence on external policy decisions. The analysis of different aspects of RCTs, e.g. their conception of the nature of societies, their design, the possibility to extrapolate their results, their narrow consequentialism, has shown that the ethical dimensions of RCTs appear to be mostly negative, or at least under-addressed by their designers.

Notes

1   The evaluation of projects, programmes or policies is indeed a structured activity, which uses a variety of methods, from qualitative assessments (e.g. borrowing from anthropology, participatory methods, focus groups, etc.) to quantitative techniques ('outcome' evaluation, 'impact' evaluation, cost-benefit, cost-effectiveness, benefit-incidence analyses, meta-analyses). Among a vast literature, a summary is provided in World Bank-Independent Evaluation Group (2015).
2   The Abdul Latif Jameel Poverty Action Lab ('JPal'), associated with MIT in Cambridge (MA): www.povertyactionlab.org. By August 2018, its website mentioned that the JPal had implemented '917 ongoing and completed randomized evaluations in 80 countries'.

References

Acemoglu, Daron (2010), Theory, General Equilibrium and Political Economy in Development Economics, *Journal of Economic Perspectives*, vol. 24, pp. 17–32.
Acemoglu, Daron, Simon Johnson and James A. Robinson (2004), *Institutions as the Fundamental Cause of Long-Run Growth*, Cambridge, MA, NBER working paper 10481.
Alatas, Vivi, Abhijit Banerjee, Rema Hanna, Benjamin A. Olken and Julia Tobias (2012), Targeting the Poor: Evidence from a Field Experiment in Indonesia, *American Economic Review*, vol. 102, n 4, pp. 1206–1240.

Angrist, Joshua D. and Jörn-Steffen Pischke (2010). The Credibility Revolution in Empirical Economics: How Better Research Design Is Taking the Con Out of Econometrics, *Journal of Economic Perspectives*, vol. 24, n 2, Spring, pp. 3–30.

Armand, Alex, Orazio Attanasio, Pedro Carneiro and Valerie Lechene (2018), *The Effect of Gender-Targeted Conditional Cash Transfers on Household Expenditures: Evidence from a Randomized Experiment*, London, University College London, Department of Economics, Institute of Fiscal Studies, CEMMAP working paper 33/18.

Arthur, W. Brian (1994), Inductive Reasoning and Bounded Rationality, *American Economic Review*, vol. 84, n°2, May, pp. 406–411.

Backhouse, Roger and Beatrice Cherrier (2017), The Age of the Applied Economist: The Transformation of Economics Since the 1970s, *History of Political Economy*, vol. 49, n°5, pp. 1–33.

Banerjee, Abhijit V. and Esther Duflo (2017), *Handbook of Economic Field Experiments*, vol. 1 and 2, Amsterdam, North Holland-Elsevier.

Battaglini, Marco, Salvatore Nunnari and Thomas R. Palfrey (2016), *The Political Economy of Public Debt: A Laboratory Study*, Cambridge, MA, NBER working paper 22406.

Bauer, Michal, Nathan Fiala and Ian Levely (2018), Trusting Former Rebels: An Experimental Approach to Understanding Reintegration after Civil War, *Economic Journal*, vol. 128, August, pp. 1786–1819.

Belloc, Marianna, Ennio Bilancini, Leonardo Boncinelli and Simone D'Alessandro (2017), *A Social Heuristics Hypothesis for the Stag Hunt: Fast- and Slow-Thinking Hunters in the Lab*, Munich, CESIfo working paper 6824–2017.

Berg, Nathan and Gerd Gigerenzer (2010), As-if Behavioral Economics: Neoclassical Economics in Disguise? *History of Economic Ideas*, vol. 18, n 1, pp. 133–165.

Binmore, Ken (1999), Why Experiment in Economics? *Economic Journal*, vol. 109, n 453, pp. F16–F24.

Binmore, Ken and Avner Shaked (2010), Experimental Economics: Where Next? *Journal of Economic Behavior and Organization*, vol. 73, n 1, pp. 87–100.

Bowles, Samuel (2004), *Microeconomics: Behaviour, Institutions and Evolution*, Princeton, Princeton University Press and Russell Sage Foundation.

Boyer, Pascal (1986), Tradition et vérité, *L'Homme*, vol. 26, n°97–98, pp. 309–329.

Brown, Alexander L., Ajalavat Viriyavipart and Xiaoyuan Wang (2018), Search Deterrence in Experimental Consumer Goods Markets, *European Economic Review*, vol. 104, May, pp. 167–184.

Buri, Sinja, Robert Cull, Xavier Giné, Sven Harten and Soren Heitmann (2018), *Banking with Agents: Experimental Evidence from Senegal*, Washington, DC: The World Bank, policy research working paper 8417.

Camerer, Colin F., Anna Dreber, Eskil Forsell, Teck-Hua Ho, Jürgen Huber, Magnus Johannesson, . . . Adam Altmejd (2016), Evaluating Replicability of Laboratory Experiments, *Science*, vol. 351, n°6280, pp. 1433–1436.

Carneiro, Pedro, Sokbae Lee and Daniel Wilhelm (2017), *Optimal Data Collection for Randomized Control Trials*, London, Institute for Fiscal Studies, Cemmap working paper CWP45/17.

Charness, Gary and Martin Dufwenberg (2006), Promises and Partnership, *Econometrica*, vol. 74, n°6, November, pp. 1579–1601.

Chassang, Sylvain, Gerard Padro i Miquel and Erik Snowberg (2010), *Selective Trials: A Principal-Agent Approach to Randomized Controlled Experiments*, Cambridge MA, NBER working paper 16343.

Chen, Daniel L. and Martin Schonger (2016), *Social Preferences or Sacred Values? Theory and Evidence of Deontological Motivations*, Toulouse, Toulouse School of Economics, TSE working paper 16–714.

Cherrier, Beatrice (2017), Classifying Economics: A History of the JEL Codes, *Journal of Economic Literature*, forthcoming.

Christensen, Johan (2017), *The Power of Economists within the State*, Stanford, Stanford University Press.

Cohen-Cole, Ethan B., Steven N. Durlauf and Giacomo Rondina (2012), Nonlinearities in Growth: From Evidence to Policy, *Journal of Macroeconomics*, vol. 34, pp. 42–58.

Craig, Peter, Marcia Gibson, Mhairi Campbell, Frank Popham and Srinivasa Vittal Katikireddi (2018), Making the Most of Natural Experiments: What Can Studies of the Withdrawal of Public Health Interventions Offer? *Preventive Medicine*, vol. 108, pp. 17–22.

Cusolito, Ana, Ernest Dautovic and David McKenzie (2018), *Can Government Intervention Make Firms More Investment-Ready? A Randomized Experiment in the Western Balkans*, Washington, DC, The World Bank, policy research working paper 8541.

Deaton, Angus (2009), *Instruments of Development: Randomization in the Tropics, and the Search for the Elusive Keys to Economic Development*, Cambridge, MA, NBER working paper 14690.

Deaton, Angus (2010), Instruments, Randomization, and Learning about Development, *Journal of Economic Literature*, vol. 48, June, pp. 424–455.

Deaton, Angus and Nancy Cartwright (2016), *The Limitations of Randomised Controlled Trials*, 9 November. https://voxeu.org/article/limitations-randomised-controlled-trials

Deaton, Angus and Nancy Cartwright (2017), *Understanding and Misunderstanding Randomized Controlled Trials*, Cambridge MA, NBER working paper 22595.

Deaton, Angus and Nancy Cartwright (2018), Understanding and Misunderstanding Randomized Controlled Trials, *Social Science and Medicine*, vol. 210, August, pp. 2–21.

De Janvry, Alain, Andrew Dustan and Elisabeth Sadoulet (2010), *Recent Advances in Impact Analysis Methods for Ex-post Impact Assessments of Agricultural Technology: Options for the CGIAR*, Berkeley, University of California at Berkeley, workshop 'Increasing the rigor of ex-post impact assessment of agricultural research: A discussion on estimating treatment effects', CGIAR Standing Panel on Impact Assessment, SPIA report version 3.1.

Dickinson, David L., David Masclet and Emmanuel Peterle (2018), Discrimination as Favoritism: The Private Benefits and Social Costs of In-Group Favoritism in an Experimental Labor Market, *European Economic Review*, vol. 104, May, pp. 220–236.

Donovan, Kevin P. (2018), The Rise of the Randomistas: On the Experimental Turn in International Aid, *Economy and Society*, vol. 47, n°1, pp. 27–58.

Drago, Francesco, Roberto Galbiati and Francesco Sobbrio (2018), *Voters' Response to Public Policies: Evidence from a Natural Experiment*, Munich, CESifo working paper 6826.

Drèze, Jean (2018), Evidence, Policy and Politics: A Commentary on Deaton and Cartwright, *Social Science and Medicine*, vol. 210, August, pp. 45–47.

Duflo, Esther (2017), The Economist as Plumber, *American Economic Review*, vol. 107, n°5, May, pp. 1–26 (Richard T. Ely Lecture).

Duflo, Esther, Rachel Glennerster and Michael Kremer (2006), *Using Randomization in Development Economics Research: A Toolkit*, Cambridge, MA, NBER technical working paper 333.

Dupas, Pascaline, Dean Karlan, Jonathan Robinson and Diego Ubfal (2018), Banking the Unbanked? Evidence from Three Countries, *American Economic Journal: Applied Economics*, vol. 10, n 2, pp. 257–297.

Dupas, Pascaline and Edward Miguel (2017), Impacts and Determinants of Health Levels in Low-Income Countries, in Abhijit Banerjee and Esther Duflo eds., *The Handbook of Field Experiments*, Amsterdam, North Holland, pp. 3–94.

Durlauf, Steven N. (2012), Complexity, Economics, and Public Policy, *Politics, Philosophy and Economics*, vol. 11, n°1, pp. 45–75.

Durlauf, Steven N., Andros Kourtellos and Chih Ming Tan (2008), Are Any Growth Theories Robust? *Economic Journal*, vol. 118, n 527, March, pp. 329–346.

Easterly, William (2001), The Lost Decades: Developing Countries' Stagnation in Spite of Policy Reform, 1980–1998, *Journal of Economic Growth*, vol. 6, n 2, June, pp. 135–157.

Eble, Alex, Peter Boone and Diana Elbourne (2017), On Minimizing the Risk of Bias in Randomized Controlled Trials in Economics, *World Bank Economic Review*, vol. 31, n°3, pp. 687–707.

Engerman, Stanley L. and Kenneth Sokoloff (2002), *Factor Endowments, Inequality and Paths of Development among New World Economies*, Cambridge, MA, NBER working paper 9259.

Evans, William N., Melissa S. Kearney, Brendan C. Perry and James X. Sullivan (2017), *Increasing Community College Completion Rates among Low-Income Students: Evidence from a Randomized Controlled Trial Evaluation of a Case Management Intervention*, Cambridge, MA, NBER working paper 24150.

Fourcade, Marion, Etienne Ollion and Yann Algan (2015), The Superiority of Economists, *Journal of Economic Perspectives*, vol. 29, n 1, pp. 89–114.

Friedman, Milton (1953), The Methodology of Positive Economics, in *Essays in Positive Economics*, Chicago, The University of Chicago Press, pp. 3–43.

Gerber, Alan S. and Donald P. Green (2011), Field Experiments and Natural Experiments, in Robert E. Goodin ed., *The Oxford Handbook of Political Science*, Oxford Handbooks Online.

Glennerster, Rachel and Shawn Powers (2016), Balancing Risk and Benefit: Ethical Tradeoffs in Running Randomized Evaluations, in George DeMartino and Deirdre McCloskey eds., *The Oxford Handbook of Professional Economic Ethics*, Oxford, Oxford University Press.

Goette, Lorenz and Egon Tripodi (2018), *Social Influence in Prosocial Behavior: Evidence from a Large-Scale Experiment*, London, CEPR discussion paper 13078.

Guala, Francesco and Luigi Mittone (2005), Experiments in Economics: External Validity and the Robustness of Phenomena, *Journal of Economic Methodology*, vol. 12, n 4, pp. 495–515.

Hacking, Ian (1988), Telepathy: Origins of Randomization in Experimental Design, *Isis*, vol. 79, n°3, September, pp. 427–451 (special issue on Artifact and Experiment).

Hamowy, Ronald ed. (2008), *The Encyclopedia of Libertarianism*, Thousand Oaks, Sage Publications.

Harrison, Glenn W. and John A. List (2004), Field Experiments, *Journal of Economic Literature*, vol. 42, n 4, December, pp. 1009–1055.

Hausman, Daniel M. (1992), *The Inexact and Separate Science of Economics*, Cambridge, Cambridge University Press.

Henckel, Timo, Gordon D. Menzies, Peter Moffatt and Daniel J. Zizzo (2017), *Sticky Belief Adjustment: A Double Hurdle Model and Experimental Evidence*, Newcastle, Newcastle University Business School.

Henrich, Joseph, Robert Boyd, Samuel Bowles, Colin Camerer, Ernst Fehr and Herbert Gintis eds. (2004), *Foundations of Human Sociality: Economic Experiments and Ethnographic Evidence from Fifteen Small-Scale Societies*, Oxford, Oxford University Press

Henrich, Joseph, Steven J. Heine and Ara Norenzayan (2010), The Weirdest People in The World? *Behavioral and Brain Sciences*, vol. 33, n°2–3, June, pp. 61–83.

Ioannidis, John P.A., Tom. D. Stanley and Hristos Doucouliagos (2017), The Power of Bias in Economics Research, *Economic Journal*, vol. 127, October, pp. F236–F265.

Jatteau, Arthur (2013), *Les expérimentations aléatoires en économie*, Paris, La Découverte.

Jimenez-Buedo, Maria and Luis Miguel Miller (2010), Why a Trade-Off? The Relationship Between the External and Internal Validity of Experiments, *Theoria: An International Journal for Theory, History and Foundations of Science*, vol. 25, n 1, pp. 301–321.

Kahn-Lang, Ariella and Kevin Lang (2018), *The Promises and Pitfalls of Differences-in-Differences: Reflections on '16 and Pregnant' and Other Applications*, Cambridge, MA, NBER working paper 24857.

Kaldor, Nicholas (1963), Will Underdeveloped Countries Learn to Tax? *Foreign Affairs*, vol. 41, January, pp. 410–419.

Karaja, Elira and Jared Rubin (2017), *The Cultural Transmission of Trust Norms: Evidence from a Lab in the Field on a Natural Experiment*, New York, Columbia University, Chapman University.

Karlan, Dean, Adam Osman and Jonathan Zinman (2018), *Dangers of a Double-Bottom Line: A Poverty Targeting Experiment Misses Both Targets*, London, CEPR discussion paper 12838.

Kühl, Leonie and Nora Szech (2017), *Physical Distance and Cooperativeness Towards Strangers*, Munich, CESIfo working paper 6825.

Kumar, Anil and Che-Yuan Liang (2018), *Labor Market Effects of Credit Constraints: Evidence from a Natural Experiment*, Dallas, Federal Reserve Bank of Dallas, Research Department, working paper 1810.

Labrousse, Agnès (2010), Nouvelle économie du développement et essais cliniques randomisés : une mise en perspective d'un outil de preuve et de gouvernement, *Revue de la Régulation*, Spring. http://regulation.revues.org/7818

Lewitt, Steven D. and John A. List (2007), What Do Laboratory Experiments Measuring Social Preferences Reveal About the Real World? *Journal of Economic Perspectives*, vol. 21, n 2, Spring, pp. 153–174.

Macdonald, Kevin and Binh Thanh Vu (2018), *A Randomized Evaluation of a Low-Cost and Highly Scripted Teaching Method to Improve Basic Early Grade Reading Skills in Papua New Guinea*, Washington, DC, The World Bank, policy research working paper 8427.

Mäki, Uskali (2005) Models Are Experiments, Experiments Are Models, *Journal of Economic Methodology*, vol. 12, n 2, pp. 303–315.

Martínez A. Claudia, Esteban Puentes and Jaime Ruiz-Tagle (2018), The Effects of Micro-entrepreneurship Programs on Labor Market Performance: Experimental Evidence from Chile, *American Economic Journal: Applied Economics*, vol. 10, n 2, pp. 101–124.

Mascagni, Giulia (2018), From the Lab to the Field: A Review of Tax Experiments, *Journal of Economic Surveys*, vol. 32, n 2, pp. 273–301.

Miguel, Edward and Michael Kremer (2004), Worms: Identifying Impacts on Education and Health in the Presence of Treatment Externalities, *Econometrica*, vol. 72, n°1, pp. 159–217.

Mises, Ludwig von (2003), *Epistemological Problems of Economics*, Auburn, Mises Institute.

Morgan, Mary S. (2005) Experiments versus Models: New Phenomena, Inference and Surprise, *Journal of Economic Methodology*, vol. 12, n 2, pp. 317–329.

Moss, Todd, Gunilla Pettersson and Nicolas van de Walle (2006), *A Review Essay on Aid Dependency and State Building in Sub-Saharan Africa: An Aid-Institutions Paradox?* Washington, DC, Center for Global Development, working paper 74.

Nunn, Nathan and Nancy Qian (2011), The Potato's Contribution to Population and Urbanization: Evidence from a Historical Experiment, *Quarterly Journal of Economics*, vol. 126, pp. 593–650.

Olken, Benjamin A. (2007), Monitoring Corruption: Evidence from a Field Experiment in Indonesia, *Journal of Political Economy*, vol. 115, n 2, pp. 200–249.

Olofsgard, Anders (2014), *Randomized Controlled Trials: Strengths, Weaknesses and Policy Relevance, Stockholm, Expert Group for Aid Studies (EBA)*, report 2014-1.

Pearl, Judea (2018), Challenging the Hegemony of Randomized Controlled Trials: A Commentary on Deaton and Cartwright, *Social Science and Medicine*, vol. 210, August, pp. 60–62.

Peirce, Charles Sanders and Joseph Jastrow (1885), On Small Differences in Sensation, *Memoirs of the National Academy of Sciences*, vol. 3, pp. 73–83.

Peterson Zwane, Alix, Jonathan Zinman, Eric Van Dusen, William Pariente, Clair Null, Edward Miguel, . . . Abhijit Banerjee (2011), Being Surveyed Can Change Later Behavior and Related Parameter Estimates, *Proceedings of the National Academy of Sciences*, vol. 108, n°5, pp. 1821–1826.

Premand, Patrick and Pascale Schnitzer (2018), *Efficiency, Legitimacy and Impacts of Targeting Methods: Evidence from an Experiment in Niger*, Washington, DC, The World Bank, policy research working paper 8412.

Ravallion, Martin (2008), *Evaluation in the Practice of Development*, Washington, DC, The World Bank, policy research working paper 4547.

Ravallion, Martin (2009), Should the Randomistas Rule? *Economists' Voice*, vol. 6, February, pp. 1–5. Retrieved from www.bepress.com/ev

Ravallion, Martin (2012), Fighting Poverty One Experiment at a Time: Poor Economics: A Radical Rethinking of the Way to Fight Global Poverty: Review Essay, *Journal of Economic Literature*, vol. 50, n 1, March, pp. 103–114.

Rodrik, Dani (2009), The New Development Economics: We Shall Experiment, but How Shall We Learn? in Jessica Cohen and William Easterly eds., *What Works in Development: Thinking Big and Thinking Small*, Washington, DC, Brookings Institution Press, pp. 24–47.

Roth, Alvin E. (1986), Laboratory Experimentation in Economics, *Economics and Philosophy*, vol. 2, pp. 245–273.

Roth, Alvin E. (2002), The Economist as Engineer: Game Theory, Experimentation, and Computation as Tools for Design Economics, *Econometrica*, vol. 70, n°4, July, pp. 1341–1378.

Samuelson, Larry (2005), Economic Theory and Experimental Economics, *Journal of Economic Literature*, vol. 43, n 1, March, pp. 65–107.

Samuelson, Paul (1948), *Economics*, New York, McGraw-Hill (1st edition).

Schelling, Thomas C. (1978), *Micromotives and Macrobehavior*, New York, Norton.

Schram, Arthur (2005) Artificiality: The Tension Between Internal and External Validity in Economic Experiments, *Journal of Economic Methodology*, vol. 12, n 2, pp. 225–237.

Sindzingre, Alice Nicole (2004), 'Truth', 'Efficiency', and Multilateral Institutions: A Political Economy of Development Economics, *New Political Economy*, vol. 9, n°2, June, pp. 233–249.

Sindzingre, Alice Nicole (2016), *'Policy Externalisation' Inherent Failure: International Financial Institutions' Conditionality in Developing Countries*, Lisbon, University of Lisbon, Lisbon School of Economics and Management (ISEG), Research in Social Sciences and Management CSG), CEsA, working paper CEsA-CSG 142/2016.

Sindzingre, Alice Nicole (2017), Understanding the Concept of Gift in Economics: Contributions from Other Social Sciences, *Eidos: A Journal for Philosophy of Culture* (University of Warsaw, Institute of Philosophy), vol. 2, pp. 4–20.

Sindzingre, Alice Nicole (2018), Concept and Causation: Issues in the Modelling of Institutions, *Forum for Social Economics*, forthcoming.

Stage, Jesper and Claudine Uwera (2018), Social Cohesion in Rwanda: Results from a Public Good Experiment, *Development Policy Review*, vol. 36, n°5, pp. 577–586.

Subramanian, S.V., Rockli Kim and Nicholas A. Christakis (2018), The "Average" Treatment Effect: A Construct Ripe for Retirement: A Commentary on Deaton and Cartwright, *Social Science and Medicine*, vol. 210, August, pp. 77–82.

Sugden, Robert (2005) Experiments as Exhibits and Experiments as Tests, *Journal of Economic Methodology*, vol. 12, n 2, pp. 291–302.

Svorencik, Andrej (2015), *The Experimental Turn in Economics: A History of Experimental Economics*, Utrecht, University of Utrecht, Utrecht School of Economics dissertation 29.

Svorenčík, Andrej (2017), Allocating Airport Slots: The History of Early Applied Experimental Research, *History of Political Economy*, vol. 49, n°5, pp. 240–263.

Tittle, Peg (2005), *What If . . . Collected Thought Experiments in Philosophy*, New York, Pearson.

Vicente, Pedro C. (2007), *Is Vote Buying Effective? Evidence from a Randomized Experiment in West Africa*, Oxford, University of Oxford, Department of Economics, working paper 318.

Vicente, Pedro C. (2010), Does Oil Corrupt? Evidence from A Natural Experiment in West Africa, *Journal of Development Economics*, vol. 92, n 1, May, pp. 28–38.

Wantchekon, Leonard (2003) Clientelism and Voting Behavior: Evidence from a Field Experiment in Benin, *World Politics*, vol. 55, April, pp. 399–422.

World Bank-Independent Evaluation Group (2015), *Managing Evaluations: A How-To Guide for Managers and Commissioners of Evaluations*, Washington, DC, The World Bank, Independent Evaluation Group.

Ziliak, Stephen T. and Edward R. Teather-Posadas (2016), The Unprincipled Randomization Principle in Economics and Medicine, in George DeMartino and Deirdre McCloskey eds., *The Oxford Handbook of Professional Economic Ethics*, Oxford, Oxford University Press.

8 The making of an ethical econometrician

Stephen T. Ziliak and Edward R. Teather-Posadas

The empirical economist in search of publication and promotion is understandably wary of bringing ethics closer to the center of econometric training and research. They know what pays in the market, at least in the short run (and you know what Joan Robinson said about the long run: it's just a longer string of short runs). Compared to the mathematical objective of maximizing expected utility subject to a budget constraint, the ethical objective of the philosopher or poet or student-activist on the street seems to many of our mathematical tribe like a gigantic error term – ethics is too messy, they believe, too loosely defined, too normative and subjective, and ultimately "someone else's call." The ethics of econometric research – from the design of a fully funded field experiment to the seminar interpretation of the most classical, virginal, linear regression – is frequently said to be the reader's business, or the government's business, or the sponsor of the experiment's business, not the econometrician's.

The econometrician who thinks this way – like Anne Krueger (2017) seems to think, or like Steve Leavitt and John List (2009) and other *randomistas* think – is making a serious category mistake (DeMartino and McCloskey 2018; Ziliak and Teather-Posadas 2016).[1] A category mistake with economic and ethical implications. Ethics is here in economics already, including right here at the center of the econometric enterprise, students must be made to understand. The ethical formation of a quantitative researcher is taking place always already, we are not the only ones to observe, from lectures on the strictly frequentist chapter on probability theory to the highly misleading and oversupplied Fisherian lectures on statistical significance testing. In empirical research, there are ethical judgments being made more or less constantly, from the definition of the problem to the selection of data and posterior evaluation of econometric output. But today, the malformation of an applied econometrician is costing us more than jobs, justice, and lives (Ziliak and McCloskey 2008).

We sympathize with budgetary, temporal, and other constraints faced by econometrics instructors who complain they "can't cover everything on the syllabus" as it is. And we are not like those soft-chair philosophers from Vienna or Virginia who'd just as soon throw the probabilistic baby out with the econometric bathwater. We ourselves are applied econometricians who believe nevertheless that there are several easy ways to improve the ethical formation of today's econometrician (Ziliak 2014).[2]

Jonathan Wight (2015) has recently observed that ethical concerns divide naturally into three main categories or approaches, with some overlap: *outcome*-based ethics, *duty*- or *rule*- or *procedure*-based ethics, and *virtue*-based ethics (compare and contrast Rawls [1971], Sen [2010], and McCloskey [2006]). Outcomes, procedures, and virtues, with occasional overlap. It's a simplification, but the model works.

"Outcomes" are what Adam Smith (1759 [2009]) calls "fortune" (throughout), the end result of some action or set of actions that is both deliberate and random. Changes in utility or income or wealth from a treatment-controlled field experiment are examples of outcomes with both deliberate and random properties; likewise, an outcomes-based ethic (though not only that) might include attention to increased poverty, illness, and disutility from that same experiment.

Examples of rule- or duty- or procedure-based ethical considerations – call them "procedures," for short – include voting rules (such as the rules regulating University Senate or Rawls's "original position" or, in politics itself, democratic majority rules). A procedure-based ethic in statistics is using Student's table of *t* if and only if one has a valid and repeated experiment or series of samples. Procedure-based ethics also include such things as disparate as family honor, military honor, obligations to others, and queuing rules (such as "women and children first" or, on the literal battlefield, medical "triage" and discovery of equipoise).

Examples of virtues from virtue-based ethics run the gamut from Adam Smith's justice, prudence, and benevolence (as determined by the impartial spectator) to being honest about statistical outliers in economic data and Martin Luther King Jr.'s practice of non-violent protest for social change (King 1963; for discussion of alternative approaches to virtue-based ethics, see McCloskey 2006).

Our point is that an *ethical* econometrics teaches the economics and ethics of *outcomes, procedures*, and *virtues* – all three. Yet in today's academy, the ethical formation of an econometrician is, we argue, blunted and distorted by insufficient attention to each of these three, mainly through incorrect teaching and misplaced material incentives for:

- Null hypothesis significance testing
- Completely randomized and placebo-controlled experiments
- Frequentist probability theory applied to one set of data

The null value of null hypothesis significance testing

Our first ethical problem – rather easy to solve – comes from teaching students of econometrics to use null hypothesis statistical significance testing without a loss function – "a test that avoids asking, How Big is a Big Loss or Gain from the null?" (the following section draws from Ziliak and McCloskey 2016). Outcomes, procedures, and virtues would rise and improve if the highly flawed null procedure were to completely vanish from the econometrics curriculum.

Statistical significance is not equivalent to economic significance, nor to medical, clinical, biological, psychometric, pharmacological, legal, physical, nor any other kind of scientific significance – those functions of gain and loss. The mistake in the falsely made equation is evident when one reflects that the estimated payoff from a gamble (of, say, one million British pounds) is not the same object as the odds of winning that gamble (of, say, one in two million chances, if the gamble in question is a national lottery, for example). Yet a widespread and pervasive failure to make the distinction between an estimate of human consequence and an estimate of its probability – between the meaning of an estimated average and the random variance around it – is harming people in medicine and impoverishing people in economics (Ziliak and McCloskey 2008). The ethical problem (or more precisely the *procedural*-ethical problem) created by a test of statistical significance is made worse by the method's blatant illogic at its core – broken at its very roots, a fact that is unacknowledged by the bulk of decision makers depending upon it.

In sciences from accounting to zoology, the errors from null hypothesis significance testing without a loss function – without some quantitative standard of meaningful gain or loss, separate from the bald probability of its occurrence – continue to mount. Long before Wight's fine book, Adam Smith himself noted that "whatever praise or blame can be due to any action, must belong either . . . to the. . . affection of the heart . . . or . . . to the external action . . . which this affection gives occasion to . . . or to the . . . consequences which . . . proceed from it" (Smith 1791, Pt II, Sect iii). How *much* unemployment, or inflation, or toxic asset bailout, is too much? That is the scientific, and ultimately the ethical, question. We are not doubting "the affection of the heart" of the average econometrician. We find them instead neglecting Smith's second and third elements of an ethical judgment. Most significance testers – for instance, 80% in economics and 90% in breast cancer epidemiology, Ziliak and McCloskey (2008) and by now many others have found – fail to take the correct "external action" with their evidence. And they neglect the ethical, economic, and other "consequences." They are testing by an ethically irrelevant criterion. By asking a question without acknowledging that size matters, they are turning a blind eye to *outcome*-ethics.

The central problem is that statistical significance is neither necessary nor sufficient for testing an ethical, scientific, commercial, or material fact in a court of law or before the academy. It is little more than a proof of existence, and a narrow one at that. An insignificant coefficient can be substantively significant, important to real people, communities, or ecosystems. Why? For example, if the possible loss from ignoring it (which, at the urging of Fisher, is the path most taken) is large enough. A statistically significant coefficient might be economically speaking irrelevant to the problem at hand, as if, for example, the significance is caused by merely having a very large sample size, or if the variable to which the coefficient is attached is not in any case a policy tool.

What people want from the analyst is a demonstration of what McCloskey and Ziliak call "oomph," that is a standard for and interpretation of meaningful size of effects, measured by probable levels of loss or gain, whether large or small. In the sizeless sciences, to which economics currently and tragically belongs, the method of null hypothesis statistical testing ignores a loss function. The analyst asks about the likelihood of occurrence for a deviation larger than the deviation actually observed, assuming a null hypothesis to be true. But they fail to ask about the size or scope or further human meaning of the deviation.

Meanwhile, the scientific culture is shifting before the economists' eyes, in a large deviation from the cult of statistical significance. There is hope on the horizon. For example, the American Statistical Association in 2016 convened a committee to discuss the status of statistical significance and *p*-values in scientific reasoning (one of the present authors, Ziliak, was a member of the committee and lead author of their proceedings). The committee would go on to release the "ASA's Statement on Statistical Significance and P-Values," an extraordinary document and blueprint for change that has not yet had the effect on economics it ought to:

> Good statistical practice, as an essential component of good scientific practice, emphasizes principles of good study design and conduct, a variety of numerical and graphical summaries of data, understanding the phenomenon under study, interpretation of results in context, complete reporting and proper logical and quantitative understanding of what data summaries mean. No single index [i.e., Fisher's rule] should substitute for scientific reasoning.
>
> (Wasserstein and Lazar, eds., 2016, p. 132)

The statement was accompanied by a series of six principles to help guide researchers as to the proper use and interpretation of *p*-values. The attempt here is not to banish *p*-values from the social sciences, but to better understand their limits and correct applications – highly relevant to *procedural*-ethics but also virtues and outcomes, as we learned during the Vioxx and Zicam debacles.

The Zicam debacle represents another hopeful and major shift in the culture of significance testing. Bright-line rules of statistical significance (such as $t > 1.96$ and $p < 0.05$) were rejected by the US Supreme Court in the 2011 decision on *Matrixx v. Siracusano* (Ziliak and McCloskey 2016; Supreme Court of the United States 2011). In a 9–0 ruling, the Supreme Court rejected Fisher's arbitrary rule, but how did this come about? Matrixx Initiatives, a pharmaceutical company, had created a homeopathic cold remedy called Zicam, a zinc-based nasal spray. As a side effect of its use, Zicam has a chance of causing anosmia, a permanent loss of smell (and therefore taste as well). The incidence of anosmia was not *statistically significant* and so went unreported, the adverse events being hidden from patients as well as shareholders. When the facts were revealed on national television, a revelation that sent Matrixx stock prices plummeting, a lawsuit was filed and was pursued all the way to the Supreme Court. The result was a ruling that stated,

> We [the nine Justices of the Supreme Court of the United States] con-clude that the materiality of adverse reports cannot be reduced to a bright-line rule. Although in many cases reasonable investors would not consider reports of adverse events to be material information, respondents have alleged facts plausibly suggesting that reasonable investors would have viewed these particular reports as material. . . . Matrixx's argument rests on *the premise that statistical significance is the only reliable indication of causation. This premise is flawed.*
>
> (Supreme Court 2011, p 1–2, emphasis added)

Gosset estimation, not Fisher "tests," is now the law of the land (Ziliak 2018). The ethical econometrician would do well to follow the examples of the ASA and Supreme Court and learn from the debacles. The tragedy itself is a failure of all three types of ethics here discussed: *outcome*-based, for the possibility of harm was known but ignored; *procedure*-based, for it was a blind adherence to statistical significance that gave "justification" to Matrixx; and *virtue*-based, for the chance of anosmia was ignored entirely, just as Fisher and Fisher School unethically recommend.

Despite all the evidence to the contrary, researchers continue to cling to Fisherian significance testing. George Cobb, Professor Emeritus of Mathematics and Statistics at Mount Holyoke College, posted the following exchange on an American Statistical Association (ASA) forum:

> Q: Why do so many colleges and grad schools teach $p = 0.5$?
> A: Because that's still what the scientific community and journal editors use.
> Q: Why do so many people still use $p = 0.05$?
> A: Because that's what they were taught in college or grad school.
>
> (Cobb 2014, quoted in Wasserstein and Lazar, 2016, p. 129)

Econometricians are creatures of ritual. Procedure, but sadly not *procedural-*ethics, has primacy. *P*-values are just another ritual to perform in economics, a set of motions to go through in order to become "valid" in the eyes of the community. Ziliak and McCloskey (2008, p. 9) recount the sociological pressures of the ritual in an anecdote from 2002 where

> we [Ziliak and McCloskey] gave together a talk at the Georgia Institute for Technology, where Ziliak was teaching, on the significant mistakes in economics. Three researchers from the nearby Centers for Disease Control [and Prevention] (CDC) attended. They agreed with us about "the cult of *p*," as they put it. But they feared that their mere presence at a lecture against Fisher's "significance" would put their jobs at risk and made us promise not to reveal their names.

The anti-pluralist nature of the cult of statistical significance is on full display here; deviations, standard or otherwise, from the normal ritual must not be tolerated, the CDC declared and enforced. Ethics must then take a back seat to methodology, and ritual – however vacuous and costly – trumps reality, even at the CDC.

All that glitters is not gold

Often we see ethics embodied within the symbolic and the ritual, in technical actions and formulations. This separates artificially the econometrician from ethical concerns. It is not they who are charged with being ethical. Rather, so long as they follow the precepts of the null ritual, all ethical concern can be safely discharged to the socially sanctioned "method." Ethics then becomes a secondary action, an effect, rather than a root concern. That is thin protection for a society and an applied science, such as economics, which requires vigilance and questioning now more than ever, or at least since 1776 or 1834 or 1980. Nowhere, perhaps, is this more evident than with the so-called "gold standard" of economic experimentation, the randomized controlled trial (RCT) (for example, Varian 2011).

The *randomistas* (Deaton 2007) of today draw their authority from a blind faith in the randomization of "treatments" and "controls" espoused by the influential statistician Ronald A. Fisher (1890–1962). Randomistas bank on the idea that

> the validity of our estimate of error for this purpose is guaranteed by the provision that any two plots, not in the same block, shall have [through the application of complete randomization of controls, treatments, and varieties] the same probability of being treated alike, and the same probability of being treated differently in each of the ways in which this is possible.
>
> (Fisher 1935, p. 429)

Yet for all its supporters, from the World Bank to preeminent economists, the randomized controlled trial suffers from many big losses (Ziliak and Teather-Posadas 2016; Ziliak 2013). The rational econometrician and statistician would be cautious and judicious in its use, and the moral social scientist would think carefully on the ramifications of what they were about to implement.

Ethically and morally, randomized controlled trials are highly suspect. Randomization, in its guise as an impartial allocator of treatments and controls, does not an ethic make. It is a weak facsimile of *procedure*-ethics. Consider the following scenarios that you, a development economist, must decide between in order to measure the effects of providing eyeglasses to poor children in a developing country:

Option 1: You supply a pair of prescription eyeglasses (costing $15) to all sight-defective children you encounter in your study given that they do not have eyeglasses of their own. You follow them in school and note the improvement.

Option 2: You flip a fair coin each time you meet a sight-defective child in the study. If the coin turns up heads, give the child a pair of eyeglasses; if tails, do not supply the glasses; instead, spend the money tracking and reporting on untreated students.

(Ziliak and Teather-Posadas 2016, p. 435)

Does Option 2 make sense, ethically, anywhere other than within the economic académie? No. It is a violation of *outcome*-ethics. Rather than striving for the common good, it seeks only to answer a technical question. Yet it is the option that would be chosen most often by the *randomistas*. Then why do we tolerate it? What ethical ground do we stand upon? What drives economists to reach that conclusion?

The *randomistas* claim that in adopting randomized controlled trials, they are merely adopting best practice methods from other sciences, particularly that of medicine. However, in medicine, the justification of randomized controlled trials (particularly those with "no-treatment" or placebo controls) rests upon a belief in the idea of "equipoise" (Freedman 1987). Equipoise, which we would classify as part of *procedure*-ethics, is the concept that given two types of treatment, "A," which represents the industry standard (the "best practice"), and "B," the new experimental treatment, it is a necessity that the experimenter be in a true state of uncertainty as to the superiority of one over the other in order for any experiment to progress. If the experimenter has any reason to believe that these two treatments are not equivalent, then "ethics requires that the superior treatment be recommended" (Freedman 1987, p. 141). This is true of an experiment with two treatments or twenty treatments. Equipoise must exist between all of them or the experiment should be discontinued and the superior treatment offered to all participants. Beyond even that,

> if equipoise is disturbed during the course of the trial, the trial may need to be terminated and all subjects previously enrolled (as well as other patients within the relevant population) may have to be offered the superior treatment. . . . Although equipoise has commonly been discussed in the special context of the ethics of randomized clinical trials, it is important to recognize it as an ethical condition of all controlled clinical trials, whether or not they are randomized, placebo-controlled, or blinded.
>
> (Freedman 1987, p. 141)

The question then becomes, does Option 2 – offering no treatment when treatment is both possible and feasible – satisfy the requirements of equipoise, our measure of *procedure*-ethics?

No. Emphatically no. Yet our eyeglass example is no mere literary device. It is an actual randomized controlled trial that was run in China: "Visualizing Development: Eyeglasses and Academic Performance in Rural Primary Schools in

China" (Glewwe et al., 2012). The economists running this experiment wished to know if wearing corrective eyeglasses might allow those children who were sight-defective (and therefore in need of corrective glasses) to perform better in school. Out of the participants, up to one-half of them were sorted into the "control" group, a group that was recruited, followed, and tracked, but from whom the corrective eyeglasses available to those in the treatment group were withheld (Glewwe et al., 2012, p. 8). The answer to their question should be obvious to any individual who wears corrective eyeglasses. Why then did such lofty groups, including the World Bank and the National Institutes of Health (NIH) (among whose ranks surely exist individuals who wear corrective eyeglasses), find the need to test such a blindingly obvious hypothesis?

Randomized controlled trials are often run in poor, vulnerable, and often underserved communities, ones that are particularly open to exploitation. The use of placebo or non-treatment controls is possibly damaging within these communities, creating inequalities of entitlements where none existed before. To give treatment to some while simultaneously withholding it from others on the basis of randomization, to the whims of an experimental design, is unethical. To return to the question of equipoise, it is rare that we truly think an intervention will have no effect compared to doing nothing. If we truly thought it would do nothing, why would we do it? Take, for instance, the work of Fairlie and Robinson (2013, p. 215). Fairlie and Robinson wanted to test if having access to a computer at home helps improve students' academic success. In explaining the logistics of the randomized controlled trial to the administration of the school, the experimenters were met with a situation where

> school principals expressed concern about the fairness of giving computers to a subset of eligible children. For this reason, we decided to give out computers to *all* eligible students. Treatment students received computers immediately, while control students had to wait until the end of the school year. Our main outcomes are all measured at the end of the school year, before the control students received their computers.

Note the phrase "*for this reason.*" It was at the behest of the community, which saw the problems of creating an inequality of entitlement between children, that extra computers were requisitioned.

This is an expression of the utilitarian ur-text in the ethical thought of economists. The group, the body academic, the population is given primacy, the totality of the machine before its constituent parts. The very "gold-standard" nature of randomized controlled trials – the pedestal they are placed upon – helps to perpetuate the ethical problems they create. As mentioned before, the act of randomized controlled trials is a ritualistic one. It follows a prescribed set of motions and actions. As long as the ritual is followed correctly, the randomized controlled trial is legitimized, given its gold star, and set forth into an unsuspecting world. The very act itself then forms a wedge between the experimenter and their ethical concerns. This allows for a rejection of equipoise and a blurring of ethical lines because the requirements of the randomized controlled trials have been satisfied. The treatment and control are "random" – here in the sense of being "non-biased" or indifferent – so are considered fair. Any randomized controlled trial is imbued with the legitimacy of all other randomized controlled trials.

As many issues as there are with RCTs, there have been movements to try to curb some of their abuses. The American Economic Association, for one, has worked to create an "RCT Registry." The AEA claims:

> Randomized Controlled Trials (RCTs) are widely used in various fields of economics and other social sciences. As they become more numerous, a central registry on which trials are on-going or complete (or withdrawn) becomes important for various reasons: as a source of results for meta-analysis; as a one-stop resource to find out about available survey instruments and data.
>
> (AEA RCT Registry)

This is a move in the right direction, as increased transparency in the planning and execution of randomized controlled trials will assist in the spread of better practices, a welcome boost in *virtue*-ethics. With even greater aplomb, we should turn our attention to the increased focused on the necessity of informed consent within these trials. Informed consent is nothing new within any discipline that has human subjects within their experiments – medicine, psychology, economics, and the like. So critical is informed consent that it is codified into US federal law where

> except as provided elsewhere in this policy, no investigator may involve a human being as a subject in research covered by this policy unless the investigator has obtained the legally effective informed consent of the subject or the subject's legally authorized representative. An investigator shall seek such consent only under circumstances that provide the prospective subject or the representative sufficient opportunity to consider whether or not to participate and that minimize the possibility of coercion or undue influence. The information that is given to the subject or the representative shall be in language understandable to the subject or the representative. No informed consent, whether oral or written, may include any exculpatory language through which the subject or the representative is made to waive or appear to waive any of the subject's legal rights, or releases or appears to release the investigator, the sponsor, the institution or its agents from liability for negligence.
>
> (45 CFR 46)

Informed consent is in place to avoid the horrors of historical abuses of human experimentation, like the shame of the Tuskegee Syphilis Experiment (1932–1972). In Tuskegee, doctors under the employ of the US Department of Public

Health, under the auspices of advancing medical knowledge, withheld syphilis treatments from African American men in Macon County, Alabama (Gray 1998); a horrific abuse of the trust. Many scholars may chafe under informed consent guidelines, such as List, who writes that there are "certain cases in which adhering to rigid ethical rules can affect the very issue that is being studied, such that it becomes quite difficult to conduct the research" (List 2008, p. 672), yet relaxing ethical rules when things become difficult is problematic. Ethical rules are not intended to make the life of the researcher easier; they are designed to protect the general public and to maintain a level of trust between the academy and the general public.

Wanted: more frequent frequency

The third ethical malformation of an econometrician is deceiving in both its simplicity and ubiquity. The problem lies in teaching economists to use frequentist probability models and tests of significance on a single set of data, that is, on a single sample or unrepeated experiment. "One and done" is not science, and economists should be forthright in saying so. Frequentist models of probability and tests of significance do have a place in ethical econometrics. But admittedly, the old confusion begins with the very word "significant." It's not like it sounds. "Significant" in the statistical sense does not mean "important." And "insignificant" does not mean "unimportant." This elementary point should be more common knowledge than in reality it is.

Of course, some of the observed variance of numerical observations will be random, some systematic. For example, in agricultural economics, the estimated level of a farmer's yield per acre when growing barley "A" will not always surpass the yield of barley "B," grown on the same or different fields. But notice that to get to these answers, you have to actually *repeat the observations. You have to repeat the experiment.* Some of the difference in yield will occur for random reasons – from uneven occurrence of rabbit holes or bird attacks, for instance. The other part of the variance might be explained by systematic reasons – from differences in the yield of "A" and "B" caused by genetic or soil differences or by differential access to water and sun.

Why did Student's *t* become Fisher's *p*?

Since the 1908 article by Student, the *nom de plume* of William Sealy Gosset, the head experimental brewer for Guinness, on "The Probable Error of a Mean," it has proven helpful to estimate how likely the observed differences might be, given the sample size, and by how much. The most commonly used test is called Student's test of statistical significance, or "Student's *t*." The *t*-test produces a *t*-statistic that one may use as an input for judging the likelihood of events. Commonly, the test assumes one has a random sample of independent and repeated observations exhibiting a normal "bell-shaped" distribution. Note again: repeated and independent observations.

The *t*-statistic is a ratio that divides observed mean differences between phenomena under comparison (such as the average difference between barley yields A–B) by a measure of its own variation, called the standard error. By convention, in most of the life and human sciences, if Student's *t* rises to twice the level of observed variation in the data (twice the standard error), then the finding is called "statistically significant"; if not, it is not.

The "*p* value" estimates something more abstract and difficult to grasp: *p* measures the likelihood that the value of Student's *t*-statistic will be *greater* than the value of *t* actually observed, assuming to be true the assumptions of the model and the stipulated null hypothesis of "no average difference" between the things being compared.

Assuming that there is no average difference between the two barley yields – or between two pain relief pills or two star clusters or two investment rates of return – the *p* value calculates the likelihood that we would observe a deviation in the data at least as large as the deviation, measured by Student's *t* statistic, that is actually revealed. (In many testing situations, scientists are comparing more than two things at once.) Prior knowledge does not figure into the calculation of *p* – a fact that both Frequentist and Bayesian Schools rail against – one more reason to consider all of the available information, both inside and outside the model. If the calculated value of *p* is low – below the overused and arbitrary 0.05 level, for example – convention claims the data on hand are not consistent with the null hypothesis of "no difference" between the objects being compared and concludes the result is "statistically significant," that is, statistically significantly different from the null hypothesis; if not, it is not. To our folly, much of economics, and indeed other fields in the social and physical sciences, ends its investigations there.

That is, if the *p*-value rises to $p = 0.06$ or 0.20, a convention enforcing the bright-line rule of $p < 0.05$ would declare "insignificance" and ignore the finding – however important the effect size might be in other regards. For example, in the clinical trial on Vioxx, the heart attack variable came in at about $p = 0.20$. Following convention (and by extension the ritual of significance testing), the dangerous side effects were thus neglected by its marketer – an unfortunate fact that was finally brought to the attention of the US Supreme Court (McCloskey and Ziliak 2010, pp. 14–18). Here, *virtue*-ethicists should be wailing and gnashing their teeth. The data are too noisy, and there might not be an effect different from the null, convention claims. But that is not so.

If there are so many issues with *p*, both technical and commonsense, then why should we measure differences between objects using *p*? By all indications, it appears we should not. As the eminent Bayesian and geo- and astrophysicist Harold Jeffreys (1961, p. 385, italics added) observed long ago:

> If P is small, that means that there have been unexpectedly large departures from prediction [under the null hypothesis]. But why should these be stated in terms of P? The latter gives the probability of departures, measured in a particular way, equal to *or greater than* the observed set, and the contribution

from the actual value [of the test statistic] is nearly always negligible. *What the use of P implies, therefore, is that a hypothesis that may be true may be rejected because it has not predicted observable results that have not occurred.* This seems a remarkable procedure. On the face of it the fact that such results have not occurred might more reasonably be taken as evidence for the law [or null hypothesis], not against it. The same applies to all the current significance tests based on P integrals.

The errors became more pervasive when they began to spread beyond researchers and into the work of lawyers, bureaucrats, policymakers, and the like. These individuals began to misinterpret larger p-values (most commonly $p > 0.05$) as the probability that the null hypothesis is true. But a large scale replication confirmed by James Berger (2003, p. 4) and others found that when p "is near 0.05, at least 72% and typically over 90%" of tested null hypotheses are "true." Statisticians have long recognized the large and important difference between a p-value and an actual calculation of the probability of the null hypothesis (Student 1938).

The origin of the controversial p-value is itself remarkable and, sadly, little known – an historical tale in which the savvy brewer (Gosset, again of "Student" fame) was outmaneuvered by the calculating academic (Fisher). In 1925, R. A. Fisher transposed and inverted "Student's" t table to produce what are now called p-values (Student 1925, p. 106; cf. Fisher 1925, pp. 22, 139, Appendix). In fact, Fisher's p-values are still found in interval form by consulting "the table of t." Exactly why Fisher took the liberty to change the table – and thus the method of estimation and interpretation – is a matter of historical and ethical (at least in terms of *procedure*-ethics) debate (Pearson 1990, p. 83; Ziliak and McCloskey 2008, pp. 227–233).

Econometricians should be explicit regarding how prior information is or is not incorporated; this is *virtue*-ethics in practice. Gosset himself was a philosophical Bayesian with a need to learn things fast, meaning he often resorted to the most powerful of frequentist methods: power (Student 1938; Pearson 1938). The cost of being wrong is not simply the Type II error, or a lesser reputation for the principal scientist, should your model or prediction be far off the mark. This rings particularly true in an age where the work of econometricians becomes more and more influential within policy circles, where their models now have the potential to impact the lives of thousands of individuals.

The confidence we place in Student's t or Fisher's p depends on the probability of one or more relevant "alternative hypotheses" perhaps being more laden with meaning, with purpose. Naively accepting the singular null hypothesis involves a loss – "but *how much do we lose*?" Student asked Egon Pearson in 1926.[3] Economics, health, and even life itself (in medicine, pharmacology, and related fields) might be lost, and are often at stake (Ziliak and McCloskey 2008 discuss dozens of real-world examples.)

Many years ago, Freiman et al. (1978, emphasis added) published in the *New England Journal of Medicine* a study entitled "The Importance of Beta, the Type II

Error and Sample Size in the Design and Interpretation of the Randomized Control Trial." The abstract reads:

Seventy-one "negative" randomized controlled trials were re-examined to determine if the investigators had studied large enough samples to give a high probability (>0.90) of detecting a 25 per cent and 50 per cent therapeutic improvement in the response. *Sixty-seven of the trials had a greater than 10 per cent risk of missing a true 25 per cent therapeutic improvement,* and with the same risk, *50 of the trials could have missed a 50 per cent improvement.* Estimates of 90 per cent confidence intervals for the true improvement in each trial showed that in 57 of these "negative" trials, a potential 25 per cent improvement was possible, and 34 of the trials showed a potential 50 per cent improvement.

Better statistics with Bayes

Perhaps the most commonly used alternative to classical t and p is the Bayes factor (Carlin and Louis 2008; Press 2003). For discrete data and simple hypotheses, the Bayes factor represents the ratio between the probability assigned to the data under an alternative hypothesis and the null hypothesis (discussed by Ziliak 2016, Johnson 2013). One big advantage of Bayesian analysis is that one can compute the probability of a hypothesis, given the evidence, whereas with the null hypothesis test of significance, measured by a p value, one can speak only to the probability of seeing data more extreme than have actually been obtained, assuming the null hypothesis of "no difference" (or whatever) to be true. An improvement in *outcome*-ethics if there ever was one; we can test for the hypothesis itself rather than the possible shadow it casts on the data. As the Bayesian Jeffreys noted (1961, p. 409):

Whether statisticians like it or not, their results are used to decide between hypotheses, and it is elementary that if p entails q, q does not necessarily entail p. We cannot get from "the data are unlikely given the hypothesis" to "the hypothesis is unlikely given the data" without some additional rule of thought. Those that reject inverse probability have to replace it by some circumlocution, which leaves it to the student to spot where the change of data has been slipped in [in] the hope that it will not be noticed.

Jeffreys went on to explain that if one assigns prior odds between the alternative and null hypotheses, multiplication of the Bayes factor by these prior odds yields the posterior odds between the hypotheses. From the posterior odds between hypotheses, scientists can compute the posterior probability that a null hypothesis is true (or in any case useful or persuasive) relative to an explicit alternative. Classical tests of significance, measured by t and p, cannot.[4]

Unfortunately, the use of Bayes factors in hypothesis testing is considered by the old school, the entrenched gatekeepers of econometrics, to be controversial –

"too subjective," they say. "We don't know our priors" or "How do we know what the alternative hypothesis should be?" Common usage is about the only recommendation for the old debate about subjective versus objective statistics. As Yogi Berra said, "No one goes there anymore; it's too crowded."

In fact, Johnson (2013) observes that in certain hypothesis tests, the alternative hypothesis can be specified so that an equivalence between Bayes factors and *p*-values can be established. Technically speaking, Johnson and others have shown, in one parameter exponential family models in which a point null hypothesis has been specified on the model parameter, that specifying the size of the test is equivalent to specifying a rejection threshold for the Bayes factor, provided that it is further assumed that the alternative hypothesis is specified so as to maximize the power of the test. The correspondence between Bayes factors and *p*-values in this setting is just one example of the false demarcation line between objective and subjective.

When an alternative hypothesis exists – and that's the usual situation of science: otherwise, why test? – Bayes factors can be easily reported, and so little reason exists *not* to report them. Bayes factors permit individual scientists and consumers to use prior information or the principle of insufficient reason together with new evidence to compute the posterior probability that a given hypothesis, *H*, is true (or, to repeat, useful or persuasive) based on the prior probability that they assign to each hypothesis. After all – fortunately – we do not have to begin every new observation or experiment from *tabula rasa*; we know some stuff, but we want to know more stuff, however imperfectly. Bayes factors add that information into the calculation comparing the likelihood of alternative hypotheses. For example, Bayes factors provide a clear interpretation of the evidence contained in the data in favor of or against the null. A Bayes factor of 10 simply means that the data were 10 times more likely under the alternative hypothesis than they were under the null hypothesis. That's a real advance over mushy *p*'s and fuzzier ethics.

A few easy fixes

Thus, the beginning of better scientific inference entails a synthesis of Bayesian and Frequentist ideas. But prior to that inevitable paradigm shift, a few easy changes in the quantitative program could go a long way toward overcoming current malpractice. Here we suggest a humble, and by no means exhaustive, list of suggestions to improve the ethical side of econometrics within the realms of procedure, outcomes, and virtue.

Economists should be schooled in ethics at both the undergraduate and graduate levels

The first, and most obvious, of the recommendations is simple enough in its direction. If you want ethical economists, you must first *train* ethical economists. Ethics should be taught to all students of economics, from undergraduates to graduates. Here we understand the limits of the modern economics curriculum, strained as it is with the amount of expectations and weights placed upon it. We do not necessarily suggest the adoption of a whole curriculum or class revolving around ethics (though a class devoted to economic ethics is a worthy goal), but rather the inclusion of conversations about ethics in already established economic classes. Principles courses could confront the urtext of utilitarianism in economics (*outcome*-ethics), econometrics courses could discuss the issues of economic versus statistical significance (*procedure*-ethics), and graduate students wishing to run RCTs of their own could sit down and grapple with the concerns raised by randomization (*virtue*-ethics). A conversation is necessary – one that should be confronted at the earliest possible moment. Ethics should not be considered a barrier or hurdle to be faced in your research, but a dialogue of trust between the researcher and the community at large.

Placebo-controlled randomized controlled trials (RCTs) should be seen for what they are, a last-ditch effort – and possibly unethical if there is no equipoise – to learn about strata; RCTs are not a cure-all "gold standard" or method to boast about

The discipline's current obsession with randomized controlled trials, driven by the *randomistas* in the World Bank and elsewhere, should be curtailed. RCTs have moved from an experimental tool to a panacea, being implemented in areas where they are neither necessary nor warranted in the name of "formalization" (that is, the Chinese eyeglasses experiment). We are not saying "thou shalt not randomize." Rather, we are saying "thou shalt not randomize without cause." Consider first, as it were, the ethics of your proposed outcome. There are instances where RCTs may be warranted, such as in a situation of clinical equipoise, but they shouldn't be used with reckless abandon. Nor should they hold the status of the only road to causality. Other avenues need to be explored and may be a better fit in many circumstances, such as more balanced experiments like Gosset's ABBA method (Ziliak and Teather-Posadas 2016, pp. 432–433).

Economists should embrace economic significance and Gossetean estimation and reject bright-line rules of statistical significance and Fisherian "tests"

This is not a new call. McCloskey and Ziliak have been making this point for decades. Time and time again it seems they have been right, most recently with the victorious denouncement of p-values made by the American Statistical Association (2016). So far, the American Economic Association has neglected their research, the ASA Statement, and the Supreme Court, continuing to plod along under Fisher's circumscribed rule of $p < 0.05$. More than 15 years ago, Ziliak and McCloskey (2004b) drafted their own Statement of properties for

Substantive Significance (or "SpSS," later revised by Ziliak and McCloskey 2008, p. 250):

(1) Economists should prefer confidence intervals to other methods of reporting sampling variance. (2) Sampling variance is sometimes interesting, but is not the same thing as scientific importance. (3) Economic significance is the chief scientific issue in economics; an arbitrary level of sampling significance is no substitute for it. (4) Fit is not a good all-purpose measure of scientific validity, and should be deemphasized in favor of inquiry into other measures of importance.

That is still good advice for the ethical formation of an econometrician, and it is not rocket science.

Notes

1 We admit to being pleased, however, when Professor Krueger pointed to Ziliak and Teather-Posadas (2016) as one of the best contributions to the DeMartino-McCloskey (2016) book on ethics in economics.
2 See also McCloskey (1985); McCloskey and Ziliak (1996, 2010); Ziliak and McCloskey (2008, 2016); Cranor, McCloskey, and Ziliak (2016); and Ziliak and Teather-Posadas (2016), who wrote the current essay.
3 Quoted in E. S. Pearson 1939, p. 243.
4 Lavine and Schervich (1999) caution that Bayes factors can sometimes lead to incoherence in the technical statistical sense of the term.

References

Berger, J. 2003. "Could Fisher, Jeffreys, and Neyman Have Agreed on Testing?" *Statistical Science*. 18(1): 1–32.

Carlin, B. and Louis, T. 2008. *Bayes and Empirical Bayes Methods for Empirical Analysis*, 3rd Rev. ed. London: Chapman and Hall/CRC Press.

Cranor, C., McCloksey, Deirdre N., and Stephen T. Ziliak. 2016. Brief of Amici Curiae [Explaining the Importance of Distinguishing Economic and Medical Significance from mere Statistical Significance], United States Court of Appeals for the Fourth Circuit, *In re: Lipitor Marketing, Sales Practices and Products Liability Litigation, Plaintiffs v. Pfizer, Inc.*, No. 17-1140(L), filed on April 2017.

Deaton, A. 2007. "Evidence-based Aid Must Not Become the Latest in a Long String of Development Fads." In A. Banerjee (ed.), *Making Aid Work*. Cambridge, MA: MIT Press, pp. 60–61.

DeMartino, George. 2011. *The Economist's Oath: On the Need for and Content of Professional Economic Ethics*. New York: Oxford University Press.

DeMartino, George F. and Deirdre N. McCloskey. 2018. "Professional Ethics 101: A Reply to Anne Krueger's Review of *The Oxford Handbook of Professional Economic Ethics*." *Econ Journal Watch*. 15(1): 4–19.

Fairlie, Robinson and J. Robinson. 2013. "Experimental Evidence on the Effects of Home Computers on Academic Achievement Among Schoolchildren." *American Economic Review: Applied Economics*. 5(3): 211–240.

Fisher, R.A. 1925 [1928]. Statistical Methods for Research Workers. New York: G.E. Stechart.

Fisher, R.A. 1926. "Arrangement of Field Experiments." *Journal of Ministry of Agriculture.* 33: 503–13.

Fisher, Ronald A. 1935. *The Design of Experiments.* Edinburgh: Oliver and Boyd.

Freedman, Benjamin. 1987. "Equipoise and the Ethics of Clinical Research." *New England Journal of Medicine.* 317(3): 141–145.

Freiman, J., T. Chalmers, H. Smith, et al. 1978. "The Importance of Beta, the Type II Error and Sample Size in the Design and Interpretation of the Randomized Control Trial." *New England Journal of Medicine.* 299: 690–694.

Glewwe, P., A. Park, and M. Zhao. 2012. "Visualizing Development: Eyeglasses and Academic Performance in Primary Schools in China." Working Paper WP12–2 (January) Center for International Food and Agricultural Policy Research, University of Minnesota.

Gray, F.D. 1998. *The Tuskegee Syphilis Study.* Montgomery: New South Books.

Jeffreys, H. 1961 [1939] *Theories of Probability.* Oxford: Oxford University Press.

Johnson, V. 2013. "Revised Standards for Statistical Evidence." *Proceedings of the National Academy of Sciences.* 110(48): 19313–19317.

King, Martin Luther, Jr. 1963 [1981]. *Strength to Love.* Philadelphia: Fortress.

Krueger, Anne O. 2017. "Review of 'The Oxford Handbook of Professional Economic Ethics' edited by George F. DeMartino and Deirdre N. McCloskey." *Journal of Economic Literature.* 55(1): 209–216.

Lavine, M. and Schervish, M. 1999. "Bayes Factors: What They Are and What They Are Not." *The American Statistician.* 53(2): 119–122.

Levitt, S.D., J.A. List. 2009. "Field Experiments in Economics: The Past, the Present, and the Future." *European Economic Review.* 53: 1–18.

List, John A. 2008. "Response: Informed Consent in Social Science." *Science.* 322: 672.

McCloskey, Deirdre N. 1985. "The Loss Function Has Been Mislaid: The Rhetoric of Scientific Tests." *American Economic Review.* 75(2): 201-205.

McCloskey, Deirdre N. 1994. *Knowledge and Persuasion in Economics.* New York: Cambridge University Press.

McCloskey, Deirdre N. and Stephen T. Ziliak. 1996. "The Standard Error of Regressions." *Journal of Economic Literature.* 34(1): 97–114.

McCloskey, Deirdre N. and Stephen T. Ziliak. 2010. Brief of Amici Curiae by Statistics Experts Professors Deirdre N. McCloskey and Stephen T. Ziliak in support of respondents, Vol. No. 09–1156, Supreme Court of the United States, Washington, DC. Edward Labaton et al. Counsel of Record (ed.), Matrixx et. al. v. Siracusano and NECA-IBEW Pension Fund, filed Nov. 12, 2010.

Pearson, E.S. 1938. "Some Aspects of the Problem of Randomization: II. An Illustration of Student's Inquiry into the Effect of 'Balancing' in Agricultural Experiment." *Biometrika.* 30: 159–179.

Pearson, E.S. 1939. "Student as Statistician," *Biometrika.* 30 (3/4): 210–250.

Pearson, E.S. 1990. *Student: A Statistical Biography of William Sealy Gosset.* R. L. Plackett and G. A. Barnard (eds.). Oxford: Clarendon Press.

Press, S.J. 2003. *Subjective and Objective Bayesian Statistics.* New York: Wiley.

Rawls, John. 1971. *A Theory of Justice.* Cambridge: Belknap Press.

Sen, Amartya. 2010. *The Idea of Justice.* London: Penguin.

Smith, A. 1759 [1791, 2009]. *The Theory of Moral Sentiments.* New York: Penguin. Introduction by Amartya Sen.

Student. 1911. "Appendix to Mercer and Hall's Paper on 'The Experimental Error of Field Trials'." *Journal of Agricultural Science*. 4: 128–131. In: Student. Student's Collected Papers, pp. 49–52. Pearson, E. and J.Wishart (eds.).

Student. 1923. "On TestingVarieties of Cereals." *Biometrika*. 15: 271–293.

Student. 1925. "New Tables for Testing the Significance of Observations." *Metron*. V(3): 105–108.

Student. 1938. "Comparison Between Balanced and Random Arrangements of Field Plots." *Biometrika*. 29(3–4): 363–378.

Supreme Court of the United States. 2011, March 22. Matrixx Initiatives, Inc., et al., No. 09–1156, Petitoner v. James Siracusano et al., On Writ of Certiorari to the United States Court of Appeals for the Ninth Circuit. 25pp., Syllabus.

Varian, Hal. 2011, April 27. "Are Randomized Trials the Future of Economics? Federalism Offers Opportunities for Causal [sic] Experimentation." *The Economist*. Available at www.economist.com/node/21256696

Wasserstein, Ronald L. and Nicole A. Lazar, eds. 2016. "The ASA's Statement on *p*-Values: Context, Process, and Purpose." *The American Statistician*. 70(2): 129–133.

Wight, Johnathan B. 2015. *Ethics in Economics: An Introduction to Moral Frameworks*. Los Angeles: Stanford University Press.

Ziliak, Stephen T. 2013, June 10. "Junk Science Week: Unsignificant Statistics." *Financial Post*.

Ziliak, Stephen T. 2014. "Balanced versus Randomized Field Experiments in Economics: Why W.S. Gosset aka 'Student' Matters." *Review of Behavioral Economics*. 1(1/2): 162–208.

Ziliak, Stephen T. 2016. "Statistical Significance and Scientific Misconduct: Improving the Style of the Published Research Paper." *Review of Social Economy*. LXXIV (1): 83-97.

Ziliak, Stephen T. 2018. "How Large Are Your G-values? Try Gosset's Guinnessometrics When a Little 'p' Is Not Enough." *The American Statistician* (forthcoming).

Ziliak, Stephen T. and Deirdre N. McCloskey. 2004a. "Size Matters: The Standard Error of Regressions in the American Economic Review." *The Journal of Socio-Economics*. 33: 527–546.

Ziliak, Stephen T. and Deirdre N. McCloskey. 2004b. "Significance Redux." *The Journal of Socio-Economics*. 33: 665–675.

Ziliak, Stephen T. and Deirdre N. McCloskey. 2008. *The Cult of Statistical Significance: How the Standard Error Cost Us Jobs, Justice, and Lives*. Ann Arbor: University of Michigan Press.

Ziliak, Stephen T. and Deirdre N. McCloskey. 2016. "Lady Justice Versus Cult of Statistical Significance: Oomph-less Science and the New Rule of Law." In George DeMartino and Deirdre McCloskey (eds.), *Oxford Handbook of Professional Economic Ethics*. Oxford: Oxford University Press, pp. 352–364.

Ziliak, Stephen T. and Edward Teather-Posadas. 2016. "The Unprincipled Randomization Principle in Economics and Medicine." In George DeMartino and Deirdre McCloskey (eds.), *Oxford Handbook of Professional Economic Ethics*. Oxford: Oxford University Press, pp. 423–452.

9 Economists, their role and influence in the media

Wim Groot and Henriette Maassen van den Brink

Introduction

"Someone who asks for the meaning gets hit by the Zen Master" is (our own translation of) a quote from Joop Klant's book *Spelregels voor Economen* (Rules for Economists), an influential book for generations of economics students in the 1980s in the Netherlands, including the authors of this chapter. The book provides an introduction to the philosophy of economics (Klant 1979). The quote expresses a question that many economists ask themselves every now and then: What is the purpose of economic research? Does economic research contribute to science by increasing our knowledge and understanding of how the economy works?

Most economic research barely makes an impact, at least not when we measure it by the use of research results by colleagues. A large share of scientific articles in economics journals are never cited by others. Laband and Tollison (2003) find that 26% of the articles in economics journals are "dry holes": they are never cited in the five years after publication. About 70% of economics articles are cited only once, and many of the citations to papers with only one or two citations are self-citations. Less than 1% of the papers are cited more than 50 times in the five years after publication (Laband & Tollison 2003). Similarly, in a sample of economists from 68 universities among the top 104 research universities in the US, Hilmer et al. (2015) find that the average number of citations per article is 12.84 (with a range from 0 to 4256), and the average number of citations per year per article is 0.89 (with a range from 0 to 157.63). The median article had only three citations and was cited only about once every four years. More than 30% of all articles in the sample of Hilmer et al. (2015) were never cited at all, a figure that is rather similar to the figure presented by Laband and Tollison (2003) using another dataset. Even among articles that were published more than six years before sampling the citations, 25% were not cited at all. Hilmer et al. (2015, p. 440) conclude that "an article that has been cited 10 times is very successful, and one that has been cited more than 50 times is quite remarkable." Hilmer et al. (2015) also calculate the Hirsch index (or h-index). In their sample, they find that for the average economist with 20 years of experience who has written about 21 articles (and has an average salary of \$122,000), the h-index varies from 0 to 31, with a mean of 6. The average h-index of the top 5% of economists is 17. Even research published in the most prominent economic journals sometimes remains unnoticed. Hamermesh (2015) finds that of the papers published in the top five economics journals, 5% remained uncited in the 40 years after publication. He concludes that "most papers, even in these prestigious outlets, are very rarely if ever cited, with relatively few articles accounting for the overwhelming attention that scholars devote to these journals."

Many research publications that have taken months of hard work disappear in the fog of oblivion of economic science. For the researchers who have worked on these papers, this might raise questions about the meaning of being an economist. Is there more to being an academic economist than publishing papers in academic journals? For the tax payer who pays for the research and preparation of these articles, there is the question of whether there are ways to increase the effectiveness of the money spent on economic research.

A scientific article used and cited by more than 10 other scientists is seen as a top cited article – many months of labor that ultimately matter to only about 10 other scientists. A column or piece on a newspaper's editorial page almost always reaches a larger audience, gets more attention and reaction, and has more impact than a research paper in an academic journal. As King et al. (2017) convincingly show, media attention increases discussion about a topic and influences opinions people have about a topic. More specifically, they find that an article published in news media increases social media posts on that topic by 10.4% over the week relative to the average number of social media posts on that specific topic over the week. Isn't it more effective for an economist, then, to present his ideas via (social) media rather than through (somewhat obscure) academic journals that are hardly read?

A major difference between (social) media publications and publications in academic journals is that the latter have an elaborate system of quality controls through peer review and a strong selection of papers where a significant percentage of papers submitted is rejected for publication that the former lacks. This raises the question that if (social) media publications are a more effective way of disseminating the knowledge economists have, do we need quality controls for media appearances of economists, and if so, how do we organize this?

The above quote from the book *Rules for Economists* by Professor Klant continues: "If so, he [the economist] can point out his social utility. The public and economists themselves are interested in knowing what use economic theory has." Economics is a social science. Economists provide insight into how incentives and changes in allocation can contribute to greater social prosperity. Economics is therefore primarily a science that aims to give practical recommendations for a better society. Or, as Tirole (2017, p. 8) puts it: "The role of economists is not to make decisions, but to identify the recurring patterns structuring our economies, and to convey economic science's current state of knowledge."

If evidence from economic science contributes to improving social welfare, this evidence should be used, and decision makers need to be informed about the existence of this evidence. Since the decision makers in our society – politicians, policymakers, managers of companies and institutions and the population at large – rarely or never read a scientific journal, an economist who wants to be useful has to find other outlets for the transfer of knowledge and insight. To utilize economic knowledge, academics need to be visible in (social) media by writing columns, blogs and articles in newspapers and by being available to give expert opinions on radio television and through new media like podcasts. This, to paraphrase Joop Klant, may offer more meaning to the professional life of an economist.

Economists can be tempted to allocate less time to academic work and more time to the media, to paraphrase Tirole (2017, p. 72), "for good (knowledge transfer) and bad (attention seeking)." In this chapter, we look at the good and bad aspects of media appearances by economists. In doing so, we combine our personal experiences with the media with some more general observations and insights from the academic literature on the topic. The central topic of this chapter is what ethical issues arise from the involvement of economists in (social) media. We address this question by looking at the normative case for media appearances by economists and the ethical issues surrounding appearing in the media. And, like virtually all economists, at the end of this chapter, we provide some recommendations – in our case, recommendations about media behavior by economists.

From an ethical perspective, this chapter tries to make two points. The first is that economists have an obligation to disseminate their knowledge and insight to the public at large. If the knowledge they possess can contribute to the greater good and increase our welfare, economists need to share their insights with the rest of the world, and one effective way of doing that is through the media. The second point we want to make is that there are "dos and don'ts" to media appearances by economists. This latter point is also the main recommendation we want to give. In recent years, codes of conduct for ethical behavior in science have been developed. These codes of conduct primarily describe what a scientist should and should not do within academia. A code of conduct for media behavior of scientists, or, more specifically, economists, is lacking. We believe developing a code of conduct for media behavior of economists would be useful.

Before we continue, a few words about our own position in this discussion. As we – the authors of this chapter – are economists working in academia, the discussion of the role of economists in the media is about ourselves as well. It is therefore relevant to disclose our own role as economists in the media. Some economists make frequent media appearances; others hardly or never appear in the media. We belong to the first category. We are frequently approached by journalists to comment on current issues in the economics of education and health care, our fields of specialization. We have written a biweekly column for the major business newspaper in the Netherlands – *het Financieele Dagblad* – for eight years. We still regularly contribute op-ed articles to newspapers and magazines in the Netherlands. We usually get contacted by journalists one or more times per week to comment on current issues within our area of expertise. We estimate that we spend two to three hours per week dealing with the media this way. So when discussing the ethical issues of media appearances by economists, our contribution is not merely academic; we speak from our own experience as well.

Finally, we note that we use the word "economist" to refer to researchers in the field of economics who work in academia. Of course, economists work in many other professions as well, and economists working outside academia appear in the media as well, but here we limit ourselves to the media appearances by economists working in academia.

The (normative) case for media appearances

Contributing to the public debate surrounding media appearances may provide not only meaning to the professional life of an economist but also a moral argument for economists to engage in the public debate. As noted by Hamermesh (2004, p. 371): "Professors in public universities – the large majority of economists – have a direct obligation to use their knowledge on a broader stage: They are paid by the public, and it behooves them to try to educate the entire public, not merely the subset who are their students, in whatever way they effectively can." The social value of economists may be enhanced if they participate in the public debate and in the media. Media appearance is also a source of accountability for economists. The public – or more specifically the fundholders for economic research – increasingly asks for accountability from economists. As the figures regarding the use of economic research papers and their contribution to the advancement of economic science suggest, the social value of purely academic work is limited. Media appearances then serve as an additional form of accountability.

A third normative argument for economists to be active in media has to do with the aim of economic science. As stated above, economic science studies how incentives and changes in allocation can contribute to the greater prosperity of society. If this claim is true, economists have a moral obligation to share knowledge and insights that may increase the prosperity of the rest of society, and the media are most suited for that.

The role of the expert who "educates the public" fits well with the view economists have of themselves. As noted by Fourcade et al. (2015, p. 90), "Economists see themselves at or near the top of the disciplinary hierarchy," at least within the social sciences. Many of them also believe that economics attracts the best and brightest of the generation. In sum, economists are frequently rather self-satisfied, and this also provides them with the necessary self-confidence to speak out.

This self-confidence provides economists with justification, at least among themselves, for stating their opinions on a wide range of social issues. This has led some academics from other social sciences to complain about economic imperialism. This economic imperialism is not limited to the scope of economic research but also includes topics on which economists think their views are valuable to a wider audience. Consequently, many economists believe there is a wide range of topics on which they have something meaningful to say and about which they think they should express themselves in public.

This self-reinforcing circle of self-confident economists or, as some may say, arrogant economists whose opinions are sought out by the media, bolsters their sense of self-importance and is summarized by Fourcade et al. (2015, p. 110) as follows: "Thus most economists feel quite secure about their value added. They are comforted in this feeling by the fairly unified disciplinary framework behind them, higher salaries that many of them believe reflect some true fundamental value, and a whole institutional structure – from newspapers to congressional committees to international policy circles – looking up to them for answers, especially in hard times." Economists therefore do not usually shy away when approached by the media.

Despite these (normative) reasons for economists to engage with the media, the incentives for economists to do so are limited. Although there is no evidence to prove this, it does not seem that media appearances play an important role in academic promotions or contribute much to salary. Also, status and recognition among peers do not seem to depend much on media appearances. Direct evidence on this is – as far as we can tell – absent. However, Hilmer et al. (2015) find that more than half of the variation in log salary of academic economists is explained by the h-index, a measure of academic achievement (through citations). They also find that – after controlling for the number of citations through the h-index – articles that are not published in elite or excellent academic journals (including articles in non-academic journals) contribute very little to salary. Ten articles that are not published in elite or excellent journals increase salary by only 1.3% to 2%.

There are roughly two reasons why an economist is approached by the media: (a) to discuss his/her own research findings and (b) to comment on a topic of general interest within his field of expertise. The latter includes a macroeconomist who comments on the recession, a professor of finance who comments on the banking crisis or, as in our own case, an economist who comments on issues in health care and education.

The first of the two occurs relatively rarely. The findings of economic research are not very frequently reported in the media. Most serious newspapers have a science section in which new research findings and breakthroughs are being reported. Most articles in the science section of newspapers report on medical research or natural sciences like physics and chemistry. Among non-medical sciences, history and archeology get quite some attention, while among the social sciences, findings from psychology are sometimes reported. However, economic research is hardly ever reported in the science news section of newspapers. The same holds for science programs on TV or radio. Hamermesh (2004) gives some examples of economic research that has attracted attention in the media, such as "the incentives to die provided by the estate tax . . . the impact of previous abortion rates on crime rates . . . the value of Christmas gifts" and Hamermesh's own work on the economics of beauty. All of these examples are attention-grabbing topics. Some of them are even on a topic that is a bit weird. But none of them are part of the mainstream research agenda of economic science.

Consequently, media attention for economists mostly consists of commenting on current economic issues or developments. The absence of economic research in the science section of newspapers says something about how serious journalists take economic research. There appears to be some discrepancy between the self-perception of economists of the importance and relevance of their research and the perception of others – at least the value journalists attach to findings of economic research. As a result, most of the discussion surrounding economic science is not about new findings of economic research, but rather the differences in opinions economists have about general or current economic topics and policies.

As indicated above, for economists, contributing to the public debate, rather than the utilization of new and innovative economic research findings, is the most common way of appearing in the media. For an economist, this raises the question of what incentives economists have to appear in the media. As we have argued above, the financial pay-off of media appearances, in the form of a higher salary, does not seem to be very significant, as salaries are mainly determined by academic achievement (measured through citations). Aside from the opportunity to express one's knowledge and insights and the ego boost that comes from knowing that you and not your colleague has been approached by a journalist as the expert on the topic, media appearances provide other benefits as well. For the writer, a piece in a newspaper or interview for radio or television offers a form of instant gratification. It offers the ability to convey knowledge and insights in a fast way and, if done well, receive immediate praise and recognition by the general public (including journalists). If an article in a scientific journal is a dinner in a three-star restaurant, a piece on the opinion pages of a newspaper is a form of fast food: you can sometimes feel a craving for it, but the satisfaction it brings is fast and not very long lasting. It is also cheap (and the salary effects small) and not always healthy. Colleague researchers sometimes react negatively out of envy or disagree with what you have said. The media may also be hard on economists who appear in the media too often in their opinion. We personally heard a journalist describe a respectable and reputable economist, who was asked for his expert opinion frequently, as being "media horny" and someone who circles the television studios in his Saab, waiting for a call from a radio or TV show for a media appearance.

Economists who actively contribute to the policy debate are sometimes looked down on. In the Netherlands, the word "policy economist" is used primarily to qualify someone with low academic status and achievement among economists. In the United States, this is different. Almost all top US economists engage in the policy debate by writing columns and opinion pieces or by working for a while as advisor to the government. Nobel laureates like Paul Samuelson, Milton Friedman, Gary Becker and Joseph Stiglitz were all closely involved in policy advice. A Nobel Prize winner like Paul Krugman is on a personal crusade against Republican presidents and senators in his *New York Times* column twice a week. And, as Weinstein (1992, p. 75) puts it, they are appreciated for it: "Overall, the economics profession deserves applause for its efforts in communicating with the public through the media."

Another reason why media appearances become important is that funding agencies increasingly use knowledge dissemination and knowledge utilization as criteria in evaluating and funding research proposals. The large research subsidies by the Dutch science foundation NWO use three criteria for evaluating research proposals: the quality of the applicant, the quality of the research proposal and the knowledge utilization. For economists, knowledge utilization frequently includes reporting on research findings in the media. The greater emphasis on knowledge dissemination and utilization in research funding illustrates the importance attached to media appearances.

Aside from that, media appearances may add to the status of economists as academics as well. Especially by outsiders, i.e., non-economists, the quality and status of an economist are frequently determined by his/her frequency of appearance in the media. A star economist is for many laymen an economist whose opinions are frequently sought by the media. This may create some tension between the internal hierarchy and status among academic economists and the perceived hierarchy by outsiders based on media appearances. American economists may have understood Karl Marx better than their Dutch and other European colleagues: it is not about understanding the world but changing it. Or, better put, the main role of an economist columnist is telling others how to change the world.

Media appearances in general increase the relevance and status of the economic profession in the eyes of the general public. However, there is also a risk attached to that. Media appearances of economists have an element of common good to them. As an economist, you not only represent yourself but also speak to some extent for the profession at large. Or, stated otherwise, what you say not only reflects on yourself but also on the profession of economists and on economics as a science. This has normative explanations as well. Behaving "badly" in the media not only does reputational damage to yourself, but there are also externalities in the damage done to the profession at large. These potential social costs may be seen to impose an obligation on economists to behave in the interest of the profession at large.

By addressing the general public through the media, economists spread their interpretation and worldview to a wider public as well. The worldview of economists is relevant to consider when discussing media behavior, as it corresponds to one of the conclusions by Hirschman and Berman (2014), who argue that "the spread of the economic discourse reshapes how non-economist policymakers understand a given issue." The way economists analyze and interpret the world influences decision-making by politicians and other policymakers. As economists share (at least to a large extent) a common framework for interpreting the world – economic theory – the way economists interpret the world contributes to shaping general opinion and sets the agenda for policies and interventions that change the world.

Economists have been influential in imposing their worldview on the public, as informing or educating the public sometimes becomes confused with indoctrination of the public. According to Tirole (2017, p. 65), economists are accused of "all thinking the same thing." This contradicts another complaint that is frequently lodged against economists, namely that they never agree on anything. The latter opinion is fairly frequently illustrated by a quote by Winston Churchill on John Maynard Keynes: "If you put two economists in a room, you get two opinions, unless one of them is Lord Keynes, in which case you get three opinions."

Whatever the case may be, it does suggest that economists are set to impose their worldview, or, as some would say, ideology, on society. Not only have they contributed to shaping policies, but the impact economists have is even more profound in imposing their worldview and perspective on society. The individualistic approach in economics, with its emphasis on the role of (financial) incentives and its philosophy that the rationale of government intervention can (only) be found in market failure – i.e., in cases where the market fails to provide optimal outcomes – has been the basis of policies of deregulation and increased use of the price mechanism as a policy instrument. At the heart of climate change policies, to name just one example, are policies related to road pricing and pricing of CO_2 emissions. In this way, the world is governed by the philosophy, or ideology, of economic science as practiced by economists.

Ethical issues in media appearances by economists

Media appearances by economists take various forms. Interviews on radio or television enable economists to directly express their opinions. So do op-ed articles in newspapers. Op-ed articles are increasingly being replaced by blogs on the internet. Quotes or interviews in newspapers are also a regular way for economists to express their opinions. These outlets differ in the control economists can exercise over the presentation of their opinions. The various ways of appearing in the media can be classified into two groups: the outlets where you, as an economist, have control over the way your thoughts are being presented to the audience and the media outlets where an intermediary – usually a journalist – determines whether and how your thoughts are being presented to the audience. Of course, most people prefer to have control over what is being presented in the media. However, a larger audience is frequently reached if the message has passed through an intermediary. A few seconds on the evening news or a few quotes in a national newspaper reaches more people than an op-ed piece or a blog on the internet.

Increasingly, media refers to social media. Social media ethics is also necessary to pay attention to, especially because of the direct communication social media provides between an academic – economist – and the audience. This not only refers to the wider audience but, in the case of academic economists, also primarily to the use of social media and its relation with students. Social media ethics guides have been developed. On the internet, many examples of codes of conduct for the ethical use of social media can be found. One example is the ethical code created by the Royal Dutch Pharmacists Association (Koninklijke Nederlandse Maatschappij ter Bevordering van de Pharmacie; see www.knmp. nl/professie/professioneel-handelen/social-media-code). The code includes recommendations such as use your common sense on social media; treat and respect others on social media like you would in normal social relations; realize that the boundaries between professional and private behavior can easily be crossed, as social media is informal and public; check your facts before you post them on social media; hold back on personal and emotional statements; do not react too hastily; respect promises about confidentiality and every now and then check what is being said about you, your colleagues and your employer on social media (for example, by googling yourself). As far as we know, there is no code of conduct for social media use for economists, although it might be useful to develop one.

Our first media experience was in the early 1990s. For a well-known and respectable professional journal in the Netherlands, *Economisch Statistische Berichten*, we wrote about the relationship between childcare and labor participation of women. Our conclusion was that childcare helped increase the labor force participation of women with young children (see Groot & Maassen van den Brink 1992). This was also reflected in the title of the article: "Childcare Improves Income of Mothers." However, we also noted in the article that a quarter of women who used subsidized childcare had no paid job. This immediately drew the attention of the media. The article was summarized in various newspapers. However, some journalists gave it their own spin by saying that subsidized childcare was abused by women using it to drink coffee and play tennis. This led to a profound reaction. A member of Parliament asked of the minister: "How is it possible for childcare subsidies to be so abused?"

Soon we learned that the attention of media and politicians is determined by the way in which results are presented. The message of our study – childcare is good for female employment – was drowned out by a loose but factually correct sentence in the story that not all women who used childcare actually had a paid job. Later on, we used the same research results in another story. We did not write that 25% of childcare users had no paid work, but that 75% had a paid job (Groot & Maassen van den Brink 1994). The memory of journalists is usually short, and this also attracted the attention of the media. This time, the reactions were diametrically opposed to those to the original article. Everyone was impressed by the large number of paid working women (the average female participation rate in the Netherlands at that time was just over 40%).

In 2005, we made a list – based on our own experience with the media – of the qualities an economist columnist and television expert should have (Groot & Maassen van den Brink 2005). These qualities still hold. A first requirement for a media appearance is to have an opinion. Not just any opinion, but rather an opinion that opens up a discussion or contributes to an ongoing discussion. Editors often measure the quality of their columnists or guests on radio or TV shows by the number of e-mails and other (social media) responses received from readers and viewers. The more, the better. A somewhat controversial opinion is especially appreciated. The columnist who writes and speaks in platitudes and "on the one hand, on the other hand" opinions does not last long in the media. Clarity is appreciated. However, an opinion must also be well founded and based on economic facts (or what passes for facts).

A second requirement is good writing skills. Economists use facts (or what counts for facts) to tell a story. Only a well-told story convinces an economist. Unfortunately, many economists do not understand that and think that economics is mostly a game with mathematical equations. Being clear and to the point are therefore major assets of an economist who wants to make a career in the media.

Brightness is also important. A column with mathematical formulas and abstract jargon is not suited for the average newspaper reader. The ability to explain complex problems in an easy to understand manner is a skill not everyone has. Or, as Weinstein (1992, p. 74) phrases it (in somewhat less positive words): "In the business of news analysis, titillating but shallow beats wise but equivocal nearly every time."

When appearing in the media, it is also important to remember not to underestimate your audience. There is nothing more irritating than an expert who explains to you the obvious. Your audience has to learn from you. You are the expert, so you should tell them things they do not already know. But you have to explain it in a way that is understandable for everyone. So be clear, but do not state the obvious.

Also, be up-to-date with current affairs and policy discussions and be prepared for journalists calling about your opinion on a range of topics much broader than you might focus on in your research or teaching. You have to be knowledgeable about current events and the hot topics in the media if you want to play a role in it and contribute to the public debate.

Furthermore, an interest in economics and society is useful. This may seem a self-evident trait for an economist, but this is not always the case. Some knowledge about what is happening in the real world outside the economic models helps as well (again, something that is not self-evident to all economists), and originality, an awareness of the contributions of others (has someone else not already expressed this opinion?) and a measure of politeness and grace toward others are also helpful.

What an economist who acts in the media also needs is the ability to deal with deadlines (a columnist needs a new fresh and thought-provoking opinion every week). Some things you can do without as a columnist – humor, for example (unless you're a comedian, and even then). Rancor is also bad inspiration for a column. In general, as an economist, you must behave as a professional and an academic. Or, as Tirole (2017, p. 70) puts it: "Academics must maintain a delicate balance between necessary humility and the determination to convince their interlocutors of both the usefulness of the knowledge they have acquired and its limits." When appearing in the media, this is all the more important to remember, especially as frequent media appearances may make an economist overconfident, lead to a sense of self-importance and make him or her perhaps even a bit arrogant.

Hamermesh (2004) presents a long list of "dos and don'ts" and behavioral advice on media appearances by economists. We will not repeat the long list of sensible and useful tips he provides; for this, we refer you to the very readable source itself (Hamermesh 2004). One of his useful pieces of advice is that when appearing on television, economists should be dressed appropriately: "If they are dressed very informally such as in a t-shirt people will have difficulty taking them seriously." Tirole (2017, p. 76) summarizes the media ethics for economists with two important rules of conduct that deserve to be repeated here: "1. Debate ideas, never persons (not ad hominem arguments), 2. Never say anything you are not prepared to defend before your peers in a seminar or at a conference."

Twenty-five years after the publicity of our study on childcare, we know better how to deal with the media. We also know better what to expect from the media. A lesson we have learned is that you should avoid being used by journalists. Be wary of journalists who know it all so well and have their conclusions ready before they have talked to you. Often they use you to provide their own story with the right quote and to endorse their opinions. Sometimes journalists only call for confirmation of their own beliefs and try to get you to go along with that. It is better to turn things around. Try to steer the journalist in the right direction. Point them to aspects that are apparent to an economist, but not to a layman. Keep track of your own story and do not agree with a journalist's judgment too quickly. Try to be your own person and not the extension of authority for the journalist. Journalists often try to seduce you into engaging in wild speculation. Keep to the facts. Simple (but still unknown) facts and figures are always good in a newspaper article or on radio or TV.

Be modest. Economists sometimes overestimate themselves. Their self-esteem is sometimes higher than the esteem outsiders have for economics and economists. The fact that economists sometimes contradict each other does not help to increase the authority of economists. Journalists often help with that and exaggerate contradictions a little. Remember that economists think about many things the same way but often emphasize different aspects and express themselves in different ways.

Do not say yes to all invitations and avoid overexposure. Also, do not go to entertainment programs; only accept invitations from serious news programs.

You are, after all, an economist, not an entertainer – unless, of course, you are contemplating a career switch.

Build a relationship of trust with journalists. If you trust them, it is less likely they will betray you by putting words in your month or by taking statements out of context. Accept that journalists will pick your brain and use it to their own advantage. Calling an expert is a widely used tool by journalists to obtain quicker insight into a problem; then they do not have to read anything. Sometimes they try to make you feel good by suggesting that you express your views on TV or radio or by saying they will quote you in their article. If they say at the end of the phone call that they will call you back to let you know, you know you have been used. Usually, you will hear your own arguments as the interviewer's questions that evening on television. What frequently happens is that the journalist picks the brains of a scientist and then puts this opinion into the mouth of a well-known television presenter. Editors do not like to announce in advance that they are looking for a particular opinion.

Conclusion and recommendations

Economists are fond of policy recommendations. Many media appearances by economists end with the answer to the question, what do you recommend should be done? We want to end our chapter by providing a few recommendations as well. Should economists be better prepared for the media and receive media skills training? Should media training and media presentation training become part of the economics curriculum or become part of PhD training programs? Perhaps yes. This should include training in how to present yourself in the media and how to deal with journalists and interviews. We must add to this, however, that we once participated in a one-day media training course but did not have the impression afterward that we had learned much from it. Media training should also include education in media ethics. A best practice guide for the use of media, including the use of social media, might be useful as well. Economists could perhaps also be more proactive and regularly update journalists about the economic perspective on current affairs or inform them about new and interesting research findings. Another recommendation is that economists should learn how to write well. Clear writing skills are not yet common among economists. A general writing skills course should be part of every graduate training program in economics.

The importance of economics in our daily lives and well-being can hardly be overestimated. Economists who appear in the media should be aware of the consequences and impact their statements may have. We gave an example of our own experience with the media when we were still young and inexperienced in dealing with it. Or, as Keynes expresses in his General Theory: "The ideas of economists and political philosophers, both when they are right and when they are wrong, are more powerful than is commonly understood. Indeed the world is ruled by little else." Practical people, who believe themselves to be quite exempt from any intellectual influences, are usually the slaves of some defunct economist. Madmen in authority, who hear voices in the air, are distilling their frenzy from some academic scribbler of a few years back. If economics wants to be a relevant science, economists have a moral obligation to make their insights and results accessible to policymakers and other interested parties. For yourself, a newspaper article or policy advice forces you to think about current social issues. This increases your economic insight. You will learn more about the practice of the field by responding to current social issues.

References

Fourcade, M., E. Ollion & Y. Algan (2015), 'The superiority of economists', *Journal of Economic Perspectives 29* (1), pp. 89–114.

Groot, W. & H. Maassen van den Brink (1992), 'Arbeidsmarktparticipatie en kinderopvang', *Economisch Statistische Berichten 3870*, pp. 731–734.

Groot, W. & H. Maassen van den Brink (1994), 'Kinderopvang verbetert inkomenspositie van vrouwen', *Economisch Statistische Berichten 4003*, pp. 304–307.

Groot, W. & H. Maassen van den Brink (2005), 'De econoom, de columnist en de zenmeester', in: W. Dolfsma & R. Nahuis (eds.), *Media en Economie: Markten in Beweging en een Overheid die Stuurt Zonder Kompas*, Preadviezen van de Koninklijke Vereniging voor de Staathuishoudkunde, pp. 157–162.

Hamermesh, D. (2004), 'Maximizing the substance in the soundbite: A media guide for economists', *Journal of Economic Education 35* (4), pp. 370–382.

Hamermesh, D. (2015), 'Citation in economics: Measurements, uses and impacts', *NBER Working Paper 21754*.

Hilmer, M., M. Ransom & C. Hilmer (2015), 'Fame and the fortune of academic economists: How the market rewards influential research in economics', *Southern Economic Journal 82*, pp. 430–452.

Hirschman, D. & E. Popp Berman (2014), 'Do economists make policies? On the political effects of economics', *Socio-Economic Review 12*, pp. 779–811.

Keynes, J.M. (1936), *The General Theory of Employment, Interest and Money*, London: Macmillan, p. 383.

King, G., B. Schneer & A. White (2017), 'How the news media activate public expression and influence national agendas', *Science 358*, pp. 776–780.

Klant, J. (1979), *Spelregels voor Economen: De logische Structuur van Economische Theorieën*, Stenfert Kroese, Leiden.

Laband, D. & R. Tollison (2003), 'Dry holes in economic research', *Kyklos 56*, pp. 161–174.

Tirole, J. (2017), *Economics for the Common Good*, Princeton University Press, Princeton.

Weinstein, M. (1992), 'Economists and the media', *Journal of Economic Perspectives 6* (3), pp. 73–77.

10 Intervention, policy and responsibility

Economics as over-engineered expertise?

Jamie Morgan

Introduction: the lack of silence is deafening

It is widely agreed that economists disagree, but it is also acknowledged that they do so according to common commitments. Perhaps the most peculiar, and thus uncommon, commonality is that economists take it as a given that the role of the economist extends to intervention in public discourse and public policy. If socialised as an economist, it is easy to miss how odd this is. A sense of mission and entitlement is built into economics, and this contrasts with sociology and political science. It has some superficial resemblance to fields found within business schools, but economics has a kind of secular zealotry they cannot match.[1] This transcends other dividing lines. Methodologists and metaphysicians categorise economists in various contrastive ways: neoclassical and not, mainstream, orthodox, heterodox and so forth. These categories are ways to group the many and the few according to ontology, theory and methods.

Sociologists and critics currently single out mainstream economics as peculiarly disciplined, exhibiting a high degree of consensus regarding norms and practices, produced and reproduced through professional associations, department recruitment, PhD supervision, national research monitoring exercises and journal publication rankings.[2] This mainstream exhibits a kind of diffident diversity, impatient of pluralism. Positioned in this way, the mainstream is the mainstream by virtue of the material consequences of recognition, that is power, though power is not a mainstream concept of the world it inhabits. Yet the interventionist drive is not restricted to the mainstream; it is shared by the rest. Where policy is concerned, there is no discourse of economic deferment, no economics of silence. Intervention is, tacitly at least, considered intrinsic to economics, a right and a duty. Whether counselling humility or inadvertently extolling hubris, whether invoking Keynes's dentist or Lucas's vanquishing of the business cycle, economists differ only about who and what to speak on behalf of: universal economic man, woman, labour, capital, the entrepreneur, the demos or the planet. Economists' policy credo might well aptly be phrased as "put up *and* don't shut up".

Having nothing to say is no crime in economics, but saying nothing is. Economists can be accomplished arrogationists but also willing recruits.[3] Being an economist, and especially an economist of note, provides a platform that bundles status, authority and legitimacy without quite testing the ties that bind these three together. Economists are enthusiastic commentators, and the media, government, corporations and NGOs are keen to translate this predilection into organisational form and content: op-eds, regular columns, ad hoc and formal board advisory roles, panel chairs for inquiries and reports and revolving door employment between academia and the rest. The full range is open to few but aspired to by the many. Paul Krugman and Joseph Stiglitz are perhaps the most famous of the omnipresent and, thanks to *Inside Job*, Frederic Mishkin the most infamous of those who have previously been so.

There are many others. This matters, and does so in various ways. For example, when the UK government commissioned a report on climate change in 2005, its primary concern was economic, and its choice of chair was Nicholas Stern, a prominent former World Bank economist well known to then Chancellor of the Exchequer Gordon Brown. As an economist, Stern was not at that time a longstanding expert in environmental issues. It was not necessary that the report was headed by an economist, and that positioning carried consequences over and above the subsequent interminable debates regarding discount rates. The report would have been differently framed had it been headed by climate scientists or social policy experts. The economy would have been a subordinate issue rather than the priority through which all else was filtered, caveats and concerns notwithstanding.

Stern has subsequently been critical of the role of economists in creating complacency regarding climate change and broader ecological problems, but that is not the point. Economists have become first port of call consultants, professional privateers and the preferred public intellectual. They are society's go-to voice, never shy in putting themselves forward, and the inclination and invitation to do so often spread far beyond the confines of the original substantive expertise of the particular economist. Yet this is ambiguous because what determines the contemporary value of the economist as a policy animal is often the amorphous understanding that what they offer is a skill set, a toolkit and a frame of mind. Of course, one might reasonably ask would "we" (society in some abstract thought experiment sense) want economists to shut up. This is not a simple question to answer because societies crave answers: opinion, evidence, explanations, ideas and solutions. Yet one can imagine a sociologist or political scientist saying, "I have nothing to say about that", "don't ask me" or "ask someone else". However, one can far more readily imagine an economist pausing long enough to flick some internal switch and then beginning a reply with "speaking as an economist".

The implication is that the economist speaks in a way that transcends all other boundaries. The economist is universally relevant. Again, economists will see nothing odd about this. The difference is as much a matter of socialisation for the psychology and anthropology of economics as it is a matter of epistemological difference between disciplines. This is not least because the differences have been developed rather than discovered. Economists *feel* competent to speak and *expect* to be heard, and this in turn cannot be unrelated to what economics has become in terms of the comprehension of what it means to be an economist and the competencies she embodies.

None of this is neutral, yet most of it is normalised (see, for example, Campbell-Verduyn, 2017, chapter 4). From "speaking as an economist" flows framing analytics, constraining theoretical formulations and a seal of approval. Economists' expertise saturates social inquiry, and this in turn is saturated by small "p" politics through the way values are treated in knowledge formation. This is as significant as large "P" political ideas. It percolates into policy from the ways economics is situated. This is *one* important way in which responsibility becomes an issue, and it is this I address in what follows.

Responsibility, aresponsibility and irresponsibility

A society of subjects is a society of conscious activity and can no more operate efficaciously without responsibility than it can without trust (see Colledge et al., 2014; Reiersen, 2017). Consciousness without this facet of conscientiousness is alien to how we reflect upon the world in which we live, and it is through reflexivity as a basic human capacity that we have (through materially consequential practice) created societies in which it is a key constituent (so there is some circularity here). Responsibility is both a condition of and contingent content within society. It is intrinsic to the reliability and durability of relations in general and relations in particular. It is a quality, not a thing; one does not hold it in one's hands, but builds it into conduct and works to make it a condition of conduct. However, it is because contexts and conduct vary that responsibility is not an unambiguous universal term. At the same time, since operative in ordinary language use, it has some signposts, a vague intuitive sense that it involves an acknowledgement of and subsequent due attention paid; a sensitivity to, a cognisance of. . . . But responsibility is given more meaning by how it is synonymised, situated, used, associated with other terms and internalised into practices, and this is revealed through the way question forms applied to responsibility direct our attention (see later section; for background range, see Fingarette, 2004; Ricoeur, 2000; McKeon, 1957).[4]

Recognition of responsibility starts to shift from vague intuitive phenomenological resonance to something more nuanced when we start to consider matters of lack of responsibility. A society without a concept and practice of responsibility would be one unconcerned by failure and reckless of harms. It would be undermined in its capacity to contest intentional forms of both of these, and it would be unable to coherently make sense of how these attach to conditions and activity (whether intentional or not). Yet it is not in general considered illegitimate to deny responsibility for some *given* action, outcome or consequence.

To deny responsibility is to contest the grounds of, and specific direction of, an attribution, most often in terms of fault or blame. But to contest the grounds, one does not reject the concept, but rather the terms in that instance. This is instructive. There is no similar licence granted to irresponsibility as a facet of character or action. "It is not *my* responsibility" is not an issue of the same order as "I *am* irresponsible". One may expect and accept irresponsibility in certain circumstances from particular categories of person (the young, the impaired or the mentally ill), but it is not an attribute that is in general deemed desirable or condoned or cultivated in a socially competent adult (it is, rather, one of the competencies that causes us to categorise an adult as socially competent).[5] Moreover, responsibility does not seem to be a concept that is conducive to a mediated term equivalent to the range moral, amoral and immoral. Arguments are made that in some spheres morality does not apply, but it is not clear one can readily try to construct a similar case for "aresponsibility", although care is required to explain why this might be so.

In economics, Milton Friedman's amorality of markets and of business in particular has had many adherents. Amorality is the claim that the moral dynamic of conditions, conduct and consequences is not the concern of some party, that is, persons, agents occupying roles and named collectives that create and contain such roles. Nor is it a relevant concern to some practice, activity, situation or circumstance circumscribed for the multiplicity of those parties. However, it does not seem plausible to state as a general characteristic of some domain that "the way in which I/we conduct myself/ourselves and the consequences of my/our conduct are not and should not be my/our concern", that is, I/we am/are "aresponsible". Any attempt to do so seems tacitly to degenerate to a claim that we are not or should not be held responsible, and so this is, in effect, a denial of responsibility, rather than a claim that responsibility does not apply to the domain. This is a matter where pronouns sit uncomfortably with propositions. Moreover, it seems likely to be a denial of some specific form of responsibility, and it is this that Friedman's argument invokes: amorality is the repudiation of moral responsibility as a relevant form of responsibility.

I am by no means suggesting Freidman's and similar claims are well justified. The denial of moral responsibility is not a refutation that a situation has a moral form and ramifications, but rather of the relevance of these for some or all participants under some description of participation. Furthermore, it remains the case that the argument has an implicit and explicit moral form, encapsulated in value claims regarding capitalism: society is served by the activity for which moral responsibility is repudiated, and in consequentialist terms, there is some assessable good, so the argumentation form is tacitly a subset of moral theory and provides also a moral legitimation to the claim that morality is not a concern in market practice *for the parties*.[6] Many discourses are set up to counter this (notably in recent years, though highly problematically) corporate social responsibility. In any case, amoral markets, etc. typically delegate responsibility to government as the appropriate locus for moral deliberation (albeit one often already shaped by the idea of implicit justice in markets and where freedom is augmented because of markets, which informs the claim that minimal government serves democracy best, which then forms an imperative that restricts the scope for the state and society to intervene in markets and capitalism; that is, to take or exercise moral responsibility through legal and regulatory construction and action). So, Friedman's claims are contestable based on alternatives, tensions in his argument and the implied continued relevance of moral reasoning, insofar as one can counter that norms are ineluctable and should not be neglected in their significance, not least because this itself has consequences (see, for example, Wilber, 2004; Sandel, 2013).

The above may seem convoluted, but the point is simple. It illustrates that the denial of moral responsibility is a denial that parties can be held responsible under particular claims regarding the context. Amorality is unstable as an argument but, even if allowable, does not seem to licence the claim that parties can be aresponsible in some more basic way. To state that parties can be aresponsible amounts to the claim that responsibility need not be a concern under *all* possible descriptions rather than any given possible description. This seems to violate the sociality which is basic to human society.[7] More prosaically, we do not expect, articulate or defend aresponsibility or irresponsibility in the ordinary course of human affairs.

Why is this worth stating?

Economics, responsibility and the socially competent adult

Reflecting upon irresponsibility in order to develop an appropriate awareness and practice of responsibility has become a significant issue in economics in recent years. The role of economists in the global financial crisis has made this an issue of contemporary concern, though the claims made about different aspects of that role highlight that the issue has enduring aspects and relevance. Individualised scandal and recrimination have played a prominent role, but whilst there may be column inches in accusations of ill-advised, venal, mendacious, avaricious or unscrupulous behaviour, of greater concern has been the critique that problems may not be isolatable to egregious instances of individuals only, but involve collective conditions and persistent potential because of the way the profession and its approach to knowledge formation and intervention in the world have developed. Though the American Economic Association has been prompted to respond (for example, AEA, 2018), it is other organisations, such as the Association for Social Economics, that have done the most to progress this and a few academics, most notably George DeMartino, who have thought deeply about this (see, for example, DeMartino and McCloskey, 2016; Davis and Dolfsma, 2015; DeMartino, 2013, 2011; Blok, 2013).[8]

Responsibility is a problematic concept for economists. Insofar as economists have become society's go-to voice, its first port of call consultants, professional privateers and preferred public intellectuals, they have arguably *accepted* responsibility, and yet economists do not clearly *take* responsibility. This seems an odd conjoining of meanings. However, tacit acceptance need have no conscious current recognition by relevant parties, but requires only the claim that those parties have put themselves in a position of acceptance (an order of argument akin to and subject to the same weaknesses as – but without being identical to – Locke's classic social contract case for consent in his *Second Treatise*). At the same time as putting themselves in this position of acceptance, much of the development of economics, and most notably mainstream economics, has created blindspots and practices that operate to limit the degree to which economists hold themselves responsible, creating a, for all intents and purposes, background denial of responsibility. There are many mutually reinforcing ways in which this operates.

For example, training as a mainstream economist involves a set of knowledge production practices that emphasise clarity of and quantification in expression, from which the implication flows that the construction of knowledge as a product is open to contestation and replication based on that clarity and quantification, and this is considered a hallmark of scientific method, something intrinsically objective because of the process. Concomitantly, economists develop theory that has a set of stated assumptions and a basic mathematical-symbolic expression (or is able to refer back to this through reference as authority – a set of theorems that act as "proofs" located somewhere); they then also construct models and use statistical analysis in combination with datasets, where the dataset tests the model and the model extracts information from the dataset. The whole may then (but need not if it is purely econometric) be formally interpreted in accordance with theory (but in any case presupposes an operation of an economy that is theory by any other name). Conclusions and findings rarely amount to more than descriptions of the tests and of the extracted information, with some discussion of the technical limitations and methods present for the model as well as how these challenges were managed through modifications of the model or methods. Read any mainstream economics journal, and one will recognise this archetype.

Importantly, innovation in economics tends to involve diversity that is still recognisable in terms of the archetype. For example, randomised controlled trials have become popular in recent years. More generally, experiment has become a common approach. This can take the form of laboratory condition testing of human subjects to confirm some atomised relation or trait conceived as a deviation from the economically rational agent and the efficient market (e.g. loss aversion), or it can be multiple simulations run on a constructed dataset to find some fit for claims about the effect of a given feature (e.g. replication for tasks by robots for job displacement). The point, however, is that these are approaches that conform to the prior narrative of clarity and quantification. They are diversity subject to assimilation that takes the archetype as a point of departure, creating deviation as variation on a theme.[9]

Clearly, the knowledge production practices are open to contestation and have been both contested and defended (for the range, see Cartwright and Davis, 2016; Lawson, 2015; Rodrik, 2015; Syll 2016; Mary Morgan, 2012; Caballero, 2010; Milonakis, 2017). It may well be that the whole misspecifies the argumentation structures economists actually construct and how they persuade (see McCloskey, 1998), but the point I want to emphasise is that the whole (modernist or not, in McCloskey's terms) affects the identity of economists and how they are socialised with respect to responsibility. Most mainstream economists will self-identify as social scientists, with reference to their field of inquiry, e.g. behavioural finance, but with a heavy emphasis on the science in social science.[10] The concept of science economists have in mind is a claim of objectivity as clarity reinforced by method, and this in turn is conditioned by the skill set that forms the basis of their expertise. The whole is hazy because economists are rarely required to reflect upon this. This, too, is important because clarity and objectivity are not necessarily negatives if appropriately pursued and justified (the terms of contestation hinge on whether they are or can be justified, e.g. the problems of ontology, realism, realisticness, and the sacrifices involved in tractability that reduce to the metaphor of using a hammer to cut hair).[11] But consider that academic economists rarely explicitly invoke the positive-normative divide and in debate are apt to be more sophisticated in their definition of economics than Robbin's study of the allocation of scarce resources. However, the influence of both of these is still built into mainstream economics.[12] They remain shibboleths.

Early training and attitude formation matter since any future recognition of problems deriving from ingrained positions rarely transcends them. There is not the space to go into any detail here, but I would note that mainstream economics has in some ways improved its recognition of issues of values. Most textbooks now have some equivalent of "thinking like an economist" in Mankiw and Taylor's *Economics* (2014, chapter 2), which clearly sets out how economists pursue a "positive" agenda of explanation (which claims to conform to scientific method), whilst also operating as normative advocates, as policy advisors who disagree amongst themselves. This is ostensibly quite sophisticated. However, problems are not transcended if issues are juxtaposed, rather than reconciled and effectively integrated, since some aspect of the non-integrated whole is liable to overwhelm the rest. This affects how and whether economists are socialised to take responsibility. The point I want to emphasise is that this feeds into the concatenation of economics as ontology, methodology, theory and practice that frames responsibility, and this in turn has fundamental consequences for how economists are positioned in relation to intervention and policy.

Though economists would resist being labelled as technocratic, by virtue of expertise, the economist is offering something technical, and by virtue of conditioning, responsibility for that is separated, not least because norms are in some ways separated out (others are responsible for discussing them – a Pontius Pilate abnegation), and in other ways norms are reformulated in a different language that disguises what they are. Norms or values become predicates or postulates and testable hypotheses within theory and models. Responsibility for what is done is then ultimately *placed* with a recipient; this is especially so if economics is broadly conceived as a "decision set science" that analyses how choices are made, whilst presupposing this is prior to any advocacy of particular ways of choosing (muddying the longstanding problem that economists' primary claim is that they describe a world but have ultimately sought to shape it in the name of those "descriptions" – a profound tension in what it means to be a science). So, the form of economics and the language by which it is expressed tend to socialise economists in ways that insulate them from taking responsibility, insofar as, in the last instance, responsibility is shifted ("here are our theories and models and findings based on the data; this is clear; do with it what you will; however, any rational person might . . ."). At the same time, the absences that accompany that form do not encourage economists to *think about* responsibility, including the way it is, for all intents and purposes, separated and placed through the development of a skill set and frame of mind that attaches to that skill set.

The elimination of philosophy, methodology, history of economic thought and ethics from the education of the economist is a longstanding concern among critics for many reasons. An important one is that the absence is both indicative of and influential for a more instrumental and narrowed curriculum that harms the reflexive capacities that pedagogy could inculcate. This narrows the skill set of many economists by denying other skills the potential to be part of their socialisation whilst at the same time relegating the issues that arise based on these subjects to sub-disciplinary groups. The more a core skill set denuded of these subjects dominates the education of the economist, the less familiar and comfortable they become reflecting upon the values and consequences of the field later. At the same time, it is this narrowed skill set that becomes the primary source of authority for economists to become intervenors and, more specifically, policy participants. This is, for example, intrinsic to Rodrik's core argument in *Economics Rules*. It is implicit in Krugman's frequent "what we all are as economists" arguments. For example,

> as you probably know, I am not exactly an evolutionary economist. I like to think that I am more open-minded about alternative approaches to economics than most, but I am basically a maximization-and-equilibrium kind of guy. Indeed, I am quite fanatical about defending the relevance of standard economic models in many situations. . . . In economics we often use the term "neoclassical" either as a way to praise or to damn our opponents. Personally, I consider myself a proud neoclassicist. By this I clearly don't mean that I believe in perfect competition all the way. What I mean is that I prefer, when I can, to make sense of the world using models in which individuals maximize and the interaction of these individuals can be summarized by some concept of equilibrium. The reason I like that kind of model is not that I believe it to be literally true, but that I am intensely aware of the power of maximization-and-equilibrium to organize one's thinking – and I have seen the propensity of those who try to do economics without those organizing devices to produce sheer nonsense when they imagine they are freeing themselves from some confining orthodoxy.
>
> (Krugman, 1996)[13]

In conjunction with the narrowed skill set, it is the corollary positioning and neglect that (arguably, obviously) ground and create the drive we might describe as attitudinal in economics, leading to "speaking as an economist".

Of course, economists are limited, not lobotomised. It would be absurd to baldly assert that economists have no sense of responsibility, nor that they are unwilling to think about it. However, responsibility has become elusive. Much of the way in which economics has developed over recent decades, especially the mainstream, has shifted and placed responsibility elsewhere whilst hindering the capacity of economists as economists to reflect upon responsibility. This is not in addition to what economics currently is. It is a consequence of what economics has become – hence the genuine value in this set of essays and in longstanding work by DeMartino and others and hence the slow changes and recognition that economics as a profession is beginning to experience (including the AEA code of conduct, bromide though it may ultimately be). Still, given the societal pervasiveness of "speaking as an economist", it is ironic that the socialisation of the economist has hindered her, when occupying the role of an economist, in conforming to an expectation and standard we have of any socially competent adult.

Responsibility and expertise as the conditioning feature of intervention

At the end of the introduction, I suggested that economists' expertise saturates social inquiry and this in turn is saturated by small "p" politics through the way values are treated in knowledge formation. I also suggested that this is as significant as large "P" political ideas, and that it percolates into policy from the ways economics is situated. There are, of course, many things one might say about policy, but there is also a point one can make that shapes how we think about the possible gaps between what economists have become and the roles they can play in terms of policy. The key term here is *expertise*.

Economics, particularly the mainstream, has become a social science that is uncomfortable with its own sociality. This is built into knowledge production, and so affects attempts to address this and confront the underlying commitments and general tendencies that shape knowledge production. The small "p" politics of economics involves the shedding of value discussion (and the suppression of value influence) in the way economics constructs and presents knowledge. To be clear, this does not mean economists do not discuss or think about values. They do so in conceiving work and when informally arguing about it. Economists disagree and will argue values using ordinary language between themselves and in the press, etc. but will also argue in a discourse-specific common language (assumptions, axioms, etc.). And economists *do* write works explicitly informed by values. Seminal or founding works that become the basis of new schools, theories, etc. often involve trenchant methodological critique that has a value dynamic (often brought forth regarding some contemporary problem – for

example, Keynes and involuntary unemployment, where neoclassical economics was a special case and Say's law incoherent). Economists of all walks write
commentaries on the state of economics and books on contemporary issues.

However, sophistication, nuance and openness based on the above are closed
down when the economist is required to *be* an economist. There is some circularity here.[14] It is the asociality and form and features of the archetype I noted,
as well as the characteristics, that lead to issues over responsibility (which
I invite you to recognise as evidenced by experience, if you are an economist,
since I can offer no definitive smoking gun or buried bodies), which define
being an economist, and this results in an externalisation of the rest. This is, of
course, unstable. The current role of the economist draws them back to theory,
models and methods within the archetype. This has become economic expertise, and expertise then becomes the transition term that situates economists'
policy influence. It is what the economist offers, and it is this that is sought out
and creates authority (including the authority to transgress the boundaries of
that expertise). The point I want to make here is that one primary and ongoing
policy issue is that economics has become society's engineer, and this creates
problems based on the nature of expertise as "engineering".

Intervention and over-engineered economics

As Mirowski and many others have noted, in combination with physics as a reference point, engineering as a shaping metaphor and inspiration for the development of economics is not new. It begins with classical political economy,
imbues Marshall's neoclassical transition and has extended into the modern
mainstream in various ways. Bernanke's response to critique of economics' role
in the global financial crisis is illuminating here:

> Some observers have suggested the need for an overhaul of economics as
> a discipline, arguing that much of the research in macroeconomics and
> finance in recent decades has been of little value or even counterproduc-
> tive. Although economists have much to learn from this crisis, as I will
> discuss, I think that calls for a radical reworking of the field go too far. In
> particular, it seems to me that current critiques of economics sometimes
> conflate three overlapping yet separate enterprises, which, for the purposes
> of my remarks today, I will call economic science, economic engineering,
> and economic management. *Economic science* concerns itself primarily with
> theoretical and empirical generalizations about the behavior of individu-
> als, institutions, markets, and national economies. Most academic research
> falls in this category. *Economic engineering* is about the design and analysis of
> frameworks for achieving specific economic objectives. . . . *Economic man-
> agement* involves the operation of economic frameworks in real time. . . .
> The recent financial crisis was more a failure of economic engineering and
> economic management than of what I have called economic science.
>
> (2010)[15]

Bernanke essentially provides a defence of contemporary mainstream economics that confirms some of its more problematic aspects. The science and engineering distinction reformulates the positive-normative divide whilst also separating out the consequences of engineering as a matter of specific failures, in effect separating out and displacing responsibility. At the same time, the authority of economics is confirmed, and the source of that authority is economics as science. But Bernanke's concept of economic science is of one separable from values despite the fact that it is a social science. It is one of generalisations. But generalisations are of specific propositional forms that are in essence isolations of an x and y. This becomes a science that offers universally relevant insight based on theory and method, and so is universally applicable. Its point of reference is the archetype I have previously referred to. Importantly, when the whole is justified in this way, the capacity to engineer flows from (and so is not really distinct from) economics as a science (as described). It offers control, but here the engineering metaphor bleeds into management since in many instances control is to pull levers of one sort or another in a short-term world that can be mastered because the models of intervention are well understood in terms of the shape of an economy that can in turn *be shaped*.

Adherents of the type of control referred to in the previous paragraph might respond that they claim no precision and what they offer is steering, but the underlying principle remains the same. Moreover, as a defence, there is surely a contradiction here. The failure of mainstream economics is isolated as a matter of engineering specifics, but this is *not* a problem of the understanding of an economy if by this we mean its science, yet this understanding is presupposed in the way engineering has been pursued. To a critic, there is not a failure of economic engineering separate from economic science, but a failure of an over-engineered economic science, leading to a concept of how an economy is to be controlled. In practice, this is different than to suggest an economy can be advocated and one can seek to construct that economy since this involves an integrated social scientific economics, rather than a separation within economics, which creates authority and provides a dubious basis of expertise in society. To be clear, there is no clear entailment that follows from this critique, if by this one means what should be done. There is, however, a clear implication that for economics to be responsible it must first reconsider its expertise, and it is only then that it can also open up the issue of responsibility in regard to policy because this is required in order for economics to become a *social* science.

Put another way, the first step in taking responsibility is a transitional recognition that there are problems in common aspects that underpin what it means to be an economist, and it is only in accepting this that responsibility can genuinely be accepted. In some respects, this should not be a controversial claim. It has been made in other ways and also spans the political spectrum as an *a priori* to policy. For example, both Austrians who follow Hayek and structural and post-Keynesians question the basis of the mainstream concatenation (e.g. Morgan and Negru, 2012; Morgan and Sheehan, 2015). Both argue that mainstream economics fundamentally misunderstands the social world, which is one of cumulative causal processes. Colander, Davis and others, of course, add some nuance to this in terms of distinctions between neoclassical and mainstream, and also the degrees of innovation within the mainstream, but ultimately the dividing line remains ontology, methodology, methods and theory that are more than mere deviations as variations on a theme from the problematic aspects of economics as "science", which has for critics become, following Hayek, "scientism". Moreover, the point is catholic since it extends potentially to all economists; Lawson, for example, has argued both sides of this regarding what might unite heterodox economists and what equally unravels this unity based on mismatches (contrast Lawson, 2015, chapters 3 and 4). This is important insofar as the interventionist drive is not restricted to the mainstream; it is, as noted in the introduction, shared by the rest, and society craves answers.

Economics as a *social* social science

So, my primary point is that economics cannot reasonably be said to be in a position to take responsibility until it becomes a social science, and this begins from a reconsideration of its *adequacy* as a social science.[16] Put another way, one cannot evade the fundamental questions: what are the features of an economy, and how can these be investigated? And yet Bernanke's comments are indicative of the evasion that has been the main recent response to problems, and I have already set out that this has further and enduring context. Though there is no definite policy frame that follows from the methodological aspect of this, there is a further extension here that prefigures how economists might approach policy in terms of grasping the sociality of a social science. This is intrinsic to a responsible social science. What I mean by this will become clear as we proceed.

In general, economists have not been encouraged to think about:

1   Who they are responsible *to*;
2   What they are responsible *for*;
3   What it means to *be* responsible through 1 and 2.

Not thinking about these is dangerous because thinking about these is not and should not be easy. Thinking about them has exercised, if not tortured, philosophers (under different terms since *responsibility* is quite a new one) for thousands of years.

There is not the space here to reprise the history of thought regarding this, and other chapters in this collection provide some of this material. However, who we are responsible to and what for can be explored as a retrospective matter, which orients on a particular action and judges whether a given person ought to be held particularly responsible (among the many causes that arise for any given action) for an event or consequence, either for the purposes of attribution of praise or blame in actual cases (which may then lead to juridical explorations or moral ones) or for the more analytic purpose of extracting, testing or inferring characteristics of persons for typologies and for learning, leading then to prospective responsibility issues – that is, the identification or development of rules, duties or obligations that can condition future circumstances for all persons or for persons as significant agents, notably through the capacities that are enabled or constituted through the powers attached to and expressed in roles. Both "to" and "for" presuppose but also allow challenges to be made regarding the nature of responsibility, creating complex overlapping developments of what it means to "be" responsible: does it arise and is it/can it be governed by principles of rationality, or is it developed through convention subject to sentiment or emotion in the form of guilt, shame, resentment, etc. (how is responsibility governed by what we are?).

Clearly, since activity is social and humans are socialised, the whole scales up to how traits can be cultivated and activity preferred and fostered collectively through communities of one kind or another (including professions), and this shifts the focus to responsibility as a virtue, without restricting the problem of responsibility to virtue ethics (since reason-driven approaches can still be deontological, as they are in the case of Kant, or consequentialist, as they are in many modern forms). Issues do not just scale; they also shade into matters of collective responsibility (more in terms of prospective issues than retrospective, though the latter are not beyond the purview of possible concern).

Ultimately, however, the practical point of a focus on responsibility is to avoid irresponsibility and to encourage *more* responsibility, and this presupposes that the latter can be both cultivated and realised, which in turn assumes that the standards set are achievable and the persons to whom they apply have the capacities to achieve them. Moreover, integrating these two seems to require responsibility (or some synonym) to itself become a subject for reflexivity. It may be possible to delegate responsibility in some ways, but it does not seem to be desirable to delegate thinking about responsibility. This being so, it would be harmful to conflate "developing good habits" with the substitution of recursivity for reflexivity where responsibility is concerned. Thinking about responsibility is a good habit if by this is meant no more than "it is a good practice that is in fact practiced in the ordinary course of events". DeMartino's professional ethics are essentially this, and framed this way, one might say that economists have as a profession developed poor habits.

For the individual economist, good habits involve the cultivation of multiple virtues that coalesce into and feed an adequate practical form of taking responsibility, where responsibility itself is an expressive virtue (for the philosopher, the coalescence demonstrates that responsibility has been taken "seriously" and so passes some test): humility, open-mindedness (perhaps pluralism), leading to learning and contributing to truth-seeking, honesty, integrity and so forth. Listing these immediately seems patronising and accusatory. Yet they are fundamental and, of course, are facilitated or impeded, since conditioned, and so there is a collective responsibility to cultivate conditions appropriate for effective conditioning (the duty we owe each other and the mechanisms we accept that encourage good practice: transparency, accountability, etc.). This is intrinsic to any adequate concept of a profession and of professionalism, including economics. This in turn raises the question of what it is that economics has been inadequate in its development of.

Arguably, a key inadequacy has been the sociality of a social science, and by this I mean the integration, rather than separation, of normativity that has been associated with expertise. Place this in the context of the skill set and toolkit of the economist, and she becomes a policy participant, able to parse out the alternatives of a given situation, but one with a restricted view of what that context is and what is relevant to it. This can readily provide technical support for "there is no alternative" policy frameworks. Moreover, even if it seems to be more open to possibilities, these can be of limited scope in terms of what can be done or what should be considered. For example, fiscal responsibility is a loaded term rooted in a whole set of commitments and understandings. Amongst other things, it conditions approaches to associated issues with equally loaded language use, including, as Dean Baker argues, "entitlements" when referring to Social Security and Medicare in the US system.

Clearly, these are deeply normative issues about which it is possible to disagree. The point is that the nature of expertise in economics can preconfigure how discourse is dominated prior to any disagreement being played out. This is important to keep in mind when thinking about what it means to be responsible as an economist and what it means for economics to be a social science. It creates tensions and problems for any articulation. For example, Krugman has to reconcile his "proud neoclassicism" with social equity. This is not impossible, but it is awkward because his values are in addition to what constitutes economics as economics rather than integral to what it means for economics to be social. Andrew Sayer expresses some of this within the (quasi) naturalistic ethical tradition:

> It seems that becoming a social scientist involves learning to adopt this distanced relation to social life, perhaps so as to be more objective as if we could be more objective by ignoring part of the object. . . . Values and objectivity need not be inversely related. For many social scientists, assessing well-being is a step too far, a dangerous importation of the researcher's own values. But well-being and ill-being are indeed states of being, not merely subjective value-judgements. . . . The very assumption that judgements of value and objectivity don't mix – an assumption that is sometimes built into the definition of "objectivity" – is a misconception. . . . How people can live together is not merely a matter of coordination of the actions of different individuals by means of conventions, like deciding which side of the road to drive on, but a matter of considering people's capacities for flourishing and susceptibilities to harm and suffering. . . . I have often encountered the strange idea that values are not only subjective but synonymous with "bias" or distortion. It is further assumed that they are personal biases that one ideally should confess to, so that others will at least be able to "take them into account", that is, *discount* them. . . . As social scientific spectators we tend to talk about behaviour in terms of what *explains* it, usually by reference to existing circumstances and meanings, but as participants, we tend to *justify* what we do, and implicitly invite others to accept or reject our justification.
>
> (2011: 6–11)

One might argue that well-being is just one way to pose the problem of integration for a normative social science. Perhaps this is so. But it is a fundamental one in terms of responsible intervention. It ripples outwards to issues that bring into question basic facets of how economics is currently conceived, and this is a contemporary matter of controversy that economics could do more to address, rather than evade, and which is centrally policy related in the most fundamental way: how should we/can we live?

The core focus of mainstream economics has configured around relative scarcity and decision sets and has then addressed activity at the margin to seek out optimums implicitly assumed to be reproducible in perpetuity (subject to shocks). For ecological economists, speaking on behalf of the planet, this is spectacularly irresponsible. Most recently, Kate Raworth has sought to synthesise a new framing for economics that mediates between ecological limits and well-being based on her *Doughnut Economics* metaphor (2017). This is an intervention within economics that contests the form of authority that economics has acquired. It is an attempt to transform what it means to speak as an economist and to reposition economics as policy relevant, though one might argue the position taken on growth is agnostic-complacent.

Conclusion

I began this chapter by noting that it is widely agreed that economists disagree, but it is also acknowledged that they do so according to common commitments, and that economists take it as a given that the role of the economist extends to intervention in public discourse and public policy. In this chapter, I have argued that in order to place themselves in a position to take responsibility as intervenors or policy contributors, economists must first reconsider what it means to be expert and what a social science is and can be. There is a great deal more to say that space does not allow. But it seems to me that these are primary. Without them, economics cannot address its adequacy as knowledge, its competency in research and its claims to policy credibility. It cannot be consistently capable of exercising the virtues that lead to dialogue in a democratic society regarding how we can and want to live, which are fundamental to any responsible social science. Of course, one might respond that this is just one more example of an economist leveraging expertise and not knowing when to shut up, and perhaps the only response to that is silence.

Notes

1 This is difficult to avoid when dealing with matters basic to the way we live, and the point applies no less to myself than others (e.g. Morgan, 2017; Morgan and Sheehan, 2015). However, the argument here concerns how the inclination is prompted, positioned and directed rather than merely that it exists, including how it is recognised, reconciled or perhaps limited. For example, Varian claims that the fundamental "attraction and the promise of economics is that it claims to describe policies that will improve peoples' lives" (Varian, 1997: 486), and that economics is a "policy science" where theory and research should be judged according to their contribution to effective policy, from

which he infers that the methodological context of comparison for economics should be engineering, not physics. Clearly, this is itself open to dispute (see Zouboulaki, 2017, and later sections).

2 For a sense of the range of methodological and philosophical critique and argument (a matter that overlaps with the drive to intervene), see Colander and Su (2018); Lawson (2017); Boumans and Davis (2016); Fine (2013); Mäki (2001); McCloskey (1998); and Caldwell (1994). For sociology, including pedagogy, see, for example, Fourcade (2009), Fourcade et al. (2015); Mearman et al. (2018a, 2018b); Morgan (2015); Negru (2010); and Colander (2009).

3 Arrogation often has negative connotations, but its root is to claim for oneself, and its form flows from the absence of clear articulated justification, rather than necessarily deceit or subversion, since these are matters of how and what is arrogated and to what effect.

4 For example, both McKeon and Ricoeur explore the etymology of the term and its diversity, but McKeon essentially sets out to find some common aspects, and also suggests that philosophers should pay more attention to the social reality of the term's use (the fact of responsibility); whilst Ricoeur places greater emphasis on the transitions in its dominant modes of use (political, cultural, moral and juridical) with reference to language and power.

5 Including via the self-awareness inherent to the acknowledgement "I *was* irresponsible", which acts as apology where fault or blame is attributed.

6 Whether one agrees with Friedman or not, there is a great deal more nuance to Friedman's *Capitalism and Freedom* than can be provided here or is distilled in the aphorism "the business of business is business", as a means to summarise his 1970 *New York Times Magazine* article.

7 It would seem incompatible with a human sense of past, present and future, able to reflect and plan in terms of these, and where reasons for acting are possible within a broader milieu of effective and material causation. The powers and capacities of humans and the constitution of society would not make sense.

8 For example, Colander's 'Creating humble economists: a code of ethics for economists' appears in Colander and Su (2018); DeMartino and McCloskey (2016). An ad hoc committee was formed by the AEA in October 2017 to explore the possibility of a code of professional conduct and published an interim report and draft code in January 2018 with an emphasis on promoting integrity, transparency, non-discrimination and free expression of ideas (that is, equality and plurality; arguably, this will suffer, according to DeMartino's (2013), critique): www.aeaweb.org/resources/member-docs/draft-code-of-conduct.

9 Similar points have been made about game theory and also neuroeconomics (as neuroscientists acknowledge they can scan the brain but not enter the mind, there is no easy mapping of thought, action, location, illness, etc.).

10 This tends to affect development and the nature of commensuration. For example, in a retrospective, Robert Shiller uses Samuelson as a mediating figure and states, "The distinctions between neoclassical and behavioral finance have therefore been exaggerated. Behavioral finance is not wholly different from neoclassical finance. . . . [Its models share some rules for construction, but] the best way to describe the difference is that behavioral finance is more eclectic, more willing to learn from other social sciences and less concerned about elegance of models and more with the evidence that they describe actual human behavior" (Shiller, 2006: 4). The question then is the degree to which common points of departure and understandings affect the adequacy of both neoclassical and behavioural finance.

11 Argument here tracks a moving target. The claim that economics is in crisis is not new; it has recurred many times, but with familiar themes, and timing matters with regard to how persuasive different stances on this are. In 1986, McCloskey stated, as part of an argument that methodology would be unlikely to provide scientific advance (whilst

rhetorical awareness would improve communication and the conversation of economics), "Economics at present is, in fact, moderately well off. It may be sleep walking in its rhetoric, but it seems to know in any case approximately where to step. The criticism of economics for being 'too mathematical' or 'too static' or 'too bourgeois' are [*sic*] not very persuasive" (1986: 174).

12 Ambivalence is not the same as resolution, and this is also a problem of long standing. Robbins stated (as a matter of contemporary description rather than unequivocal approval – something that is often forgotten), "Economics is not concerned at all with ends *as such*. It is concerned with ends insofar as they affect the disposition of means. It takes the ends as given scales of relative valuation and enquires what consequences follow in regard to certain aspects of behavior" (1932: 29). However, Kenneth Boulding notes both "the economist's duty is to raise his voice in defence of the proposition that *if resources are limited, what goes to one thing must be withdrawn from another*" (1958: 101, italics in original) and "no economist of any reputation has managed to construct an economics so bloodless as to be utterly indifferent to the ends of the system which it describes. All the great schools . . . have had definite views on the objectives of economic life and policy" (1958: 105).

13 I thank Philip George for this source; it is available at http://web.mit.edu/krugman/ www/evolute.html.

14 And some resemblance to Jacob Viner's philosophically unsatisfactory definition of economics as "what economists do" (see Buchanan, 1979).

15 Consider how this functions to restrict the degree and the way in which economists can be held responsible for the GFC in the context, for example, of Barack Obama's original fighting talk when endorsing the Volcker Rule that would become part of Dodd-Frank: "I welcome constructive input from folks in the financial sector. But what we've seen so far, in recent weeks, is an army of industry lobbyists from Wall Street descending on Capitol Hill to try and block basic and common-sense rules of the road that would protect our economy and the American people. So if these folks want a fight, it's a fight I'm ready to have. And my resolve is only strengthened when I see a return to old practices at some of the very firms fighting reform; and when I see soaring profits and obscene bonuses at some of the very firms claiming that they can't lend more to small business, they can't keep credit card rates low, they can't pay a fee to refund taxpayers for the bailout without passing on the cost to shareholders or customers – that's the claims they're making. It's exactly this kind of irresponsibility that makes clear reform is necessary" (Obama, 2010). Obama, of course, ultimately delivered considerably less in terms of effective change than seemed to be implicit in his early criticism of finance.

16 This variety of intervention can be far-reaching, though no less disputable for that, as, for example, is the case with Colander and Kupers' *Complexity and the Art of Public Policy* (2014), or it can be small scale (see, for example, Morgan and Patomäki, 2017).

References

AEA. (2018) 'Draft AEA code of professional conduct', January 5th www.aeaweb.org/ resources/member-docs/draft-code-of-conduct

Bernanke, B. (2010) 'Implications of the financial crisis for economics', speech delivered September 24th, Princeton University, Federal Reserve: www.federalreserve.gov/newsev ents/speech/bernanke20100924a.htm

Blok, V. (2013) 'The power of speech acts: Reflections on a performative concept of ethical oaths in economics and business', *Review of Social Economy* 71(2): 187–208.

Boulding, K. (1958) *The Skills of the Economist* London: Hamish Hamilton.

Boumans, M. and Davis, J. (2016) *Economic Methodology* Basingstoke: Palgrave Macmillan, second edition.

Buchanan, J. (1979) *What Should Economists Do?* Indianapolis: Liberty Press.

Caballero, R. (2010) 'Macroeconomics after the crisis: Time to deal with the pretence-of-knowledge syndrome', *Journal of Economic Perspectives* 24(4): 85–102.

Caldwell, B. (1994) *Beyond Positivism* London: Routledge, revised edition.

Campbell-Verduyn, M. (2017) *Professional Authority After the Global Financial Crisis* Basingstoke: Palgrave Macmillan.

Cartwright, N. and Davis, J. (2016) 'Economics as science,' pp. 43–55 in Skidelsky, R. and Craig, N. editors, *Who Runs the Economy?* Basingstoke: Palgrave Macmillan.

Colander, D. (2009) *The Making of an Economist Redux* Princeton: Princeton University Press.

Colander, D. and Kupers, R. (2014) *Complexity and the Art of Public Policy: Solving Society's Problems from the Bottom Up* Princeton: Princeton University Press.

Colander, D. and Su. H. C. (2018) *How Economics Should Be Done: Essays on the Art and craft of Economics* Cheltenham: Edward Elgar.

Colledge, B., Morgan, J. and Tench, R. (2014) 'The concept(s) of trust in late modernity, the relevance of realist social theory', *Journal for the Theory of Social Behaviour* 44(4): 481–503.

Davis, J. and Dolfsma, W. editors (2015) *Elgar Companion to Social Economics* Cheltenham: Edward Elgar, second edition.

DeMartino, G. (2011) *The Economists Oath: On the Need for and Content of Professional Economic Ethics* Oxford: Oxford University Press.

DeMartino, G. (2013) 'Epistemic aspects of economic practice and the need for professional economic ethics', *Review of Social Economy* 71(2): 166–186.

DeMartino, G. and McCloskey, D. editors (2016) *The Oxford Handbook of Professional Economic Ethics* Oxford: Oxford University Press.

Fingarette, H. (2004) *Mapping Responsibility: Explorations in Mind, Law, Myth and Culture* Chicago: Open Court.

Fine, B. (2013) 'Economics: Unfit for Purpose', *Review of Social Economy* 71(3): 373–389.

Fourcade, M. (2009) *Economists and Societies* Princeton: Princeton University Press.

Fourcade, M., Ollion, E. and Algan, Y. (2015) 'The superiority of economists', *Journal of Economic Perspectives* 29(1): 89–114.

Krugman, Paul (1996) *What Economists Can Learn from Evolutionary Theorists* Talk: European Association for Evolutionary Political Economy, November.

Lawson, T. (2015) *Essays on the Nature and State of Modern Economics* London: Routledge.

Lawson, T. (2017) 'What is wrong with modern economics, and why does it stay wrong?' *Journal of Australian Political Economy* 80: 26–42.

Mäki, U. editor (2001) *The Economic World View* Cambridge: Cambridge University Press.

Mankiw, G. and Taylor, M. (2014) *Economics* Andover: Cengage Learning, third edition.

McCloskey, D. (1998 [1986]) *The Rhetoric of Economics* Madison: University of Wisconsin, second edition [first edition].

McKeon, R. (1957) 'The development and the significance of the concept of responsibility', *Revue Internationale de Philosophie* 11(39): 3–32.

Mearman, A., Berger, S. and Guizzo, D. (2018a) 'Whither political economy? Evaluating the CORE project as a response to calls for change in economics teaching', *Review of Political Economy* 30(2): 1–19.

Mearman, A., Berger, S. and Guizzo, D. (2018b) 'Is UK economics teaching changing? Evaluating the new subject benchmark statement', *Review of Social Economy* 76(3): 377–396.

Milonakis, D. (2017) 'Formalising economics: Social change, values, mechanics and mathematics in economics discourse', *Cambridge Journal of Economics* 41(5): 1367–1390.

Morgan, J. (2015) 'Is economics responding to critique? What do the UK 2015 QAA Subject Benchmarks indicate?' *Review of Political Economy* 27(4): 518–538.

Morgan, J. (2017) 'Taxing the powerful, the rise of populism and the crisis in Europe: The case for the EU Common Consolidated Corporate Tax Base,' *International Politics* 54(5): 533–551.

Morgan, J. and Negru, I. (2012) 'The Austrian perspective on the global financial crisis: A critique', *Economic Issues* 17(2): 27–55.

Morgan, J. and Patomäki, H. (2017) 'Contrast explanation in economics: Its context, meaning, and potential', *Cambridge Journal of Economics* 41(5): 1391–1418.

Morgan, J. and Sheehan, B. (2015) 'Has reform of global finance been misconceived? Policy documents, and the Volcker Rule', *Globalizations* 12(5): 695–709.

Morgan, M. (2012) *The World in the Model: How Economists Work and Think* Cambridge: Cambridge University Press.

Negru, I. (2010) 'Plurality to pluralism in economics pedagogy: The role of critical thinking', *International Journal of Pluralism and Economics Education* 1(3): 185–193.

Obama. B. (2010) *Remarks by the President on Financial Reform* The White House Office of the Press Secretary, January 21st.

Raworth, K. (2017) *Doughnut Economics* London: Penguin.

Reiersen, J. (2017) 'Trust as belief or behaviour?' *Review of Social Economy* 75(4): 434–453.

Ricoeur, P. (2000) 'The concept of responsibility: An essay in semantic analysis', pp. 11–36 in Ricoeur, P. editor *The Just* Chicago: Chicago University Press.

Robbins, L. (1932) *An Essay on the Nature and Significance of Economic Science* London: Palgrave Macmillan.

Rodrik, D. (2015) *Economics Rules: The Rights and Wrongs of the Dismal Science* London: Norton.

Sandel, M. (2013) 'Market reasoning as moral reasoning: Why economists should re-engage with political philosophy', *Journal of Economic Perspectives* 27(4): 121–140.

Sayer, A. (2011) *Why Things Matter to People: Social Science, Values and Ethical Life* Cambridge: Cambridge University Press.

Shiller, R. (2006) 'Tools for financial innovation: Neoclassical versus behavioural finance', *The Financial Review* 41(1): 1–8.

Syll, L. (2016) *On the Use and Misuse of Theories and Models in Mainstream Economics* London: College/WEA Books.

Toulmin, S. (1970) *Reason in Ethics* Cambridge: Cambridge University Press.

Varian, H. (1997) 'What use is economic theory?' pp. 108–119 in D'Autume, A. and Cartelier, J. editors *Is Economics Becoming a Hard Science?* Cheltenham: Edward Elgar.

Wilber, C. (2004) 'Ethics and social economics: ASE Presidential Address, January 2004, San Diego, California', *Review of Social Economy* 62(4): 425–439.

Zouboulaki, M. (2017) 'Teaching relevant microeconomics after the global financial crisis', *Real World Economics Review* 82: 47–59.

11 Conclusions

Raising up private Max *U*

Deirdre Nansen McCloskey

Because orthodox economists no longer study philosophy in graduate school, or because the philosophy they might have studied as undergraduates is itself fiercely anti-ethical – a course in symbolic logic, say, or a course in social science methodology beginning and ending with logical positivism c. 1920 – they are thoughtless about ethics. Or, as Mark D. White observes in his chapter in this volume, they have merely two thoughts: Pareto and Kaldor-Hicks.

That is, if *all* relevant people are bettered by a project, it should go through. (But which people are relevant?) Or, much more weakly, if the winners *could* hypothetically compensate the losers, it should go through. (But why "could"? Why not actual compensation?) Kaldor-Hicks, formulated in the 1940s, says, in other words, that if GDP per head goes up, we should celebrate. A lucid exposition of the orthodox argument is a classic article by A. C. Harberger in 1971.

I am not outraged by the orthodox argument, as are many of my leftish friends – for example, many here. The leftists say, "Look at who is hurt by your so-called progress!" An extended example of the left's complaint is an otherwise fine collection of their newspaper articles by the historians Kenneth Pomeranz and Steven Topik, *The World That Trade Created: Society, Culture, and the World Economy 1400 to the Present* (2006). Pomeranz and Topik, honorable men of the left, tell skillful tales of the losers from scores of historical rises in GDP that might satisfy Kaldor-Hicks, if not Pareto. But the book is never about the winners, always about the losers, such as the exploited Central American workers who harvested the fiber used to bind bales in US Midwestern agriculture. It never mentions that the Great Enrichment, 1800 to the present, has increased income per head of the poorest – in Central America too – not by 100 percent, or even 500 percent, but by fully 3,000 percent (McCloskey 2016). Unlike my leftish friends, I am very willing, as was the great Hans Rosling in his posthumous volume in 2018, *Factfulness*, to praise such a commercially tested betterment arising from economic liberalism, considering that it achieved 3,000 percent for the poor (Rosling 2018, pp. 47–74). Yes, buggy whip manufacturers and their skilled workers were hurt by the invention of the automobile. To which I reply, "Not to worry. And if to worry, not to worry too much."

White points out that Kaldor-Hicks is utilitarian and therefore violates the Kantian rule against using up others against their will. Utilitarianism in its crudest form, much favored by economists, merely adds up the dollars . . . uh, interpersonally comparable utils . . . of the community and then goes to lunch. No worries about distribution. But, of course, as the economist Donald Boudreaux regularly points out, it is ethically crazy to say, for example, that the dollar loss to people unemployed by a rise in the minimum wage, such as the people left by the law earning zero dollars instead of positive dollars, is offset in dollars by the lovely gain to the people who go on holding the now higher-paid minimum-wage jobs. Under what ethical system is it acceptable to damage *very* poor people, who are very unskilled, in aid of *somewhat* poor people, who are somewhat skilled? The extreme case is South Africa, in which a high minimum wage sponsored by the Congress of South African Trade Unions leaves millions of non-unionists in unemployment – upwards of 50 percent of them – sitting in huts in the uplands of KwaZulu-Natal. Yet one hears daily from leftish economists just such a calculation of the alleged net benefit from the minimum wage, when they are not busy denying outright the law of demand for hired labor (though affirming it for purchases of cigarettes or sugary drinks). About the unethical outcomes of the minimum wage, they say, "Not to worry."

In the movie *Saving Private Ryan*, a company of seven or so US Army Rangers in the precarious weeks after the 1944 Normandy invasion is put in jeopardy going into a highly contested area in order to seek out and send home a Private Ryan, all of whose three brothers have just been reported killed in action. As one of the company points out diffidently, the expedition makes no utilitarian sense. Seven to one.

Around 1978, the Department of Economics at the University of Chicago was having its weekly luncheon at the Episcopal Theological Seminary cafeteria (amusingly, a few decades later, the expanded Department took over the churchy main building of the by-then-defunct Seminary, making God into mammon). A student of Gary Becker's had determined by regressions across US states that each execution of a convicted murderer prevented seven other murders, and Gary was telling us about it. I objected – admittedly without the ethical clarity I now claim to have achieved – that the government's official execution was not the same thing as a private murder. By permitting executions, among other coarsenings of our society, we honor an all-powerful government. After all, we could deter over-parking by executing the offenders. But execution is not in the same ethical coin as over-parking. Gary turned contemptuous, as he often did in argument. As he strode away carrying his lunch tray, he repeated angrily to me over his shoulder, "Seven to one! Seven to one!" Decades later, Alex Tabarrok had the identical encounter with him over the same issue (Tabarrok 2015). Gary's ethical thinking had not advanced.

True, as in the Trolley Problem in ethical philosophy discussed here by Andrew Mearman and Robert McMaster, sometimes seven to one is ethically decisive. Do you pull the switch between two tracks to divert the runaway trolley to kill the seven people strapped to one track or to kill the one person strapped to the other? By itself in isolation, of course, you choose to kill one, not seven. Or to kill a dog rather than a child. Simple. I remember listening to an interview on the BBC in 1967 with an animal rights advocate of an extreme sort. (Britain has long had such people. The Royal Society for the Prevention of Cruelty to Animals was founded in 1824. The Royal Society for the Prevention of Cruelty to *Children* was not founded in London until 1884. Don't beat your horse. Do beat your child.) The interviewer sought to entrap the animal rights advocate by saying, "Suppose you are speeding in your auto through a country lane on a dark night, impenetrable hedgerows on either side, and you come round a bend at top speed to find to your horror an infant child sitting on one lane of the road and a dog on the other. You have to kill one [thus the Trolley Problem]. Which do you kill?" There was a long silence. Very long. At last the advocate replied, "I hope I never have to face such a choice."

Or consider the example of protection. When the Trump administration imposes tariffs on imported steel because the Secretary of Commerce had once been a flack for the steel industry and because Trump's main adviser on trade is an economist who does not understand any economics, we savvy economists are likely to complain that the jobs saved in steel are far outweighed by the jobs lost in steel-using industries. Seven to one. Kaldor-Hicks. Though utilitarian, it is not an entirely silly argument, rhetorically speaking, considering that the protectionists are the ones who introduced the idea of the number of jobs protected in the first place.

In a typical Kaldor-Hicks calculation, for example, the economist Maximilano Dvorkin of the Federal Reserve Bank of St. Louis reckoned that the US, 2000–2007, lost from competition from China about 800,000 jobs. (It was a tiny fraction, by the way, of the jobs lost from what we all agree were desirable technological change, such as the demise of video stores and the rest of the jobs moved or made obsolete. In those seven years, out of a total labor force of 140 million, such jobs amounted to scores of millions, not a mere 0.8 million.) But according to Dvorkin, trade with China gained on the same account a similar number of *other* US jobs, for a net effect on jobs of zero. (The same is true on a much larger scale of so-called technological unemployment.) And as a result of the lower prices from such reallocation and competition in the China trade, "U.S. consumers gained an average of $260 of extra spending per year for the rest of their lives" (Dvorkin 2017; see also Caliendo et al. 2015). Expressed as a capital sum discounted to the present, free trade with China was like every consumer getting a one-time check for about $5,000. Good, not bad.

Actually, the most striking examples in the present book of unethical behavior by economists arising from utilitarianism and seven to one are not the orthodox and Kaldor-Hicks-besotted development economists whom many of the papers criticize from the left, but the science-besotted, field experiment economists. They are to be criticized not from left or right – both of which are enthusiasts for big government and therefore big violence, in differing forms – but from a liberalism of a society of free people having what Kant called equal dignity. Alice Nicole Sindzingre gives here an excellent survey of the numerous ethical problems involved, and Stephen T. Ziliak and Edward R. Teather-Posadas focus laserlike on the fetish for misapplied statistical significance and dubiously ethical randomized controls.

White mentions at one point that the criterion of all-around win-win, that is, Pareto improvement is seen as the "gold standard" of tests of welfare by economists even though ethically inadequate if lacking an answer to the question of which people are the alleged winners. Similarly, experimental economists such as Esther Duflo at MIT argue that double-blind experiments *on other people, not volunteers*, are the gold standard in medical research and therefore should be so in economics. After all, we need above all to be scientific, understood as exposited in high school chemistry. We are authorized to hurt one group to help another – though of course we do not subject *ourselves* to the experiment. Shades of the minimum wage. The ethical contrast is sharp, with the long history of *self*-experimentation in medicine, such as the courageous junior doctors and other volunteers under Dr. Walter Reed (though not Reed himself) in the 1900 confirmation that yellow fever is spread by mosquitoes (Weisse 2012; Mehra 2009).

In the dismal, if brief, history of field experiments in economics, the worst case so far is described by Ziliak and Teather-Posadas. The field experimenters gave out eyeglasses to Chinese children randomly to "test" whether being able to see Chinese characters affects the speed with which the children learn to read them – as though we didn't already know that children who can't discern characters can't learn to read them (Glewwe et al. 2012). Any normally ethical person regards such an experiment as hideously unethical, using up other people (yet not ourselves) in anti-Kantian fashion. The ethical course is to not do the experiment at all and instead give away the money collected to provide needed glasses to as many Chinese children as you can find. The using up of the near-sighted children who do *not* get the glasses ("the control group") is justified by Kaldor-Hicks, at best, seven to one, seven to one. And most especially it is justified by the juiced-up record of scientific publications by professors of economics at MIT or the University of Minnesota. In medicine, the history of unethical field experiments on involuntary subjects is long. The economists propose now to initiate their own Tuskegee syphilis experiments, sacrificing one for seven. A test: an economist actually, ethically, deeply believes in free international trade when she accepts that *her* ox may be gored, that she may lose some advantage. It is to experiment on oneself, in the style of Sen's "commitment" – that is, an act that *loses* utils or money – that registers thereby its genuine character.

In *Saving Private Ryan*, the problem is solved quite differently than from the outside of our ethical cultures by recourse to a merely utilitarian calculation of seven to one. The leader, played by Tom Hanks, and the rest of the company – and, to the present point, we the audience watching the film – understand that more is at stake. For example, the mission is about the definition of ourselves as humans sympathetic to the grieving mother. It is about our willingness to risk even death to honor such a sympathy. Or it is about being an honorable soldier and obeying honorable orders unto death, as, for example, in 1995 at

Srebrenica, the Dutch battalion charged by NATO with defending the Muslims did not. Honor is about identity. Seven to one is not.

§

The more usual remark against Kaldor-Hicks from the economic left and middle (the illiberal right says simply, "To hell with the losers") is that, after all, Kaldor-Hicks is unethical if the compensation to the losers is not actually paid. The present volume is rich with such remarks, the better to undermine a market economics the authors regard as unethical.

Yet the biggest problem with a Kaldor-Hicks utilitarian defense of a project – to build, say, a new underground railway in London – lies in the very definition of a "project." Every human action is a "project." White concludes that "if compensation is to be taken seriously, it should be incorporated into any proposal submitted to a Kaldor-Hicks test." He notes that "externalities arise from almost any social interaction with overlapping interests." Yes, *every* social interaction entails overlapping interests. If Henry David Thoreau invents new methods to make high-quality pencils, as he in fact did during the 1840s in his father's business, he harms the older makers. If actual compensation is to be paid to them, then every project of every person requires such payment. The Victoria Line, after all, has repercussions, however tiny, on the Isle of Mull.

The absurdity of such a procedure is evident. The point might be called the Boudreaux Reductio ad Absurdum, after the economist I mentioned, Donald Boudreaux of George Mason University, who uses it so often in criticizing schemes of protection. Start with the Paradox of Marketed Bread. No person is an island, entire of herself. Each person is a piece of the continent, a part of the main. That is to say, *every* person's action to buy or not buy, to offer for sale or not, to enter a trade or not, to invent or not, affects someone else in the economy, for better or for worse. If I buy a loaf of bread, someone else cannot have it. Or, to put it another way, my decision to buy the loaf will very slightly raise the price for every other buyer to the exact extent, when summed over all of them, of the price I paid. That's market economics (and the particular point is one I first learned from the great Chinese price theorist, S.N.S. Cheung).

Now the Boudreaux Reductio. Under actual compensation à la Kaldor-Hicks, you should be stopped from buying bread because you impose a tort on others in buying it. Everyone should compensate everyone else for everything, for every human action. As Boudreaux puts the defense to the Reductio: "What no person is free to do is to oblige *others* to subsidize his or her choices. I, for example, should be free to work as a poet but not empowered to force you either directly to buy my poetry or to obstruct your freedom to spend your money on mystery novels, movies, and other items that compete with my poetry" (2018). Compensation entails governmental power against freedom. It is not a voluntary choice within a framework of individual rights. Such compensation, if carried out logically, is unethical.

The terrifying phrase of Sombart's popularized by Schumpeter, "creative destruction," arouses the same fears and the same proposals for protection. Yet it is not "capitalism" that requires creative destruction, *but any progressive economy*. If you don't want innovation to happen and don't want poor people to get rich by the 3,000 percent that they have in Japan and Finland and the rest since 1800, then, fine, we can stick with the old jobs, keeping in their former employment the elevator and telephone operators, the armies of typists on old mechanical Underwoods, grocery stores with a clerk in an apron handing you the can of beans over the counter. But if innovation is to happen – Piggly Wiggly in Memphis in September 1916 initiating the self-service grocery store, or a North Carolina tobacco trucker initiating in 1956 the shipping container – then people, and also the machines and factories owned by the bosses, have to lose their old jobs. Human and physical capital has to reallocate. Of course.

How much? Fully 14% of jobs per year, according to the Department of Labor statistic. That's *every year*, in a progressing economy (see Diamond 2019; Haltiwanger 2011; McCloskey 2017b). It's a startling figure. The monthly labor reports you hear about on the news give the *net* figure – in a good month, 200,000 being the net of new jobs gained from moving or innovation minus the old jobs lost from the same. The gross figure should be more widely known. An improving economy requires the workers and the machines to move, to reallocate, to retrain, to shift, to innovate on a very large scale. Of course.

So the crudely practical problem with compensation and protection and schemes of subsidized retraining by government bureaucrats who do not actually know what the new jobs will be in five years is that we cannot "afford" to compensate 14% of the workforce every year. In a few years, half the workforce would be on the dole, or kept in their old jobs at the old pay, or trained in the wrong new jobs. For that matter, we could try to keep physical capital, too, where it began, directing subsidies to factories and neighborhoods rather than letting the people and factories move as creative destruction requires. It requires it under perfectly planned socialism as much as under commercially tested betterment. Carried out with philosophical consistency, the Boudreaux Reductio would require us to keep shoe manufacturing in Massachusetts as much as coal mining in West Virginia, economy-wide, forever.

The deeper philosophical problem is that the unethical logic of actual compensation and protection violates the rights of others. The problem is that ethics in economics has been thoughtlessly attached to Rousseau's notion of a general will. Deep in left-wing thought and in a good deal of right-wing thought about the economy is the premise, as Isaiah Berlin once put it, that government can accomplish whatever it rationally proposes to do. As has been often observed about leftists even as sweet as was John Rawls, the left has no theory of the behavior of the government. It assumes that the government is a perfect expression of the will of The People. So goes the welfare economics of Abraham Bergson and Paul Samuelson and the public finance of Richard Musgrave and behind them the (mathematically incoherent) goal of the greatest happiness of the greatest number, to be achieved by wise utilitarians in government. The liberals such as James Buchanan do have a theory of government and a good deal of empirical work to back it up. Liberalism has always been a theory against and therefore about coercion. When my left-wing friends, of whom I have many, claim with a knowing smile that in admiring markets I am "ignoring power," I have a way of replying no, dear, it is you who are ignoring power, the power of the monopoly, of violence called a government.

More generally, indeed, the ethical problem among economists is the entire program of social engineering. Jamie Morgan in the present volume is quite right to say that a peculiar "sense of mission and entitlement is built into economics, and this contrasts with sociology and political science" (p. 145). Yet it is not at all controversial among most economists – but should be – to assume that they should be unsleepingly active in devising new ones.

§

In any case, we need something to prevent the Boudreaux Reductio from being ethically required, with the ending of all human progress in science, the arts, or the economy. The usual guard rail is the notion of "rights." As John Stuart Mill put it in *On Liberty*, "Society admits no right, either legal or moral, in the disappointed competitors to immunity from . . . suffering [from successful competition]; and feels called on to interfere only when means of success have been employed which it is contrary to the general interest to permit – namely, fraud or treachery, and force" (1859 [2001], pp. 86–87). An ill-advised and under-capitalized pet store, into which the owner pours his soul, goes under. But he does not get compensation by way of Kaldor-Hicks. In the same neighborhood, a little independent office for immediate health care opens half a block from a branch of the largest hospital chain in Chicago and seems doomed to fail the test of voluntary trade. Although the testing of business ideas in voluntary trade is obviously necessary for betterment in the economy – as it is, too, by non-monetary tests for betterment in art and science and scholarship and would be in a wholly planned socialist economy as well – such failures are deeply sad, if you have the slightest sympathy for human projects, or for humans. Yet we cannot admit a right to subsidy or protection or compensation. The pet store, the health treatment office, the Edsel, Woolworth's, Polaroid, and Pan American Airlines face the same democratic test by trade: do the customers keep coming forward voluntarily? That's all you as the pet store owner or Boudreaux's poet have a right to – the right to let the customers choose you, or not, which is why commercially tested betterment is in its actual practice the most altruistic of systems.

Without such liberal rights to trade with whom we wish, we could all by governmental compulsion backed by the monopoly of violence remain in the same jobs perpetually "protected." Or, with taxes taken by additional state compulsion, we could subsidize new activities without regard to a commercial test by voluntary trade, "creating jobs," as the anti–economic rhetoric has it, venturing into the High Frontier of space, for example, at enormous expense "because no private entity will do it."

Such schemes assume that the government knows better than profit-dependent businesspeople about what customers want or should have. It is the declared premise of the economist Mariana Mazzucato's bestselling book *The Entrepreneurial State: Debunking Public vs. Private Sector Myths* (2015). But consider the possibility that the reason no private entity will venture into the High Frontier is that it makes no sense. If the assumption of governmental wisdom is mistaken, the effect of such venturing is to lower national income. And the schemes assume that there is nothing objectionable about the compulsion required in tax and regulation to do the venturing in the first place.

And anyway, to descend again to crude practical problems, the protective schemes and governmental entrepreneurship seldom work for the welfare of the poor, not to speak of the rest of us. Considering how a government of imperfect people actually behaves in practice, job "protection" and job "creation" regularly fail to achieve their gentle, generous purpose. The political decision-making means that the protections and creations get diverted to favorites. Jobs for the boys and girls running poverty programs. Spending on useless military jets, spread over every congressional district. Premature ventures into the High Frontier. In a society of lords or clan members or Communist Party officials or even voters restricted by inconvenient voting times and picture IDs, the unequal and involuntary rewards generated by sidestepping the commercial test are seized by the privileged. The privileged are good at that.

§

As White summarizes the guard rail of rights, we object to a loss "particularly [he must mean 'only'] if those losses, or harms, involve violations of their rights and are therefore wrongful, regardless of the net utility generated" (p. 78). He quotes Richard Posner (who, like him, misunderstands Ronald Coase's eponymous theorem): "But when transaction costs are prohibitive, the recognition of absolute rights is inefficient" (p. 81). Well, not always.

What exactly are the "rights" that Boudreaux, McCloskey, White, Coase, Posner, and Mill find so lovely? "The homeowner who does not take as much care of his lawn as his neighbors," says White, "is lowering their well-being and possibly their home values but is not violating any widely recognized right of theirs" (p. 83). Well, maybe, but not always.

Note "*widely recognized*." That is the key. The notion of rights is not technological (this being Coase's actual point) but irremediably social. We decide what are rights and what are not. White says, "Individuals are free to act in ways that do not necessarily increase total welfare and may even lower it; this is the sense in which, as Dworkin said, 'rights trump welfare'" (p. 84). Yes, I am free to so act. I can kill my cow just for the fun of it. But wait. Rights do *not* trump welfare in an ethical person – "widely recognized" – a person, for example, raised on a farm who views killing cows for no reason as evil. You have a right to lie in your economic research, but as an ethical person, you will not let yourself do it.

We need to raise up people like that. That is the obvious and simple solution to the ethical formation of economists – not codes or formulas that enshrine utilitarianism or constitutional constrains in black letter law. Neither side – neither the professor of economics standing for absolute utility nor the law professor standing for absolute rights – speaks of the raising up of people. It is the characteristic vice of Western ethical philosophy since Descartes that it takes a fully formed male, Western, philosophically inclined adult, who pays no attention to how people are raised, to consider others or themselves or the transcendent, ethically speaking. Modern Western moral philosophy is peculiarly masculinist and, so to speak, adultist, taking an autonomous, finished adult, preferably a middle-aged and childless bachelor, as the site of philosophizing. Feminists such as Carol Gilligan and her many followers and critics do not forget that we were all once children, and feminists such as Nel Noddings and Annette Baier do not forget that we all came from families.

Some men also do not forget it. Mearman and McMaster here praise the wise economist Kenneth Boulding, who was also a major figure in world Quakerism, for saying, in their words, that "all communities are founded on cultures that provide guidance on right and wrong" (p. 29). That's correct, and the guidance comes from the development of character in family or church or profession – a raising up. It is what the Blessed Adam Smith was about in his other book, *The Theory of Moral Sentiments*.

The philosophies of the Scholastics and of the Greeks and Romans, and of Confucians in China and of Hindus and Buddhists in South Asia, all treat raising up as crucial. The hero of the *Mahabharata*, the virtuous if flawed Yudhishthira, is asked by the mother of the Pandavas, "Why be good?" He replies, "Were *dharma* ['virtue,' among other meanings] to be fruitless. . . [people] would live like cattle" (Das 2009, p. 73). Precisely. To be raised up as human is to put on the vestments of ethics. The cynical economist will scorn, but in his actual human life, he puts them on without thinking. Yudhishthira's reply is exactly paralleled by Cicero lambasting the Epicureans – the ancient Mediterranean's version of Max U economists – as "those men who in the manner of cattle [*pecudum ritu*, literally, 'by the cattle's rite'] refer everything to pleasure" and who "with even less humanity . . . say that friendships are to be sought for protection and aid, not for caring" (Cicero 44 BCE, 32). Consult Gary Becker. The method of ethical philosophy since Hobbes has been to abandon the ancient tradition of the virtues and their program of raising a child to an ethical adult, and instead to judge the goodness or badness of actions from afar, by rule and formula. What Hobbes denied, and has been denied since by every ethicist eager to stand in judgment of actions, is that character matters and is more than a calculation of cost and benefit, even socially.

There is a way of rescuing Kaldor-Hicks that leads it in a better and more liberal direction, ultimately to character. As argued by the economists John

Harsanyi, James Buchanan, and Gordon Tullock, and the economics-influenced philosopher John Rawls, the relevant question is which society you would rather enter at birth, without knowing where in it you would end up. Choose one in which all jobs are protected, bureaucrats decide who gets the limited amount of special subsidies, journalists direct attention always to the losers and never to the winners, and the economy slides, as South Africa has, into stagnation and youth unemployment. Or choose one in which labor laws are flexible, individual workers decide their futures, journalists know some economics, and the economy lifts up the poorest among us.

The male economists are telling us an ethical story. It suggests a more radical story. Carol Gilligan long ago pointed out the male character of stories of ethical development. A standard story in tests of ethical development is the Dying Wife. A man's wife is dying of a treatable disease, but he does not have the money to buy the drug that can save her. Is he ethical to break into the drugstore and steal it? The male way of answering the question is to turn to an ethical formula, such as the one Kant proposed – in which case, no, he would not break in. But girls and women answer in a more richly narrative way. They want to know what relationship the man and wife had, what kind of a person the druggist is, what the surrounding society is like. It's not the slam bam thank you ma'am type of rules such as the categorical imperative.

We need ethical raising up, not more ruminations on slam-bang formulas.

§

What sort of ethical raising up? It is implausible to suppose that one can actually extract full justice for the handicapped, the globally poor, or the animals from a starting point that does not already include love of others and full justice, at the start, in some veiled form if you wish, as a Rawlsian or Buchananite tests before birth.

Political and economic philosophy needs to be done with all seven of the virtues, not merely with some cleverly axiomatized subset. To characterize people with one or another of the boys' own "models," said since Hobbes in 1651 to suffice for theories of justice or politics, will not do. Characterizing humans as Prudent Only, or even as prudent and just, with love of others tacked on, will not do. People also have identities (faith) and projects (hope), for which they need courage and temperance, those self-disciplining virtues. And they all have some version of transcendent love – the connection with God, the traditional object, though the worship of science or humanity or the revolution or the environment or art or rational choice models in political science has provided modern substitutes for Christianized *agape*.

And raising up through edifying stories and modeling of good mentors the entire set of seven virtues is necessary to get the ethical project going in the first place. This is important. Full human beings – not saints, but people in possession of their own wacky and personal and, alas, often idiotic versions of all seven human virtues and corresponding vices – are the only beings who would be *interested* in forming a good human society.

To put it still another way, suppose you have in mind to make fully flourishing human beings (or fully flourishing living beings *tout court*, if you include the animals, and even the trees). If this is your end, namely, a society consisting of such beings, then your social-scientific means must, as the philosopher Martha Nussbaum says, 'focus on ethical norms from the start' (Nussbaum 2006). You have to put the little rabbits of the ethics of the food society, or a good economics profession, into the hat in order to magically draw them out. Self-interest, prudence, rationality, Max *U* won't suffice. In order to have a society that shows all of them – prudence, justice, love, faith, hope, courage, and temperance – you need to arrange to have people who are prudent, just, loving, faithful, hopeful, courageous, and temperate "from the start."

The "start" is called "childhood." A political/economic philosophy needs to focus on how we get in the first place the people who are prudent, just, loving, etc., and who therefore would *care* about the capabilities of good health, emotional attachment, affiliation, etc., or about the appropriate constitutional changes to obviate prisoners' dilemmas, or about the categorical imperative, or about the greatest happiness. This is what feminist economics has been saying now for four decades and what also comes out of some development [note the word] economics, and even, reluctantly but persistently and embarrassingly, out of such unpromising-looking fields, often officially hostile to the slightest concern with ethics, as game theory, experimental economics, behavioral economics, realist international relations, the new institutionalism, and constitutional political economy.

The excellent little primer on ethics by the late James Rachels begins with a "minimum conception of morality" underlying any ethical system whatsoever. In describing "the conscientious moral agent" at which the analysis must begin, Rachels selects unconsciously from the seven virtues. The conscientious moral agent will be in part "someone who is concerned [that is, who has love, connection] impartially [who has justice] with the interests [having prudence to discover these] of everyone who is affected [justice, love, faith] . . .; who carefully sifts facts [prudence again, with temperance] . . .; who is willing to 'listen to reason' [justice plus temperance = humility] . . .; and who, finally, is willing to act on the results [courage]" (Rachels 1999, p. 19). Since all this is quite an arduous task, a *bonum arduum*, as Aquinas put it, a hard-to-achieve good, he'd better have hope too.

That is, ethics, even the political ethics we call political theory, must *start* from an ethical person imagined as The Ethicist or The Political Theorist – who turns out to have all seven of the Western virtues. The little rabbits are already in the hat. Think of how impossible it would be to come to the conclusions of Kantian or utilitarian or Sen-Nussbaum or Buchanan-Tullock political ethics if The Ethicist or The Theorist did not *already* have the character Rachels praises of concern, impartiality, carefulness, humility, courage, and so forth. Frankly, my dear, he wouldn't give a damn.

Mark White, in an earlier essay, arrived at a similar conclusion. He said that a Kantian ethical theory posits a prudential and an ethical self, the choice between them being determined by a probability, p, that one has the strength of character to follow the ethical self. This seems to fit Kant, and as White pointed out, it also fits the philosopher John Searle's notion of a "gap" in decision-making allowing for free will. One is reminded, too, of Stuart Hampshire's account of free will.

But White realizes that something is fishy. "Is the probability distribution, representing one's character, exogenously given? Though that would make things much simpler, I should think not; it is crafted by our upbringing, and even to adulthood one can act to improve his character. Of course, this... [suggests] the question: to what goal or end does one improve character?" His reply is that "in the Kantian model ... we assume that a rational agent's true goal is to be moral" (White 2005, p. 15). But that is the goal of being a virtuous person. His argument begs the question – though in this field we are going to find that good is good pretty much every time.

Annette Baier made a related point about characteristically male ethical theories: "Their version of the justified list of obligations does not ensure the proper care of the young and so does nothing to ensure the stability of the morality in question" (1994, p. 6). It is not merely a matter of demography. It is a matter of more fundamental reproduction, as the Marxists say. Somehow the conscientious moral agent assumed in the theories of Descartes and Kant and Bentham and Buchanan and Rawls and Nussbaum must appear on the scene and must keep appearing generation after generation. "The virtue of being a *loving* parent," Baier says, "must supplement the natural duties and the obligations of [mere] justice, if the society is to last beyond the first generation." Imagine a human society with *no* loving parents. We have examples in children war-torn and impoverished, boy soldiers or girl prostitutes. One worries – perhaps it is not so – that the outlook for them becoming conscientious moral agents, and making a society in which humans (or trees, for that matter) can flourish, is not very good.

The intellectual tradition of economists since Bentham and of political scientists since Hobbes and recently since Rawls does *not* wish to acknowledge – especially at the start – all the virtues in a flourishing being. It wants to start simply with a nearly empty hat, such as "Pareto optimality," and then pull from it a complex ethical world. It wants to reduce the virtues to one, ideally the virtue of prudence, and derive the other virtues, such as a just polity, from the prudence. It does not want to talk about how we arrange to have on the scene in the first place an ethical actor who by reason of her upbringing or her ongoing ethical deliberations wishes the greatest happiness for the greatest number, or the application of the categorical imperative, or the following of constitutional instructions from behind a veil of ignorance.

It hasn't worked, not at all, this boy's game, and it's time that economists and political theorists admitted so. So-called "welfare economics" has recently shown some faint stirrings of complexity in ethical thought, as in the works of Amartya Sen, and more in the works of younger economists and philosophers inspired by his overcautious forays. But most academic economists and political theorists, such as Buchanan and Nussbaum, continue working the magician's hat.

The hat does not contain a living theory of moral sentiments. Instead of a nice set of seven cuddly rabbits, the theorists have supplied the hat with a large, Victorian, utilitarian parrot, stuffed and mounted and fitted with marble eyes. Sen complained of the "lack of interest that welfare economics has had in any kind of complex ethical theory," and added, "It is arguable that [utilitarianism and] . . . Pareto efficiency have appealed particularly because they have not especially taxed the ethical imagination of the conventional economist" (1987, p. 50). Time to give the dead parrot back to the pet store – though the economist/salesman will no doubt keep on insisting that the utilitarian parrot is actually alive, that Pareto optimality will suffice, or at worst Kaldor-Hicks, that though the parrot *appears* to be dead, kaput, over, a former parrot, in fact he's merely pining for the fjords.

Nor is any one-virtue ethic going to do. Adam Smith writes in a well-known passage that if *love* for our fellow humans was all we had to depend on, then the extermination of the Chinese would trouble us less, really, than the loss of a little finger (Smith 1759 [1790], p. 136; cf. Rousseau 1755, p. 121). It takes a sense of abstract propriety, he argued, a virtue separated from love and not translatable into it, to want to give a damn for a foreign people whom you have never seen and whom you can never love. The moral sentiment impels the man within to scold a self that is so very selfish as to save the finger rather than the entire race of Chinese. "What is it," he asks, "which prompts the generous upon all occasions and the mean upon many to sacrifice their own interests to the greater interests of others? It is not . . . that feeble spark of benevolence. . . . It is reason, principle, conscience, the inhabitant of the breast. . . . The natural misrepresentations of self-love can be corrected only by the eye of this impartial spectator" (Smith 1759/90, pp. 308–313).[1]

But the same can be said of the other virtues. Take the actual person of the economist James Buchanan as a case in point. It takes a character of hope, which Buchanan actually had on his better days, to have an interest in constitutional reform. It takes a character of faith to worry about the corruptions of Me-ism in American society. It takes a character of courage to stand against the Northeastern establishment in intellectual life.

In other words, the civic republican notion that the way to have a good society is to arrange somehow to have a bunch of good people – which in the light of invisible hand liberalism seems primitive and moralistic and insufficiently social-scientific – turns out to be much more plausible and scientific than we 18th-century liberals thought. It is as true of a scientific society such as economics as of the wider society. The more seriously we take full human flourishing, the more true becomes Orwell's apology for Dickens' ethic: "'If men would behave decently the world would be decent' is not such a platitude as it sounds" (1940, pp. 150–151).

In still other words, an economics or political theory that takes human flourishing seriously should start with teaching in sing and in story the virtues – and finish with them, too, since they end up pretty much the same, and that is what we want in humans raised from childhood. To put it in terms that begin to edge toward Virginia Political Economy, the seven virtues are what a flourishing individual wants for herself. They are what she chooses, when she has the capability to choose. Maybe before she is born.

§

What to do, then, for economics? Answer: raise ethical men and women, some of whom become economists. We are not doing so now in the education of economists.

Mearman and McMaster observe that in economics, the "degree courses, at best, begin with a brief discussion of the distinction between positive and normative, and an eschewal of the latter" (p. 24). Some years ago, the Department of Economics at Indiana University required all entering graduate students to read Milton Friedman's article on positive economics *and nothing else*. Friedman once told me that he regretted writing the article. Jamie Morgan attacks, as many do, "Friedman's amorality of markets and of business" (p. 148) supposedly expressed in his famous 1970 *New York Times Magazine* essay. But Morgan needs to actually read the text, or the life. Most people who have expressed shock or pleasure at Milton's article have not noticed that he adds a side constraint to the manager's fiduciary duty to the stockholders: "make as much money as possible *while conforming to the basic rules of the society, both those embodied in law and those embodied in ethical custom*" (Friedman 1970, p. 33, emphasis added). Yet Morgan is correct that "Friedman's argument invokes: amorality" (p. 148) was clearly not his intent, though I admit it had this effect. An instance is the astonishingly amoral essay by Werner Erhard and Michael C. Jensen (McCloskey 2017a).

Milton's essay on positive economics to the contrary, graduate students, and undergraduates, too, need to be told to be as ethically driven as Milton actually was as a man and an economist. What's needed is an ethical change of attitude, or character, as George DeMartino puts it, "a practice of critical inquiry into the myriad ethical questions that arise in the context of and as a consequence of economic practice." "Professional ethics," he continues, "is not in the first instance about preventing crooks, frauds, and charlatans from acting badly" (p. 10). It's about ordinary life. It's not about incentives, as many economists instinctively suppose. It's about ethics at home. Shame.

If you want a good career, of course, you can follow the shameless script of James Watson in *The Double Helix*. For example, you can steal "Rosy" Franklin's x-rays. You can use tests of se statistical significance even though you know they're silly. "A generation of graduate students," wrote Anne Sayre (in her luminous biography of Franklin) about Watson's teaching, "learned a lesson: the old morality is dead, and they had . . . been told about its demise by . . . an up-to-date hero who clearly know more about how science was acceptably 'done' than the old-fashioned types who prattled about 'ethics'" (1975, p. 19). To the contrary, say the older economists, such as Ronald Coase (b. 1910): "My mother taught me to be honest and truthful" (1994, p. 190). In the same volume, James Buchanan (b. 1919) speaks of a teacher in graduate school who "instilled in me the moral standards of the research process, . . . something that seems so often absent in the training of economists of the post-war decades" (1987, p. 139). That's about all the methodological advice we can safely handle. As teachers of writing put it, "Be good, and then write naturally." Or as Cato the Elder said, the rhetorician is "the good man speaking skillfully." The good economist is the good person speaking intelligently about the economy.

All right, how? Wim Groot and Henriette Maassen van den Brink quote Daniel Hamermesh, who notes that "professors in public universities – the large majority of economists [he may on this be wrong: non-academic economists are numerous] – have a direct obligation to use their knowledge on a broader stage: They are paid by the public, and it behoves them to try to educate the entire public" (p. 135). (Note the ethical evocation of the cash nexus even in the profession itself.) The responsibility is taken more seriously by Continental professors. I remember seeing once a complete bibliography for the great Swedish economists of a century ago – Wicksell, Heckscher, Ohlin, Cassel, as I recall – and being startled by how much educating of the entire public they all did, each publishing a journalistic piece once every fortnight or so over their careers.

The responsibility should not be about "incentives." University professors in countries like the US or the Netherlands or Sweden make enough to put that consideration aside. The fellow Dutch economist of Groot and Maassen van den Brink, Arjo Klamer, another student of Joop Klant, does so, and contributes deeply and eloquently to the public discussion (Klamer 2006, 2016). The point is professional responsibility, not vanity or, as Groot and Maassen van den Brink say, "instant gratification." After a dozen or so appearances on the national stage, the vanity and gratification wear out. One does it for the good of one's fellow citizens.

Morgan wisely turns to the notion of "responsibility" in the rhetoricians Paul Ricoeur and Richard McKeon. These are issues of raising up. Responsibility viewed in virtue-ethical terms is something learned, and the word itself is an especially modern concept – before it was simply thought of as ethical education (education being literally *ex-ducere*, to lead out of evil and ignorance). The American historian Thomas Haskell wrote in 1999 a startling essay chronicling the new prominence of the word in a commercial America in the 18th and 19th centuries. The OED gives 1787 as the earliest quotation of "responsibility" in one of its modern senses, as merely accepting factually that one has done such and such, by Alexander Hamilton in *The Federalist Papers*, and shortly thereafter by Edmund Burke. Haskell notes that it was used much earlier in law in the sense of 'being required to respond to a legal action.' Such a "responsible" person, meaning "liable to be called to [legal] account" (sense 3a), occurs as early as 1643. The OED's earliest quotation for the favorable ethical meaning, the dominant modern sense, "morally accountable for one's actions; capable of rational conduct" (sense 3b), is as late as 1836 – which is Haskell's point, though he dates it a little earlier. The linking of "responsibility" with the market-like word "accountability" occurs in the first instance of "accountability" detected by Haskell in 1794, in Samuel Williams's *Natural and Civil History of Vermont*: "No mutual checks and balances, accountability and responsibility" (p. 169). Raise us up to responsibility, in a market or in a science of markets.

Mearman and McMaster suggest that we "become more pluralist by incorporating heterodox economics perspectives" (p. 27). Yes, we should. The medieval motto was *Audite et alteram partem*, listen even to the other side. It is especially the ethical responsibility of a scholar and scientist to listen to the other side, though most, disgracefully, do not. Mearman and McMaster say, following DeMartino, that to avoid harm "requires economists to 'integrate themselves deeply' into communities'" (p. 31). Yes. But it's not enough to speak to the unemployed. You need to understand the wider system. (I offer free advice: to understand it, you'll do better to start with Marshall than with Marx.) Jamie Morgan notes that the economic "mainstream [I prefer to call it 'orthodox' or 'Samuelsonian'] exhibits a kind of diffident diversity, impatient of pluralism" (p. 145), or of ethical considerations, an extreme example of which is Anne Krueger's astonishingly careless and slanted review in the *Journal of Economic Literature* of the collection edited by DeMartino and me (mainly, I report, by George). Anne partially apologized. Only partially.

So, yes, let the orthodox listen. But the left needs to follow its own advice. Mearman and McMaster urge "deployment of pluralism, not least from a duty of care for students" (p. 40). But I have long observed that many heterodox economists do not actually know price theory, the core of liberal economics. They think they do because they have been made to read Mas-Collel and the like. But they don't. I invite them to open *The Applied Theory of Price* randomly (it is available free on my website: no excuses) and see if they can answer any of the five hundred worked problems there.

A startling example of the left not understanding what it is criticizing is the way Thomas Piketty botches the response of supply to increasing scarcity on the bottom of page 6 of the English translation of *Capital in the Twenty-First Century*. If you don't understand that increasing scarcity entices new entrants into an industry, you do not understand much about a market economy. Craig Duckworth says that "the responsible economist must, then, not only *think like an economist* but must also reflect on what it means to think like an economist" (p. 72). I certainly agree. Duckworth does not want it narrowed to technicalities. Nor do I. And yet. . . . A good many unassuming technicalities are not understood even by many economists – for example, that the balance of payments is meaningless, that national income equals national expenditure, that trade benefits both sides, that shortage yields supply responses.

One reasonably painless way to get the price theory and the thinking-like-an-economist stright is to read Austrian economics. For decades, I have been trying to persuade my friends on the left that Austrian economics is also heterodox, though pro-market. Except for the remarkable Ted Burczak at Denison University, who urges Marxists to read Hayek, they aren't biting (Burczak 2006). If you ask me to listen open-mindedly to Marx or Myrdal or Mirowski, it is only fair that you listen open-mindedly to Mill and Menger and Mises. DeMartino does. He emphasizes the "irreparable ignorance. . . [economists face as they] try to understand, predict, and control inherently complex systems" (p. 11), and then immediately earns his pluralistic street cred by pointing out that Austrians (he cites Hayek) and Knightians and Shackleites know it too. Morgan remarks here that "the elimination of philosophy, methodology, history of economic thought and ethics from the education of the economist [means that they miss that] . . . both Austrians who follow Hayek and structural and post-Keynesians. . . [emphasize] cumulative causal processes" (p. 155–6). Yet aside from Morgan and George and Ted and some of my friends at *Rethinking Marxism*, together with once upon a time Herb Gintis and Sam Bowles, few on the heterodox left listen to the heterodox liberals of Austria, even those presently flourishing at George Mason.

Consider White in describing Kant's notion of "a *dignity*, an incalculable and incomparable worth, due to their capacity for autonomous choice – that is, the ability of make ethical choices despite inclinations or preferences to the contrary" (p. 79). Note the phrase "despite inclinations or preferences." I suggest that the economics here should focus on the Austrian notion of "human action," which is emphatically not passive. The utilitarians focus on reaction instead of action, on the utils gathered from a so-called "choice" instead of the dignity achieved by initiating the choice in the first place.

Not rules, constraints, institutions, but ethics. The proposal stands against neo-institutionalism, which merely rewrites Samuelsonian economics with rules of the game explicit. As Craig Duckworth puts it, "DeMartino . . . sees modification of behaviour within the economics profession itself as a way to improve the situation, rather than, primarily, theoretical or regulatory change" (p. 61). DeMartino himself declares that "the watchwords of professional ethics are education, elucidation, and aspiration – not regulation, legislation, or condemnation" (p. 10). That's right, and that's also what I recommend: not rules, incentives, constraints, punishments, except to the extent that they raise up, in the style of Smith's *Theory of Moral Sentiments*, the adult 'man [or woman, dear] within the breast'.

What we really need is not a social eighth-floor criterion but a ground-level one, which is to say a social agreement among actual people, down at the level of individual ethics, to participate in a liberal society willing to accept 3,000 percent enrichments of the poor. White properly attacks merely "potential Pareto improvements" when they are not defended by anything more than 10 > 9. We need an ethic or ideology of innovism – 3,000 > 1 in the long run rather than 10 > 9 in the short. The locus of ethics is not the society, but the person. "Social justice," as the Austrians say all the time, to the puzzlement of their colleagues left and right, is meaningless.

After all, it was an *ethical* change in Holland and then Britain and its offshoots from 1517 to 1789 that made liberalism and innovism possible after 1800. It is ethical change that runs the economy and causes economic development and advances science. Not money, which is ancient, and given, and obvious, and unchanging. Economists dislike ethics because they want everything to be a matter of given constraints and preexisting utility functions, not persuasion or education. But given constraints are not how we grow and discover.

What, concretely, to do? DeMartino speaks of internships, residencies, and immersions, an approach to economic science that my old friend Richard Weisskoff of the University of Miami has long advocated in economics – and practiced. I've often thought that field work would be good, though I am myself typical of academic economists in having done none of it myself. But before sending the kids out, they have to be told to be good and then to discover naturally. Mearman and McMaster want to get into the weeds of COREs and SBSE. I suggest instead a simpler proposal: reinstate as a required course in graduate programs the history of economic thought. One less econometrics course, say. That way the economists can learn what Mill and Pareto and Wicksteed actually said, largely favorable to a liberal regime of commercially tested betterment.

§

Language, speech as ethics: that is what we need. DeMartino envisions the economics initiate taking a ceremonial oath. It is an excellent idea. Economists sneer at such "mere rhetoric." They follow Hobbes, who said that words have no purchase. But Hobbes was wrong. What is needed is the person within the breast.

Duckworth here wants to drag conscience over into institutions and incentive, à la Oliver Williamson: "the taking of an oath functions, in intention, as an institutional device. The responsibilities it entails structure behaviour so as to achieve objectives towards which professions may not be naturally inclined and that are not easy to incentivise" (p. 63). Compare Douglas Allen's brilliant book on the Royal Navy in the age of sail with a similar theme absent professionalism and the man within (McCloskey 2013). Duckworth finds it "difficult to be convinced that, in this context, the act of commitment itself provides the basis of the normativity of a professional code of conduct" (p. 64). I am astonished. Duckworth doubtless runs his own professional life ethically from the man within. If the dean says, "Cheat to get a promotion," he won't do it. Duckworth says, strangely, that "commitment (being voluntary) can be withdrawn ad libitum" (p. 65). So he seems to fall for Hobbes. In Hobbes, and Duckworth, and most economists, promises are not promises, commitments not commitments, responsibility not responsibility. As someone put it recently, truth is not truth.

Well, no. Or rather, yes, we need ethics, expressed in words.

References

Allen, Douglas. 2012. *The Institutional Revolution: Measurement and the Economic Emergence of the Modern World*. Chicago: University of Chicago Press.

Baier, Annette C. 1994. Ethics in Many Different Voices. From her *Moral Prejudices: Essays on Ethics*. Cambridge, MA: Harvard University Press.

Boudreaux, Donald. 2018. "Letter to Amanda Crosslan." 23 Aug., posted to the blog Cafe Hayek.

Buchanan, James. 1987. "Autobiographical note" in: R.W. Spencer and A. Macpherson. *Lives of the Laureates*. Cambridge, MA: MIT Press.

Buchanan, James, and Gordon Tullock. 1962. *The Calculus of Consent: Logical Foundations of Constitutional Democracy*. Ann Arbor: University of Michigan Press.

Buchanan, James, and Viktor Vanberg. 1991. "Constitutional Choice, Rational Ignorance and the Limits of Reason." In *Collected Works* 16, p. 128.

Burczak, Theodore. 2006. *Socialism After Hayek: Advances in Heterodox Economic*. Ann Arbor: University of Michigan Press.

Caliendo, Lorenzo, Maximiliano Dvorkin, and Fernando Parro. 2015. "Trade and Labor Market Dynamics." Working Paper 2015–009C, Federal Reserve Bank of St. Louis, Aug.

Coase, Ronald H. 1994. "Autobiographical note" in: R.W. Spencer and D.A. Macpherson. *Lives of the Laureates*. Cambridge, MA: MIT Press.

Das, Gurcharan. 2009. *The Difficulty of Being Good: On the Subtle Art of Dharma*. Oxford: Oxford University Press.

DeMartino, George F. 2011. *The Economist's Oath: On the Need for and Content of Professional Economic Ethics*. New York: Oxford University Press.

DeMartino, George F., and Deirdre Nansen McCloskey. 2018. "Professional Ethics 101: A: Reply to Anne Krueger's Review of *The Oxford Handbook of Professional Economic Ethics* [in the *Journal of Economic Literature*]." *Econ Journal Watch*, 31 Jan.

Diamond, Arthur M., Jr. forthcoming. *Openness to Creative Destruction: Sustaining Innovative Dynamism*. New York: Oxford University Press.

Dvorkin, Maximiliaino. 2017. "Top of Form What Is the Impact of Chinese Imports on U.S. Jobs?" *The Regional Economist*. Federal Reserve Bank of St. Louis. May 15.

Friedman, Milton. 1970. "The Social Responsibility of Business is to Increase its Profits." *New York Times Magazine*, Sept. 13.

Glewwe, P., A. Park, M. Zhao. 2012. "Visualizing Development: Eyeglasses and Academic Performance in Rural Primary Schools in China." Working Paper WP12–2, Center for International Food and Agricultural Policy, University of Minnesota.

Haltiwanger, John C. 2011. "Job Creation and Firm Dynamics in the United States." *NBER Innovation Policy & the Economy* 12: 17–38.

Harberger, Arnold C. 1971. "Three Basic Postulates for Applied Welfare Economics: An Interpretive Essay." *Journal of Economic Literature* 9 (3): 785–797.

Harsanyi, John C. 1955. "Cardinal Welfare, Individualistic Ethics, and Interpersonal Comparisons of Utility." *Journal of Political Economy* 63: 309–321.

Haskell, Thomas L. 1999. "Responsibility, Convention, and the Role of Ideas in History." pp. 1–27 in P. A. Coclanis and S. Bruchey, eds., *Ideas, Ideologies, and Social Movements: The United States Experience since 1800*. Columbia: University of South Carolina Press.

Hobbes, Thomas. 1651. *Leviathan*. Everyman Edition. London: J. M. Dent and New York: E. P. Dutton, 1914.

Klamer, Arjo. 2006. *Speaking of Economics*. London: Routledge.

Klamer, Arjo. 2016. *Doing the Right Thing: A Value-Based Economy*. Amsterdam: de Brink.

Knight, Frank. 1922. "Ethics and the Economic Interpretation." *Quarterly Journal of Economics*, reprinted as pp. 11–32 in Frank Knight, ed., *The Ethics of Competition and Other Essays*. Chicago: University of Chicago Press, 1935.

McCloskey, Deirdre Nansen. 2006. *The Bourgeois Virtues: Ethics for an Age of Commerce*. Chicago: University of Chicago Press.

McCloskey, Deirdre Nansen. 2013. "A Neo-Institutionalism of Measurement, Without Measurement: A Comment on Douglas Allen's *The Institutional Revolution.*" *Review of Austrian Economics* 26 (4): 262–373.

McCloskey, Deirdre Nansen. 2016. *Bourgeois Equality: How Ideas, Not Capital or Institutions, Enriched the World*. Chicago: University of Chicago Press.

McCloskey, Deirdre Nansen. 2017a. "Comment on 'Putting Integrity into Finance: A Purely Positive Approach' (by Werner Erhard and Michael C. Jensen)." *Capitalism and Society* 12: 1–12. (Columbia University Center on Capitalism).

McCloskey, Deirdre Nansen. 2017b. "The Myth of Technological Unemployment." *Reason*, Aug.

McCloskey, Deirdre Nansen, and Arjo Klamer. 1995. [206] "One Quarter of GDP Is Persuasion." *The American Economic Review* 85 (2, May): 191–195.

Mehra, Akhil. 2009. "Politics of Participation: Walter Reed's Yellow-Fever Experiments." *AMA Journal of Medical Ethics, Virtual Mentor* 11 (4): 326–330 at https://journalofethics.ama-assn.org/article/politics-participation-walter-reeds-yellow-fever-experiments/2009-04

Mill, John Stuart. 1859 (2001). *On Liberty*. Kitchener: Batoche Books.

Noddings, Nel. 1984. *Caring: A Feminine Approach to Ethics and Moral Education*. Berkeley: University of California Press.

Nussbaum, Martha. 2006. *Frontiers of Justice: Disability, Nationality, Species Membership*. Cambridge, MA: Harvard University Press.

Orwell, George. 1940. "Charles Dickens." pp. 135–185 in Orwell, *Essays*. John Carey, ed. Everyman Library. New York: Knopf 2002.

Pomeranz, Kenneth, and Steven Topik. 2006. *The World That Trade Created: Society, Culture, and the World Economy 1400 to the Present*. London and Armonk, NY: M. E. Sharpe. Rosling, Hans.

Rachels, James. 1999. *The Elements of Moral Philosophy*. Third Edition. New York: McGraw-Hill College.

Rosling, Hans, Ola Rosling, and Anna Rosling Rönnlund. 2018. *Factfulness: Ten Reasons We're Wrong About the World – And Why Things Are Better Than You Think*. London: Hodder & Stoughton.

Rousseau, Jean-Jacques. 1755. *Discourse on Political Economy*. pp. 111–138 in D. A. Cress, trans. and ed., *Jean-Jacques Rousseau: Basic Political Writings*. Indianapolis: Hackett, 1987.

Sayre, Anne. 1987 (1975). *Rosalind Franklin, Rosalind Franklin and DNA*. New York: W.W. Norton.

Sen, Amartya. 1987. *On Ethics and Economics*. Oxford: Blackwell.

Smith, Adam. 1759, 1790. *The Theory of Moral Sentiments*. Glasgow Edition. D. D. Raphael and A. L. Macfie, eds. Indianapolis: Liberty Classics, 1976, 1982.

Tabarrok, Alex. 2015. "What Was Gary Becker's Biggest Mistake?" *Marginal Revolution Blog*. Sept. 16 at https://marginalrevolution.com/marginalrevolution/2015/09/what-was-gary-beckers-biggest-mistake.html

Weisse, Allen B. 2012. "Self-Experimentation and Its Role in Medical Research." *Texas Heart Institute Journal* 39 (1): 51–54. At www.ncbi.nlm.nih.gov/pmc/articles/PMC3298919/

White, Mark D. 2005. "A Kantian Critique of Neoclassical Law and Economics." Forthcoming, *Review of Political Economy*. MS Department of Political Science, Economics and Philosophy, College of Staten Island.

Index